DIGITAL VICTORIANS

STANFORD
TEXT TECHNOLOGIES

Series Editors

Ruth Ahnert

Roopika Risam

Elaine Treharne

Editorial Board

Benjamin Albritton

Caroline Bassett

Lori Emerson

Alan Liu

Elena Pierazzo

Andrew Prescott

Matthew Rubery

Kate Sweetapple

Heather Wolfe

DIGITAL
VICTORIANS

From Nineteenth-Century Media to Digital Humanities

PAUL FYFE

Stanford University Press
Stanford, California

Stanford University Press
Stanford, California

© 2024 by Paul Fyfe. All rights reserved.

No part of this book may be reproduced or transmitted in any form or by any means, electronic or mechanical, including photocopying and recording, or in any information storage or retrieval system, without the prior written permission of Stanford University Press.

Printed in the United States of America on acid-free, archival-quality paper.

Library of Congress Cataloging-in-Publication Data
Names: Fyfe, Paul (Paul Camm), author.
Title: Digital Victorians : from nineteenth-century media to digital humanities / Paul Fyfe.
Other titles: Text technologies.
Description: Stanford, California : Stanford University Press, 2024. | Series: Stanford text technologies | Includes bibliographical references and index.
Identifiers: LCCN 2024005568 (print) | LCCN 2024005569 (ebook) | ISBN 9781503639911 (cloth) | ISBN 9781503640948 (paperback) | ISBN 9781503640955 (ebook)
Subjects: LCSH: English literature--19th century--History and criticism. | Literature and technology--Great Britain—History—19th century. | Technology in literature. | Digital humanities—History.
Classification: LCC PR468.T4 F94 2024 (print) | LCC PR468.T4 (ebook) | DDC 820.9356—dc23/eng/20240304
LC record available at https://lccn.loc.gov/2024005568
LC ebook record available at https://lccn.loc.gov/2024005569

Cover design: Bob Aufuldish/Aufuldish & Warinner
Cover art: Queen Victoria typing on a laptop, MidJourney, June 6, 2023

CONTENTS

	Acknowledgments	vii
	Introduction	1
1	How the Internet Lost (and Found) Its Body: The Dream of Disintermediation from the Mail Coach to Transoceanic Cables	32
2	Data Ethics from Realism to the Right to Be Forgotten	66
3	Henry James, Counting Words, and Machine Reading	103
4	Jekyll, Hyde, and the Dark Side of Digital Humanities	136
5	The Archaeology of Victorian New Media	171
Afterword	The Digital Victorian Frame of Mind, 1957–2020	216
	Notes	229
	Index	275

ACKNOWLEDGMENTS

THE ROOTS OF THIS PROJECT reach back to formative years at the University of Virginia with its cohort of digitally minded Victorianists. As a twenty-something grad student who knew HTML and just needed a summer job, I did not at first appreciate how special was the opportunity to work with the Rossetti Archive under the gracious tutelage, good humor, and endless curiosity of Jerome McGann. There, I became a digital scholar and a "wombat" alongside Bethany Nowviskie, Bill Hughes, Dana Wheeles, Cory McLaughlin, Melissa White, PC Fleming, and Ken Price. Our conversations about what was becoming digital humanities were expanded by the Electronically Enabled Literary Studies group (EELS), including Andy Stauffer and Brad Pasanek. At one point, my friend Justin Neuman asked me what connected Victorian literature and digital humanities. Perhaps, with this book, I have an answer.

Even while constantly preoccupied with that question, I had to wait some years before giving fuller attention to the project. Along the way, student research assistants including Anna Bighta, Danisha

Baker-Whitaker, and John Handel helped me establish its foundations. Early versions of chapters were presented at the ADHO's digital humanities (DH) conference, the North American Victorian Studies Association, the Research Society for Victorian Periodicals, the CUNY Annual Victorian Conference, the Victorian Data conference, and the Victorians Institute. I am indebted to the many scholars cited throughout this book, but would like particularly to thank Richard Menke, Megan Ward, Adrian Wisnicki, Alison Hedley, Thomas Smits, Meredith Martin, Natalie Houston, Priti Joshi, Ryan Cordell, and Jim Mussell for their inspiration and guidance.

Research for the book was supported by a Frederick Burkhardt Fellowship for Recently Tenured Scholars from the American Council of Learned Societies, taken as a residency at the National Humanities Center. I am so grateful to the class of 2018–19 for its intellectual community and interdisciplinary perspectives, epitomized by Matt Rubery, Eleanor Courtemanche, Weihong Bao, Ling Hon Lam, Ted Underwood, and Honor Sachs. Thanks also to Brooke Andrade and Sarah Harris, comprising the NHC's indefatigable library staff, and to Tania Munz for coordinating the program.

I learned much from another cohort of scholars as part of the Andrew W. Mellon Society of Fellows in Critical Bibliography, including classes at Rare Book School. Thanks to the Mellon Foundation as well as to Michael Suarez, Barbara Heritage, and Donna Sy for orchestrating a vibrant scholarly community. As a Mercator Fellow funded by the German Research Federation (DFG), I benefited from partnerships with the "Journalliteratur" research group including Andreas Beck, Jens Ruchatz, Vincent Fröhlich, and Nora Ramtke. I am grateful to Ryan Cordell and David Smith for facilitating the grant-funded Oceanic Exchanges project on digitized newspapers, and for assembling an awesome international team, including M. H. Beals, Jana Keck, and Mila Oiva.

Sincere thanks also go to staff at the British Library, especially Ed King, Beth Gaskell, Stewart Gillies, and Mia Ridge for their generous assistance. At NC State University Libraries, Markus Wust, Darby

Orcutt, Will Cross, and Colin Keenan helped me navigate the landscape of data access, contracts, and fair use. I owe much to colleagues in the NC State English Department—including Tony Harrison, Leila May, Sharon Setzer, Sharon Joffe, James Mulholland, and Margaret Simon—for their unfailing support and friendship during this journey.

Ultimately, this book only happened because of Erica Wetter, my exemplary editor, who started improving it during an informal Zoom meeting before I'd even submitted a proposal. Many thanks also to Elaine Treharne, Ruth Ahnert, and Roopika Risam for helping develop the book for SUP's Text Technologies series. Caroline McKusick expertly steered the project through its review and production. Thanks additionally to Dawn Hall, Tiffany Mok, Melissa Jauregui Chavez, David Zielonka, and the team at Stanford University Press. I'm also incredibly grateful to the three mostly anonymous reviewers who sharpened the project's edges and cheered it along its way.

An earlier part of chapter 5 previously appeared as "An Archaeology of Victorian Newspapers" in *Victorian Periodicals Review* 49, no. 4 (2016): 546–77, © The Research Society for Victorian Periodicals. Thanks to RSVP for permission to include it here.

INTRODUCTION

The first of the leading peculiarities of the present age is, that it is an age of transition.
—J. S. MILL, "The Spirit of the Age" (1831)[1]

New media are old; and old media are new.
—ALAN LIU, "Imagining the New Media Encounter" (2004)[2]

THE NINETEENTH CENTURY UNDERSTOOD ITSELF as a time of change. Even time itself seemed changing: J. S. Mill's famous quotation spans an entire "age" and an intensified awareness of the "present." Wandering between two worlds, caught between the best and worst of times, the Victorians perceived themselves in the middle of an epochal transition, including to the ways they depicted and communicated these changes. In 1842, a journalist identified only as "W." captured the widely shared sense that communication technologies had inaugurated this new era: "The annihilation of space and time is beginning to be no fable. The broad Atlantic has been bridged by steam navigation. . . . The electric spark has been seized, and made to obey the impulse of the human will. Lightning is our news carrier—light is our portrait painter."[3] Seemingly from the realm of "fable," something was beginning. W.'s metaphors quickly sketch the dramatic shifts that technology hath wrought: the collapse of space and time, the blurring of technology and agency, the reconfiguring of arts and information. They all signal how W. grapples with an emerging concept of media.[4] Though it had yet to be named, it exemplified the transitions of the era, and everyone felt it was new.

The Victorian moment of new media is also our moment. The last few decades have brought a similar sense of living through an unprecedented age of digital transformation, for better and worse. "New media" became an industry and an experience of its platforms; the internet has bridged and divided our world; its material appetites and carbon outputs have split this epoch from the past and endangered its future. Ours is another era of a technologizing, intensifying present. Like wonderstruck Victorians, many of us have witnessed this "age of transition" in our own lifetimes. In my first proper job, I was an editorial assistant at a New York publishing company, which still produced its books in paper galleys. My tasks included photocopying line drawings to a certain scale for the compositor to glue onto cardboard. My second job, a few blocks away, was at an internet company featuring all the slogans, excess, and eventual layoffs of the dot com bubble. Then the planes hit the towers. I left to study British Victorian literature in graduate school, during which time "digital humanities" was invented. It was all happening. It was all strange and new.

Yet, as I learned, it was not new. Ironically, the self-declared uniqueness of this historical age makes it easier to recognize its ancestry. Media is always already new, as Lisa Gitelman suggests, but must forget its history to imagine and market itself as such.[5] As John Durham Peters explains, "the history of new media is old."[6] The transitions of the nineteenth century convinced Mill and others that theirs was a unique era, but they also lead directly to how we imagine *our* present as something distinctive. Among the many contexts in which we can trace a nineteenth-century inheritance—the lasting schisms of empire, climate crisis, or even historical thinking as such—this book is especially interested in the contemporary legacy of Victorian new media. This is not simply because nineteenth-century inventions like the telegraph helped establish the technologies and infrastructure for the digital present—which, intriguingly, they did. Instead, the nineteenth century sets the conceptual terms we still use to understand new media and our relationships to it. Our very sense of technological newness has a Victorian history.

As Alan Liu suggests, this road runs both ways: "new media are old; and old media are new." Looking backward from our present vantage, we can recognize aspects of the Victorian past that remained invisible at the time, and make them "new." "Old media" have latent histories that may only appear in retrospect—in our case, during another age of intense media transition. Seeing the "Victorians in the rearview mirror," as Simon Joyce put it, means not only to consider their afterlives but to project our own situation backward.[7] This kind of anachronism or "presentism" can be controversial, yet it offers a powerful tool to make the past legible, and subsequently useful, for present purposes. If we recognize digital media in the Victorian past, that does not commit us to valorizing the present or excluding other forms of historical knowledge. Making the Victorians "digital" may actually help resist the narratives of historical uniqueness that "new media" enables, then as well as now. It gives us tools to know the past and ourselves differently.

In *Digital Victorians*, I make these arguments in tandem: looking back, the history of the digital present extends to nineteenth-century encounters with media in transition; looking forward, this history reframes our own contemporary relationships with the digital, especially in contexts of the materials, interpretive practices, and professional landscape of the humanities. Several critics have already argued for a prehistory of the digital age in the nineteenth century, its technologies, and/or its concept of information.[8] But this book shifts from the generalized category of the "digital" to the emergence of "digital humanities" (DH) as a notably self-conscious discourse about what happens to text, writing, communication, culture, and work amid significant media shift—questions that had intensely preoccupied the Victorians as well. While DH has a longer history, prefixing "digital" to the humanities in the early 2000s announced something new, and simultaneously encouraged scrutiny about the relationship of its terms. As much as it delivered tools or methods, "digital humanities" prompted expansive reflections on the disciplines in an age of transition. To the Delphic riddle "what is DH," I would hazard an answer that DH is a metadiscourse about changing knowledge practices in an era of media shift. Thus, this book approaches DH as defined less by specific technologies or scholarly methods than by historical self-awareness about what they expose or shift about the humanities' purview. Put bluntly, DH made us digital Victorians, intensifying an awareness of transitions in the present age.

Like "new media," DH has a longer and more complex history than typically gets acknowledged. This book finds an alternative one in nineteenth-century encounters with its new media. Sometimes, these historical examples directly relate to contemporary DH, as in late nineteenth-century experiments to count words and analyze literature quantitatively and at scale, a kind of distant reading avant la lettre.[9] At others, they probe resonant questions about materiality, desocialization, memory, privacy, and machinic intelligence that we now see driving research in other fields, including media studies, communications, and science and technology studies (STS). One of the advantages of studying the Victorians is we can recognize genealogies of our own knowledge practices before their disciplinary enclosure and analyze how those divisions took hold from their "undisciplined culture" to ours.[10] For this reason, this book takes a broad approach to what counts as DH—whose boundaries seem ever in question anyway—to encourage the interdisciplinary conversations among digital scholars that the Victorians remind us to have. Writers from Dickens and Eliot to du Maurier and Stevenson agonized about the ephemerality of industrializing print, the consequences of social hyperconnection, the remediation of their works, and the possibilities of automated writing. If the Victorians were already digital, they might help us envision a more encompassing field or alternative futures for digital scholarship now.

The characteristic self-consciousness of DH is also why this book studies Victorian writers and literature. *Digital Victorians* is not (quite) a media history, but a history of interpretive attitudes about media in transition, for which writing and literature—broadly construed—

furnish such useful evidence. As scholars have suggested, nineteenth-century literature shows a remarkable awareness of its own changing communicative and material status *because* of the changing media landscape in which it manifests.[11] "The study of literary history is the study of media history," argues Linda Hughes.[12] The reverse can also be true: as demonstrated by media historians, including Carolyn Marvin and others, nineteenth-century writers helped shape how new mediums were conceived, represented, and operated.[13] In their medial self-awareness, these writers confronted the consequences of media shifts in ways that still define contemporary responses. As I will show, their legacy appears across a spectrum of reactions to digital media, from skeptical resistance to enthusiastic welcome of its possibilities.

Digital Victorians argues for the substantial explanatory power of Victorian literature for thinking about the digital age and reconfiguration of humanities practices within it. This book charts what Gitelman calls a "predigital history for the digital humanities," finding its conceptual roots in nineteenth-century encounters with telecommunication networks, privacy intrusions, quantitative reading methods, remediation, and their effects on literary professionals.[14] More broadly, Victorian responses to their changing media landscape continue to influence how we understand new media. With its transhistorical correspondence, this book offers a capacious and interdisciplinary approach to studying new media, including attention to the materiality of transmission, the ethics of data, the historiography of digital materials and methods, and the origins of academic fields. Ultimately, *Digital Victorians* presents an alternative genealogy for the digital turn, entangling the present with its strange Victorian inheritance to deepen our understandings of, and our critical interventions in, the relations of technology and the humanities.

Victorian New Media

Perhaps there has never been an age without transition. Why distinguish one era as such when all of history is just one damn thing after another? As Geoffrey Nunberg cautions, "the past can come to seem an unbroken stream of proclamations that man is living an epochal moment."[15] Certainly other, earlier eras also developed historical self-consciousness about their sweeping shifts; for instance, Marshall McLuhan made famous an analogy between the Elizabethan's unsettled print culture and the twentieth century's juvenile computer age.[16] Yet even Nunberg is among those scholars who credit the nineteenth century with some definitive shifts. Nunberg, James Gleick, and Toni Weller all locate the emergence of a modern concept of information at this time: "it was during the nineteenth century that the overt recognition and expectation of information that is characteristic of our own age first became evident."[17] Other scholars see related concepts taking shape concurrently. For James Carey and John Durham Peters, technologies for speaking and writing at a distance (e.g., tele-graph, telephone) changed "communication" from its older meaning of physical transfer to its modern association with transmitting messages across time and space.[18] These nineteenth-century communication technologies amount to "the introduction of new media" for Marvin, establishing the social framework for the later reception of computers: "All debates about electronic media in the twentieth century begin here."[19] John Guillory hypothesizes that late nineteenth-century technologies of communication and recording help generate the concept of "media" itself.[20]

I rehearse just a few of these arguments to suggest how strongly the nineteenth-century's "age of transition" resonates with scholars—especially those guided by a constellation of terms including information, communication, technology, and media. They also reveal a desire to recognize nineteenth-century developments as precursors to our own, as if the Victorian age transitions directly to the present. For example, in *Rethinking Media Transition*, David Thorburn and Henry Jenkins also use Mill's "age of transition" quote to introduce their entire book: "Set aside the nineteenth-century tonalities, and this passage could belong to our own era. Its apocalyptic rhetoric and its self-conscious awareness of change closely mirror the discourse of the so-called digital revolution."[21] Perhaps we all wish to see ourselves in the past. But the nineteenth-century's technological shifts seem especially seductive for recognizing digital media in the Victorian mirror. Such comparisons have popular and counterintuitive appeal, as in Tom Standage's book *Victorian Internet*, or articles that trace AI facial recognition to 1880s forensic photography, or claims that quirky Victorian technologies like the electrophone were the precursors of live streaming.[22] As "veterans of unprecedented media change," the Victorians help us grapple with our analogous era, as Alfano and Stauffer argue.[23] In a similar spirit, Bowser and Croxall trace the early 2000s surge of interest in Victorian steampunk to "our experiences of, unease with, and desires for technology in the present."[24] Steampunk allows a backward glance at the stirrings of digitality and the posthuman—perhaps even representing what Roger Whitson calls nineteenth-century digital humanities.[25] Fans and scholars alike are reclaiming the Victorian era in the present, as it helps stabilize or decode the disruptions of digital culture. As Maurice Lee argues, "debates over the fate of literature in our information age . . . are powerfully conditioned by the nineteenth century, which encountered its own information revolution with wonder and anxiety."[26]

If Victorian technologies, media, and information culture share features with the digital present, they also reveal how we *conceptualize* that present like Victorians. Consider a few phrases from the previous paragraph: "our information age," "our own era," "our own age." When exactly is the "present," anyway? And whose age or era does "ours" claim to be? Invoking a broad category like the "digital age" doesn't clarify much about specific technologies or whom they impact. Announcing "new media" doesn't necessarily help either, as it has been declaring itself new for decades.[27] Charles Acland complains that "few phrases have been evacuated of meaning, and have outlived their critical usefulness, faster than 'new media.'"[28] However, if these phrases lack precision, they accurately name the critical self-awareness about the moment of change they occasion. New media throws us into an unsettled relationship to history that we call "the present," which happens time and again. In this book, I am as interested to study this sense of the digital present as its potential origins in the Victorian past. Both are historical conditions defined significantly by media in transition, whose "newness" has less to do with technological invention and more to do with social, cultural, and professional structures in flux.

In *When Old Technologies Were New*, Marvin established how "new media" opens a window onto such shifts: "the introduction of new media is a special historical occasion when patterns anchored in older media . . . are reexamined, challenged, and defended."[29] New media provoke the scrutiny of the concepts and historical conditions they unsettle. This makes the "history of old new media" especially interesting to study, as its meanings, social protocols, and relations of power get renegotiated.[30] The "novelty years" of a new medium stir up crises that reveal the linkages between information, communication, or technology and their adjacent social and cultural domains.[31] The Victorians witnessed such new mediums in parade, from electric communication to techniques of the mass image to the capture and broadcast of sound. Yet, as Marvin and others have shown, the history of technology is social history, which is never a series of "novelty" inventions or artifacts but a discursive contest that understands itself as new, and in which writing and literature are very much involved. Victorian representations of these technologies—as in astonished journalism, telegraphic romances, stories of typewriter operators, or the fictional incorporation of recorded sound or photographs—all became part of how these technologies worked.[32]

In this sense, the nineteenth century does not just generate the media concept or deliver technologies that uncannily resemble our own. It sets the pattern for what Liu calls the "new media encounter."[33] This encounter imagines the collision of old and new and exaggerates the uniqueness of its own moment. If the Victorians understood theirs as an age of transition, they continually described it in the terms of epochal media change. That contemporary scholars, journalists, and even steampunk cosplayers have followed suit is, in many ways, evidence of the nineteenth century's own imaginative success. Narratives of such encounters are everywhere in its writing about communications technologies—and feature extensively in the chapters to come.

As in the opening excerpt from the *Westminster Review*, the Victorians envisioned the annihilation of space and time, the technological transformation of agency, the transfer of writing and picture-making to machines and electric mediums, the possibility of extrahuman senses. That rhetoric sometimes supported the Victorians' larger narrative about modernization and its economic imperatives—just as claims of "innovation" and "disruption" and more recently "artificial intelligence" have driven the financial speculations of a new media economy. Yet the new media encounter can also generate what Liu calls "whole imaginative environments," which can unsettle and promote "the scholarly and cultural potential of new media."[34] This book ranges across selected essays, illustrated journalism, novels, stories, and science writing in which the Victorians imagined a new media condition to interpret their era's significant sociotechnical changes.

The nineteenth century's imaginative environments expand the discursive reckoning with new media and thereby encourage all sorts of productive interdisciplinary exchanges among literary studies, media studies, and the history of science, communication, and technology. In my own field, scholars have used media history to theorize the role of writing and literature in setting media's conceptual horizons. What Alison Byerly calls "Victorian media studies" looks at the constitutive role of Victorian writing in the apprehension, representation, and developing protocols of historical mediums.[35] As Amy Wong argues, literary studies brings different perspectives to communication history by showing the "the historical many-sidedness of nineteenth-century media" and the "messy alternate histories" that it might generate.[36] Other critics have taken inspiration from media archaeology with its interest in "dead media" and technologies that never survived, but whose aspects reveal forgotten historical configurations or trajectories untaken. For instance, the "pianotype" machine for composing moveable type with a piano keyboard: invented in the 1840s, it never took off, but nonetheless reveals the embedding of gender and aesthetic composition into ideas about media production.[37] Relatedly, media scholars' attention to materiality and platforms has helped to reinvigorate "media-specific analysis" in literary scholarship.[38] Although textual scholarship and bibliography have long histories in the discipline, they too have been galvanized by media studies to take broader, more critical forms. For example, Richard Menke has demonstrated how thoroughly Victorian literature registers the changing conditions of telecommunications networks and material infrastructures. Gissing's novel *New Grub Street* knew very well how the "new" marketplace for mass print depended on fragile resource extraction for its paper.[39]

I understand my own work within this recent trajectory of Victorian media studies. However, though such cross-disciplinary conversations have been generative, the periodization and geographical focus of literary scholarship ("Victorian studies") does not neatly align with media history. As a consequence, researchers of the Romantic era or the eighteenth century or the early modern period or medieval and even classical contexts have all variously claimed that modern aspects of media have even *earlier* origins.[40] "New media, it turns out, is a very old tale," Liu says.[41] As much as anything, these competing claims may reflect the professional incentives of our own field distinctions, reinscribing the "new" in an ever-retreating mise en abyme. Some media historians have been more open to a gradual narrative, understanding new media through continuities rather than revolutions.[42] Scholars in media archaeology have also proposed some very different chronologies. For example, Wolfgang Ernst offers the concept of "time criticality" to emphasize media's infinitesimal processes as well as enduring, slow operations—neither quite corresponding to the chronology humans (or humanists) perceive or use to understand the past.[43] Similarly, Jussi Parrika has proposed a "geological" approach that traces the mineral histories of new media's components to the long timelines of earth science.[44] Certain approaches to "media ecology" and "environmental media" have also stretched media's history and communicative functions beyond the familiar dimensions of literary periods.[45]

For these reasons and more, literary scholars need to take care in claiming media studies under our auspice, or assuming the literary provides evidence for other disciplines. The digital age has encouraged much cross-fertilization and comparative work among scholars interested in media, book history, and text technologies. Yet, as Whitney Trettien cautions, the conceptual vocabulary of media studies has its own distinct disciplinary origins and does not always translate.[46] Kathleen Fitzpatrick has warned English departments in particular against a "colonialist approach to interdisciplinary studies: incorporating the texts and methodologies studied in other fields, but only insofar as they shed light on the still narrowly defined category of the literary."[47] This seems especially hazardous for the field of Victorian studies, given the colonial legacy of its namesake, and the field's very ambitions, announced in the first issue of its eponymous journal, of "openness to critical and scholarly studies from all the relevant disciplines."[48] Even with the best intentions, we can risk what Catherine Gallagher calls "being interdisciplinary all by ourselves."[49] As a sometime Victorianist in an English department, I take the point. Interdisciplinary work should start with a clear understanding of one's own disciplinary contribution, then interface with—rather than claim and capture—the language, ideas, and citations of media studies in common. Yet my own employment has always been in other fields: working in new media before grad school, then variously hired to teach the history of text technologies, digital media, and digital humanities. I have tried to devise *Digital Victorians* with critical openness to these fields, informed by our shared subjects and interests, while also committed to what literary studies might uniquely contribute.

When opened to these interdisciplinary conversations, Victorian studies has a great deal to offer to media history and theory. Before the modern distinctions that enclosed academic fields—itself a nineteenth-century phenomenon—the discourse of media was active across a pre-disciplinary culture of nineteenth-century writing. During the novelty years of emerging mediums, writers were scrutinizing the changing communicative, professional, and imaginative environments of their own work and the mediums in which it circulated. As a result, narratives of new media encounter in nineteenth-century literature offer what Liu calls an "elementary form of media theory" or a "metadiscourse about media" at its origins.[50] In a related sense, Menke claims that late Victorian writers articulate a "vernacular media theory" that twentieth-century scholars would inherit and formally define.[51] Following on these insights, this book identifies another metadiscourse emerging in the nineteenth century's media vernacular, articulated across a spectrum of imaginative and nonfictional writing. But, as I will argue, the implications would not fully emerge until the early twenty-first, when a related metadiscourse formed around something newly called the "digital humanities."

The Digital Humanities Moment

Digital humanities was invented in 2004. Or perhaps in 2000. Or in the 1970s. Or in the 1950s. Or—if my own book is to be believed—in the 1840s. The history of DH has a lot of competing claims about its origins. It is conventionally accepted that the 2004 publication of Blackwell's *Companion to Digital Humanities* first announced the phrase to the public.[52] That may have originated, in turn, from a master's program that John Unsworth (one of the *Companion*'s editors) attempted to propose in 2000 at the University of Virginia.[53] The editors wanted a phrase more expansive than "humanities computing," in parlance for several decades, but which no longer accounted for the broadening mediums and methodological experiments that "DH" would index. Susan Hockey's well-known "History of Humanities Computing" (published in the 2004 *Companion to DH*) noted that the journal *Computers and the Humanities* began in 1966, with regular conferences on literary and linguistic computing beginning in the 1970s. Hockey also gave the field a birthday and a founding father: "Unlike many other interdisciplinary experiments, humanities computing has a very well-known beginning" with the punch-card concordance experiments of the Italian Jesuit priest Father Roberto Busa.[54] Busa's example offered the field a durable "creation myth," but this popular origin story has been disputed if not debunked.[55] Rachel Buurma, Laura Heffernan, and Brad Pasanek have all highlighted the earlier (and unacknowledged) experiments in computational literary stylistics in the 1950s by UCLA English professor Josephine Miles.[56] Other scholars have traced the genealogy further back, for instance, to quantitative methodologies of reading, writing, and interpretation present in the practical criticism of I. A. Richards in the 1920s, to the turn-of-the-century work of Gertrude Stein and Vernon Lee, or to social scientists like Thomas Mendenhall who were publishing about stylometry in the 1880s.[57]

The history of DH is justly disputed, but its historiography shows a clearer timeline. Digital humanities does have a "well-known beginning," though not necessarily in the guise of any breakthrough practitioner or the invention of certain methodologies. Rather, DH symbolically announces its birth during a "naming moment," which Scott Weingart finds roughly in the years 1997–2005.[58] Nominated "digital humanities" by the Blackwell *Companion*, it comes to public consciousness shortly thereafter, famously declared as the "next big thing" for the humanities by William Pannapacker in the *Chronicle of Higher Education* in 2009.[59] This was followed by Matthew Kirschenbaum's important field delineation in 2010, "What Is Digital Humanities and What's It Doing in English Departments?" Each of these subsequently received so much skepticism and pushback that, in 2014, Kirschenbaum published a companion piece: "What Is 'Digital Humanities,' and Why Are They Saying Such Terrible Things About It?"[60] As DH emerged as such in the early 2010s, it was characterized by grand proclamations and fierce reactions, so much so that Matthew Gold inaugurated an influential book series with the University of Minnesota Press in 2012 simply called Debates in Digital Humanities. Gold titled his introduction to the first volume "The Digital Humanities Moment." In it, he acknowledges the surge of attention that DH has received and explains how its debates, perhaps "more than most fields," have focused much larger conversations about the institutional transformation of the academy. By contrasting innovation with tradition, the "digital" provokes unusually public conversations about changes in humanities work and produces an "introspective and self-reflexive" discourse about scholarly materials, methods, and professional practice.[61] As Élika Ortega later claimed in a special issue of *PMLA* on "Varieties of Digital Humanities," its "collection of practices and approaches ... can be viewed as a scene of media encounter" just as Liu had characterized.[62] In short, DH is the academy's new media encounter.

After being named, the novelty years of DH saw a number of attempts to refine its definition: some boosterish, some quite critical, but all marked by the narrative characteristics of a new media encounter. For example, the 2012 volume *Digital_Humanities* begins this way: "Confronting the massive transformation of knowledge, society, and culture that is underway in the digital age, this book takes stock of this new world."[63] Regardless of how old DH might arguably be, such pronouncements emphasize the difference of the "digital age" as a transition to a "new world." That rhetoric reappears in a 2015 book *Between the Humanities and the Digital*, which "reveals that a new turn—perhaps a new temporal chapter—has emerged in the relational engagement between humanities and the digital."[64] Other notable contributors in the volume echo the point: "we are now . . . in the first phase of a digital revolution in higher education," write Liu and Thomas.[65] Making a grander gesture, N. Katherine Hayles claims that "there is reason to think that human being[s] may be entering a new era."[66] This sense of a "new temporal chapter" represents its before and after as "digital" versus "traditional humanities," marked by their contrasting conditions of media.[67] Along these lines, Jonathan Sterne juxtaposes digital humanities with "analog humanities": "a nexus of methodological, technological, and institutional conditions across the humanities that have only come into clear focus in retrospect." What brings them into focus is not digital media per se, but the sense of historical transition it helps us to imagine. As these examples suggest, defining DH is largely about distinguishing a moment in time—"the 'digital era' as our present moment"—in which to scrutinize academic practices and institutional configurations.[68]

In this sense, DH has invited scholars into a moment of media in transition, defined less by new technologies than by wide-ranging contests over their uses, significance, and social organization. As Liu attempted to explain in "The Meaning of Digital Humanities," "the underlying issue is the disciplinary identity not of the digital humanities but of the humanities themselves."[69] Of course, the disciplinary identity of "the humanities" has never been so stable and has certainly never lacked for enabling crises. Yet DH has framed big debates about the politics, pedagogy, and professional implications of digital change in the academy. It has provoked what Julia Flanders calls "productive unease" about institutional and disciplinary norms.[70] Or it imports "alien paradigms" that require our reorientation to the humanities.[71] Or, as Kirschenbaum argued elsewhere, DH functions as a "tactical term" for the redistribution of material and institutional resources—and similarly becomes a "discursive construct" for those objecting to such reallocations writ large.[72] Or, as Moya Bailey and Kim Gallon suggest, DH redraws the "human" within the humanities, often exclusive of ways minoritized communities address digital media.[73] All these responses—and there are so many more—show scholars negotiating the newly declared "digital" on the alien, uneasy, and contested terrain of its significance for their fields and professions. It makes sense that "What is DH?" is an endlessly asked and unanswerable question. The question is its own answer, as DH is a metadiscourse that has prompted the humanities to vigorously reassess its purview.

The references noted here will already be familiar to DHers, and they hardly sketch the extent of definitions, debates, and alternative visions that follow DH into its maturity or its increasingly global and postcolonial reach. I have selected a few that help to underscore how I am defining DH historically and describing its self-awareness in terms of a new media encounter. Its definitions tend to reference "our present moment," roughly corresponding to the first two decades of the twenty-first century. In some ways, this period of transition shadows the crisis moments of Kuhn's scientific revolution when disputes over "normal" and emergent paradigms remain unsettled.[74] Bracketing this "digital era" in time has the advantage of seeing its constructedness, making it comparable to other historical moments, and envisioning its possible futures in the interchange. Scholars have already noted some of these parallels in defining DH. For example, Cathy Davidson claimed that the digital transformation and remediations of "Humanities 2.0" is happening at "a scale unequaled since the late nineteenth century, a comparable era of technological transformation."[75] Similarly, in a landmark article about DH in the *New York Times* in 2010, Tom Scheinfeldt compared its "methodological moment" as "similar to the late 19th and early 20th centuries, when scholars were preoccupied with collating and cataloging the flood of new information brought about by revolutions in communication, transportation and science."[76] Rising to this challenge, the late nineteenth century saw the emergence of the "big humanities," as Chad Wellmon argues, which stirred familiar anxieties about the organization and ethics of scholarly work.[77] Digital humanities may be having the nineteenth century's new media moment all over again.

Those historical correspondences will preoccupy the rest of this book. Connecting them yields some important perspectives about each. First, it helps resist the technological determinism implicit in the naming of these phenomena, including the "digital age" or "digital humanities." In a similar way, it addresses the historical amnesia of new media with its progressivist rhetoric of innovation, disruption, and replacement. Historical contrasts also invite some productive unease into our own naturalized relationships with media, whose success depends on our "inattention or 'blindness' to the media technologies themselves."[78] Second, such comparisons can expose the constructedness of each moment. Especially when attentive to the *differences* and noncorrespondences of historical contrasts, or the unsuccessful inventions or possible historical trajectories that media did *not* take. As Gitelman argues, "technologies that succeed exert a teleological tug," but a careful media history shows "technology as plural, decentered, indeterminate, as the reciprocal product of textual practices" rather than as a deterministic agent of change, or a necessary step towards the present.[79] Comparative media histories can decenter specific technologies, unsettle the dominant narratives by which the present understands itself, and potentially make space for alternatives. For these reasons, Gitelman has called for "a deeper history of sorts (there must be other such histories) for the digital humanities."[80] *Digital Victorians* endeavors to provide one.

This project joins such efforts already underway in media studies, literary studies, and DH itself. For example, Lee's book *Overwhelmed* explores the nineteenth-century's unsettled relationships between American literature and information "to expand our historical understanding of DH and the debates that surround it today."[81] Ongoing work by Mark Turner and Clare Pettitt tries to articulate a genealogy of the digital in nineteenth-century concepts of miscellaneity and seriality.[82] Yet even a "deeper history" may not go far enough to redress the disciplinary biases and contemporary exclusions that many suggest DH has helped institutionalize. Scholars stretching DH back to the nineteenth century—myself included—need to realize the risks of perpetuating the historical prejudices of that time frame into the digital "new world."[83] As Roopika Risam explains, such pronouncements can overlook "the histories and traditions of humanities knowledge production that have been deeply implicated in both colonialism and neocolonialism."[84] Pursuing "an expanded genealogy for the digital humanities," Adeline Koh and Dorothy Kim have published *Alternative Historiographies of the Digital Humanities*, which challenges not only its histories but who gets to frame them, and from what embodied, political, and institutional position.[85] Their volume collects important perspectives about Black, queer, global, multilingual, and indigenous versions of (or visions for) DH. The unease of the "digital humanities moment" includes debates about who writes its histories. I want to acknowledge these alternatives and, while not claiming them for my own, hope they have informed the arguments to follow. While I am using the Victorians to defamiliarize the digital present, this book also uses the present against that past, critiquing the Victorians' problematic yet persistent legacies, and noting how certain roads untaken might help expand DH as a field. To facilitate these transhistorical conversations, I turn to the strategic potential of anachronism.

Strategies of Presentism

Named for its structuring anachronism, *Digital Victorians* encourages its readers to think differently about each of these corresponding eras. But this gambit also comes with a few risks I want to acknowledge up front. The first is *parallelism*, or the willingness to see and identify connections just about anywhere—but without explaining the necessary, causal, or sufficient relations between them. As scholars, we excel at seeing patterns and connections, sometimes to the point of parody: "Professor Sees Parallels between Things, Other Things," says a banal yet biting headline in *The Onion*.[86] Perhaps we are constitutionally prone to apophenia, or finding patterns where none exist, in our desires to explicate the nuanced textures and submerged strata of human cultures.[87] Or, as Eve Sedgwick explained, we are acculturated to the "hermeneutics of suspicion" and "paranoid reading" whose risks are not simply being wrong, but rehearsing a critical gesture (these things = other things) at the expense of other reparative possibilities.[88] *The Onion*'s professor feels no need to answer the greatest of all critical questions: *so what?* What motivates those connections? Who does this help? And what about those other "other things" that could just as well align in parallel?

Parallelism's most familiar form may be *presentism*, which uses anachronism to make parallels between then and now. It answers "so what" with "because that's us!" Presentism comes in a variety of forms, from simply attempting to make the past relevant to uninterested parties, to the political inventions of scholars who emphasize the historical injustices that continue to structure the lived inequalities of marginalized communities. Advocates of presentism want their fields to respond to the urgencies of their own time. Skeptics tend to question whether it's an appropriate methodology for historical knowledge, "rushing to connect while forgetting to distinguish" all the contexts and complexities that do not easily transfer.[89] To privilege the present as a way of decoding history might also implicitly accept a teleology that our own age was always in the making. Especially among historians, presentism has traditionally been a bad word. As Miri Rubin writes, "the presentist is thus accused of being a confuser of categories, an offender whose crime is the historian's cardinal sin: anachronism."[90] In 2022, the president of the American Historical Association criticized presentism in his column in the AHA's newsletter—twenty years after a predecessor published a similar column, "Against Presentism," in 2002.[91]

Ironically, presentism is both an outdated problem and a new idea—whenever that happens to be. The "ism" synchronizes to the present moment of its own debates. Which is why we tend to find presentism debated at historical junctures that understand themselves as new. Almost by definition, new media has been an engine of presentist thinking, seeming neatly to distinguish breaks between technological eras. Mill's "age of transition" and awe-struck wonderment at nineteenth-century communications technologies announce the Victorians' own presentism. Just as statements about the "digital age" express ours. Of course, taking these statements at face value is a mistake: as Marvin warns, "our amnesia simply complements theirs."[92] We can learn from that complementary relationship instead, resisting "the notion that we live in a set of special and unique circumstances that our technology has created" by contrasting other historical circumstances when it also happened.[93] As Rubin suggests, "on occasion, a felicitous convergence between polemics of the past and modern sensibilities offers particular clarity."[94] New media presents just such an occasion: not to confirm its progressivist story, but to clarify how and why this story gets told. As a method, presentism allows for that comparison, but not necessarily to privilege our moment or accept claims about its uniqueness. Rather, such comparison might offer insights into how those claims emerged as well as grounds for their critique. If the new media encounter is marked by presentist thinking, a comparative approach to such encounters helps reveal their historicity. Sometimes, presentism can be useful, even strategic.

Rubin is among several historians interested in what she calls "presentism's useful anachronisms." We can accept the risks and even biases of anachronism and still use it in interesting and incisive ways. Perhaps we are always looking for ourselves in the past, but sometimes it shows unexpected differences as much as a familiar reflection. As Jay Clayton argues, anachronism is a two-way street: it can "establish a creative relationship with the received wisdom about a period" and "suggest intriguing perspectives on the contemporary world."[95] In other words, anachronism might warp the past, but it can also defamiliarize rather than validate the present. In doing so, it encourages critical habits of mind, or "thinking reflexively," as Catherine Hall argues, with the potential to reshape the contemporary:

> Embracing the possibility of thinking more critically, reflecting dialectically on the relation between past, present and future, probing the silences and absences in the archives, being self-conscious about the limitations imposed on us by the present we inhabit, engaging with a politics of changing the course of history by writing about it—that seems a kind of work worth doing.[96]

Presentism can be a political act. Debates over presentism are thus debates over the politics of a discipline and its "work," or whether historians should be "changing the course of history." James Sweet, then president of the AHA, quickly retracted his 2022 column after many scholars—especially scholars of color—objected to his dismissal of "contemporary social justice issues" as an appropriate historical framework.[97] As Christina Sharpe points out, these issues cannot be cordoned off from history or isolated within previous eras but form "the continuous and changing present of slavery's as yet unresolved unfolding." To grapple with that challenge, scholars like Sharpe are experimenting with "a method of encountering a past that is not past."[98] In these efforts, presentism has taken on a variety of strategic forms.

Victorian studies has long seen interest in the "afterlife" of the nineteenth century, including its historical legacies as well as its notion of historicity. As John Kucich and Dianne Sadoff argue, the Victorians share a "self-reflexive and periodizing temporality" with postmodernist thinking, a sense of historical rupture that has made the Victorian era attractive to adapt in our own.[99] In his related work on postmodernism, Clayton brought attention to anachronism as "an important but neglected form of historical experience" and as a scholarly method.[100] But perhaps it was not until the V21 Collective that presentism emerged as such for Victorianists, charged with political energies to confront contemporary crises. Among its points, V21's manifesto urged a new openness to *presentism*: an awareness that our interest in the period is motivated by certain features of our own moment. In finance, resource mining, globalization, imperialism, liberalism, and many other vectors, we are Victorian, inhabiting, advancing, and resisting the world they made.[101]

Members of the collective would further refine this approach as "strategic presentism," which seeks to spotlight nineteenth-century legacies (including climate catastrophe, imperial power, and racial prejudice) that continue to precipitate ecological and political crises. David Sweeney Coombs and Danielle Corialle announced in a 2016 forum on strategic presentism for *Victorian Studies* that "Now, more than ever, we need to be able to explain the importance of the nineteenth century for the twenty-first."[102] In 2020, Ronjaunee Chatterjee, Alicia Mireles Christoff, and Amy R. Wong extrapolated how that work must be done with self-conscious commitment to in/justice, connecting historical contexts to their exclusionary legacies in how Victorian studies is even practiced, affecting scholars and marginalized communities now. Confronting "a past that is not past" might mean changing the very disciplinary configurations of how we study it—or who that pronoun "we" includes or ignores.[103]

Seen this way, presentism does not triumphantly overwrite the past so much as cultivate a self-consciousness about how that past gets studied and mobilized. How did we get here? How does understanding this story help us change where we're going? Who tells the story from other viewpoints? Victorian studies as such might limit the answers we could explore. But perhaps, in its emerging forms, it can also help reshape our contemporary awareness. In an earlier discussion about "Globalizing Victorian Studies," Priya Joshi argued that we need not leave the "Victorian" behind so much as mobilize its preoccupations beyond the historical, geographical, and disciplinary conventions of its study. Joshi would renovate the term into "a set of interrelated cultural, intellectual, and social preoccupations" that recombine in its "contact zone" of global and historical encounters over the *longue durée*.[104] Presentism does not require a leap across the gulf of time: the Victorian, Joshi claims, is "a relationship that has developed *and gets reproduced* because it addresses preoccupations and practices of the moment."[105] We are reproducing it now, whether in a historian's snobby reactions to presentism or in enthusiastic proclamations of its justice. When the "Victorian" becomes what Joshi calls a "migratory practice," it also encourages scholars and students to interrogate all sorts of geographic, transhistorical, and interdisciplinary correspondences.[106] It offers a mobile heuristic to identify and analyze its configurations elsewhere. Including, perhaps, within what Sharon Marcus suggests are "historical eras yet to be named" that cross periods, geography, and language.[107]

In keeping with a period that generated significant ideas about historicism, scholars in nineteenth-century studies have been regenerating it in innovative forms. If Matthew Rowlinson urged Victorian studies to develop its own "theory of anachronism," we now have more than a few.[108] There are the "stereoscopic" historical methods of Andrew Piper, Roger Whitson's geological "deep nineteenth century," Clayton's postmodern afterlives, Lynda Nead's "pleated or crumpled time," the "problem of entangled times" noted by Dipesh Chakrabarty, Megan Ward's approach to the "historical middle," Caroline Levine's move "from the break to the loop," Devin Griffiths's "comparative historicism," the "queer historical touches" noted by Mary Mullen, the enduring "nineteenthcentricity" found by Buurma and Heffernan, Nathan Hensley's "discontinuous historicism," Wai Chi Dimock's "spectrum of affinities," Eleanor Courtemanche's "hinge points," the historical and geographical "intimacies" of Lisa Lowe, not to mention the strategic presentism of the V21 Collective.[109] Recently surveying the field of nineteenth-century studies, Adela Pinch noted that an "engaged presentism" seemed its most conspicuous trend.[110]

Presentism is the spirit of the age and a method for deepening its dialogue with the past. These critical approaches suggest a two-decades-long preoccupation in Victorian studies with the uncertain significance of our young century, running in parallel to the emergence of digital humanities but oriented toward earlier moments of challenge and change. *Digital Victorians* joins this conversation while adding other dimensions to it, especially the perspectives of media historians and communication scholars. Genealogies of media have pursued their own anachronisms, such as Hayles's "comparative media studies" or what Cronqvist and Hilgert theorize as "entangled media histories."[111] Each looks across media forms, geographical arenas, and historical periods to challenge the material, national, and temporal logics that have conventionally organized the interpretation of media. Media's historical entanglements might also challenge the disciplinary conventions of how it's studied. My version of "engaged presentism" thus reaches out to other fields also doing the work of comparative historicism, with lessons for how we understand its potentials in literary and cultural history.

Inspired by these varied approaches to presentism and transhistorical study, *Digital Victorians* entangles its two primary domains to intervene in each. Yes, this professor sees connections between things, other things. But the parallelisms and anachronisms of this book all endeavor to show different perspectives about its contributing contexts. Finding the digital in the Victorian reveals the surprisingly contemporary aspects of its historical media encounters—including some we recognize as well as differences we need to adapt. Conversely, claiming the Victorian for the digital historicizes the present, gives DH an alternate genealogy, and resists the amnesia of new media by showing its ancestry in the concepts, debates, and material legacies of the past. Is this important to do, or do now? I think so, especially in resisting an ideology of disruptive innovation by which "new" media erases its histories, material dependencies, and human consequences. And in asserting the critical value of literary studies in telling that story, about the past as well as the present.

• • •

In pursuit of these goals, the chapters to follow will oscillate between remote historical contexts, compare multiple forms of media, and trace the Victorians through the intervening frameworks that shape our access to and understanding of them. Each chapter brings examples past and present into a shared context, selected to reveal certain correspondences between them. The chapters' sequence illuminates the Victorians' emerging digital awareness and the interpretive methods and professional debates that followed. Taken together, they track the establishment of something like digital humanities in the nineteenth century, generalized as the relationship of writing, publishing, and reading to conspicuous changes in the Victorians' sociotechnical landscape, which I will describe in terms of media shift. At the same time, the chapters also show how Victorian concepts have been transmitted or regenerated in the context of "the digital age." This includes foundational ways of understanding digital im/materiality, the proliferation of information, and their effects on privacy, socialization, labor, and reading. Some of these concepts fall more into the purview of media studies than digital humanities proper—but using the Victorians to widen DH's purview is partly the point. The Victorians show us a broader range of humanistic engagements with the digital than "DH" comprises, and which it might need to take up, under whatever name. Other chapters engage the field directly, explaining how Victorian debates about literary writing and reading precipitate the methodological experiments and professional battles that defined DH in the public eye. In sum, the book traces the establishment of Victorian digitality, identifies its legacies in the present, and assesses the problems and opportunities of that strange inheritance.

In talking about the "present," this book does not necessarily mean *right now* (whenever that is for you, dear reader), but a recent era defining itself as such, largely compelled by the claims of new media. I do not take that technologizing present as a given but consider how it enables the negotiations of a new media moment, for which "the digital" or "our information age" or even "the internet" often becomes shorthand. In similar ways, the nineteenth century addressed its own new media moments often through specific technologies of telecommunications and recording whose implications were never so stable. As Gitelman suggests, "it is . . . a mistake to write broadly of 'the telephone,' 'the camera,' or 'the computer' as it is 'the media,' and of—now, somehow, 'the Internet' and 'the Web'—naturalizing or essentializing technologies as if they were unchanging."[112] For that reason, I do not track specific technologies back to their uncanny Victorian precursors but try to demonstrate corresponding moments in which their significance was negotiated. We might name that phenomenon in various ways, but "digital humanities" offers an especially useful metadiscourse in which to identify and analyze its workings. As its own historical phenomenon, DH brings the present into relief, attentive to its own declared newness. And though its boundaries are always in dispute—actually because of such dispute—it connects to Victorian concerns about the changing dimensions of writing, materiality, memory, and professional interpretive practice amid their own new media moments. Finally, as media history never exists outside of the media that transmit that history, even studying the Victorians means attending the transformations that frame our own access to those materials, which DH—in a tradition of textual studies—has well equipped scholars to do.

To tell this story, the chapters to follow appear in three sections. The first (chapters 1 and 2) establishes some general contexts for the "digital" situation in which Victorian writers found themselves. The second (chapters 3 and 4) explains how that changing media atmosphere precipitates concerns about literary composition, interpretive reading, and professional authorship, which still inform debates about DH. The final section (chapter 5 and the afterword) argues that the digitization of Victorian materials, seen in a long view, has determined the shape of academic organizations and their interpretive horizons. From nineteenth-century media contexts, to a prehistory of DH, to the ways digitization influences our materials and the questions we ask about the past: this book uses the digital to trace a historical arc from past to present. But these chapters will also move backward in time, using examples from the twentieth and twenty-first centuries to illuminate latent meanings in Victorian contexts and to demonstrate how Victorian ideas and materials have been regenerated in subsequent discourse about the impact of new media. So you can read *Digital Victorians* as a genealogy. You can also read it for the anachronisms that cast raking light across a media historical landscape, offering a different look at its ages of transition. However you read it, I hope its prehistories and provocations suggest ways of reconfiguring your own understanding of the digital age and its implications for the humanities.

Digital Victorians begins with the nineteenth-century origins of a pervasive myth about the digital: that it is somehow disembodied, or just an ethereal carrier of information that has "lost its body," as Hayles suggests.[113] Rather than countering this myth—now we tend to know better—chapter 1 explains its Victorian genesis in context of the "annihilation of space and time" of steam travel and telecommunications. This annihilation was not effected by technology but by an insistence on the human body to measure media's effects. Playing a major role in the consolidation of this myth was Thomas De Quincey, whose essay "The English Mail-coach" (1849) waxes nostalgic for preindustrial forms of messaging. Throughout the essay, De Quincey makes the affective body the measure of modern telecommunication networks, which become "alien" and unfeeling by contrast. That pattern persists across reactions to iconic nineteenth-century communications media. However, even in De Quincey's case, the disembodiment of information networks is balanced by a fascination with the material production of *print*, and a desire to market its innovations for readers. As I show with examples from newspapers, illustrated periodicals, and the distribution details of De Quincey's own essay from wheelbarrow to warehouse, "disintermediation" would ironically compete with Victorians' desire to celebrate the new production techniques and broad circulation of their texts.

What results is a dynamic between disembodiment and "infrastructuralism" that comes to pattern recent investigations of the internet—some of which take direct inspiration from nineteenth-century exemplars.[114] For instance, Neil Stephenson's famous essay "Mother Earth, Mother Board" and Andrew Blum's book *Tubes: A Journey to the Center of the Internet* each borrow specific Victorian tropes as well as conceptual frameworks in their efforts to comprehend the materiality of modern internet infrastructure. And yet, like their Victorian exemplars, they do not go far enough in addressing the politics of disintermediation. But other media scholars have suggested different ways of confronting the erasures of digital media and its infrastructures, which might offer, in turn, inspiration for returning to nineteenth-century media history on our own terms, rather than theirs. Like the nineteenth-century telegraph cables that laid future pathways for fiber optic networks, the Victorians' historical responses set an agenda for recent studies of the cloud, network infrastructure, and alienated digital labor, which still operates in the long shadow of the British empire.

The second chapter turns from the Victorians' emerging information networks to the resulting anxieties about hyperconnectivity and information overload within those networks. My opening case study is the "doxxing" of George Eliot, or the unwanted revelation of her pseudonymous identity, whose fuller consequences she explores in her gothic novella *The Lifted Veil*. In that story, Eliot considers how sympathy—arguably the keystone of her ambitions as a realist novelist—might depend on knowing relatively more or less about other people. With his uncanny omniscience and telepathy, the suffering narrator Latimer offers a cautionary tale that knowing more about people—even *everything* about them—paradoxically means sympathizing less. Critics have shown how Latimer becomes a metaphor about media at the time, but I expand these arguments to suggest how he anticipates the distributed surveillance of a data-driven culture. This context emerges even more clearly with the uncanny narrator of George du Maurier's novel *Peter Ibbetson*. A text about memory within hyperconnected networks, *Peter Ibbetson* draws on Victorian spiritual materialist theories to imagine the possibilities of remembering everything about one's life and environments, including what passes outside of focused attention. Then it goes further, envisioning the transfer of such accumulated memories from one person to another, forward and backward in time, in perpetuity.

Partly seduced by this promise, Peter Ibbetson is also anxious about a permanent memory that accumulates with his unwitting passage through the world, and over which he has no control. Together with Latimer, these Victorian narrators apprehend the psychological and ethical implications of a totalizing network. In response, they craft an ethics of forgetfulness that has persisted across intervening debates about privacy, attention, and sociability as reconfigured by twentieth- and twenty-first-century information networks. From Brandeis and Warren's landmark argument in "The Right to Privacy" to more contemporary arguments about information overload and the "right to be forgotten," Victorian writers established major throughlines in how we apprehend the consequences of memory technologies. They also model how we might ethically respond to them. I show how Victorian writers like Eliot have been (mis)appropriated in these debates and suggest what we might learn from them instead.

The material conditions of new media also shaped the conceptual horizon of what writers and readers did with their texts—a legacy we are actively seeing develop in humanities computing. In the subsequent two chapters, I argue that the literary history of nineteenth-century media sets the interpretive terms that DH rediscovers in computational methods, or which digital media claims as new. Chapter 3 traces the genealogy of a digital humanist sensibility within Victorian literary responses to connectivity, scale, and remediation. Quantitative literary stylistics, now better known as distant reading, developed in this same milieu, having been first proposed in an 1887 paper in *Science* magazine. Then as now, this approach was controversial, essentially dismissed as "counting words" by Henry James in his 1898 novella *In the Cage*. I use this story to situate debates about quantitative text analysis within a contest over predigital machine reading, rooted in late-century arguments over speed reading, literary stylistics, and gendered secretarial labor.

This offers, in part, a longer genealogy of distant reading that reaches back to the late 1800s. I join several scholars in reconsidering those origins, but I also suggest a different Victorian legacy reemerging in the predictive intelligence of machine learning. While James denigrates these capacities as characterized by the anonymous telegrapher of *In the Cage*, he ironically celebrates them in the guise of his favorite secretary, Theodora Bosanquet. When James turned to dictating his writing, Bosanquet proved exceptionally proficient in understanding his aims—to the point where, after James died, she continued transcribing his messages from the beyond. The chapter concludes with a different look at the "psychic secretarihood" of Bosanquet and her spiritual interest in automatic writing in the context of generative artificial intelligence.[115] Bosanquet's secretarial transcriptions, spiritual writings, and published scholarship on James—long dismissed by the field—raise a cluster of problems now returning with large language models. The Victorian legacy of machine learning helps shift the discourse of AI away from a superintelligent consciousness and toward the difficult questions about the authority, occluded labor, and collaborative possibilities of semiautomated writing that we have yet to resolve.

The book's final chapters extend the Victorian genealogy of DH into other modalities, looking beyond text to the audio, visual, and data forms that transmitted as well as transformed the materials and methods of literary studies over the twentieth century's historical gap. In this context, chapter 4 recasts Stevenson's *Strange Case of Dr Jekyll and Mr Hyde* as a nightmare of media obsolescence, anxious about its own potential transformations from a text into other forms. Ironically, these adaptations helped spread its fame: *Jekyll and Hyde* was among the first audiobooks ever recorded and was used to test other emerging media across the twentieth century, especially film. That makes sense, given the story's built-in fascinations with embodied transformations and its implicit questions about whether the medium changes the message—figured not only by the title characters, but by the forensic problem of Jekyll/Hyde's handwriting. As Stephen Arata and others have shown, it is a novel everywhere preoccupied with writing and its professional applications.[116] Yet a new dimension to those professional debates emerges more clearly in retrospect, as Jekyll turns writing into data and Hyde scribbles blasphemies across the sacred texts of their profession.

Jekyll and Hyde dramatizes the professional threats of media shift that have returned, in a familiar gothic guise, in prominent debates about the "dark side of digital humanities." We can find parallels between the novel and contemporary fears about the institutional transformation of DH as degenerative, data-driven, and hostile to professional norms. More interestingly, those debates adapt a late Victorian gothic genre to shift conversations about technology to spirited critiques of DH as a monstrous transformative force of neoliberalism in higher education. While a number of scholars have noted connections between nineteenth-century spiritualism and modern concepts of information and media, I suggest the surprising durability of Victorian genres and tropes in which spiritualism, the supernatural, and the gothic figured their relations to these concepts.[117] The long adaptation history of *Jekyll and Hyde*, from audiobooks to arguments at MLA, suggests how we have persistently adapted the Victorians to interrogate new media and its transformations of the humanities.

Moving from Victorian discursive legacies to databases of Victorian materials, chapter 5 tracks how Victorian texts and images were even transformed into data. By undertaking a media archaeology of a digital collection of Victorian newspapers, I recover a lost history of how they got to now, following the transmission of the British Museum's collection of nineteenth-century newspapers from bound library volumes through twentieth-century microfilming and then digitization. Looking at Victorian materials over the *longue durée* of their mediation reveals a surprising confederation of actors and institutions, well beyond Victorian sources or the scholars or public who use them. These materials were variously selected and processed by anxious museum officials, World War II intelligence agencies, wartime US cultural elites, microfilm companies, and, in their digitization phase, global IT services outsourced to India and Cambodia—all of whom affected source materials still marketed as "nineteenth-century British." These entanglements are mostly hidden yet inextricable from what we can know about the nineteenth-century past.

The long history of digitization also parallels the formation of Victorian studies as a field. While its origins are conventionally ascribed to the interdisciplinary ambitions of a group of scholars in the 1950s, I link the emergence of professional scholarly societies more specifically to the development of scholarly resource materials, including microfilm collections and the computerization of library records. Their availability exerts a strong historiographic influence on what and how scholars study, which extends through the uneven emergence of digitized materials today. As Buurma and Heffernan argue in *The Teaching Archive*, literary studies tends to narrate its history as a grand progression of intellectual movements, usually trickling down from elite institutions.[118] But the day-to-day materials and transactions of the profession can tell a different story. In the relationship of academic societies to scholarly resource materials, we find a wider array of participants and institutions who have shaped the discipline. In recognizing their contributions, we might also realize the extra-academic networks of editors, information workers, and library professionals who deserve their places in any discipline's purview.

If the introduction to this book grapples with its defining anachronism, the afterword reckons with its unavoidable limitations in writing about new media. As critics have suggested, the nineteenth-century's canonical legacy and racial exclusions have also persisted in the institutionalization of DH. We hardly need anachronism to find a digital Victorian mindset operating across the materials, methods, and institutional configurations of DH. In sketching DH's own problematic "nineteenthcentricity," I also suggest how its futures might follow a salutary pattern, in the postcolonial rupture and global expansion of its concerns. *Digital Victorians* proposes that a version of DH began in the nineteenth century: perhaps DH as such will "end" by leaving that formative mindset behind. We may already have reached the end of DH's new media moment, turning from its inaugural chapter to the next. What that will compass, and the relative usefulness of the nineteenth century in facing that future, remain open questions.

ONE

HOW THE INTERNET LOST (AND FOUND) ITS BODY

The Dream of Disintermediation from the
Mail Coach to Transoceanic Cables

... so much the roaring speed benights
All sense and recognition for a while;
A little space, a minute, a mile.
Then look again, how swift it journeys on—
Away, away, along the horizon,
Like drifted cloud, to its determined place;
Power, speed, and distance, melting into space.
  —H. R. "THE PASSING RAILWAY TRAIN" (1844)[1]

chug chug chug chug chug chug chug chug chug chug chug INTERNET!!!!!!!!

  —DREW FAIRWEATHER, "internet train" (2007)[2]

HOW DO WE GET FROM the nineteenth century to now? According to the webcomic *Married to the Sea*, we take the "internet train." As the steam engine chugs out of its shed, the whistle screams "INTERNET!!!!"—signaling where the railway and the nineteenth-century postal service (the train is a "USM[ail] Express") will ultimately arrive. This cartoon's sublimely dumb caption—"chug chug chug internet"—is wonderfully articulate about the disruptive rhetoric of these two linked eras. First, as the train departs in the nineteenth century and arrives, almost instantaneously, in the networked landscape of the twenty first, the comic collapses historical distance and replays Victorian awe at how steam travel would "annihilate time and space, and allow everybody to be everywhere at the same time!"[3] Fearful and celebratory versions of that statement circulated everywhere in response to the railway's cultural impact, seeming like nothing less than a reconfigured modernity. Second, the comic mocks the similar ways the internet has been celebrated with the rhetoric of breakthrough, disruption, and revolution. We accelerate all at once from a moderate "chug chug chug" to the ludicrous speed of "INTERNET!!!!!"—an unprecedented phenomenon, arriving with a shriek, displacing everything into "drifted cloud."

The "internet train" also makes a tidy satire of commentary that traces the epochal media shifts of the near present back to the nineteenth century—a project in which this book is also engaged. This was the dawning of the "tele-culture," as Nicholas Royle suggests, shaped by "forms of communication from a distance through new and often invisible channels, including the railway, telegraphy, photography, the telephone and gramophone."[4] Other writers make the connections explicit, fashioning this tele-culture as a precursor to our own, as in Standage's *The Victorian Internet*. The telegraph, he claims, was "the greatest revolution in communications since the development of the printing press," and "modern internet users are the heirs of the telegraphic tradition."[5] Or, as the science fiction writer Neal Stephenson similarly quips, "everything that has occurred in Silicon Valley in the last couple of decades also occurred in the 1850s."[6] Several historians and media historians effectively agree, tracing to the nineteenth century the emergence of a concept of networked information that seems "characteristic of our own age."[7] Put succinctly by Megan Ward, "the Victorians were the future."[8]

Chug chug chug internet. The "internet train" reminds us to take care in claiming analogies, connections, and genealogies that do not become cartoonish, losing nuance and difference in the process, or otherwise making arguments only validated by the degree to which they decode the present. Runaway presentism, you might call it. Ward's own scholarship models an alternative. She emphasizes the "historical middle," the flyover period ignored in some historical analogies, but which sets the conditions for the nineteenth century to become legible in informatic terms.[9] The problem of the "middle," like comic's "missing middle" joke, works on another level, too. "Middle" is the etymological root of "medium." As the "internet train" skips the historical middle, it also tells a story of medial erasure. It switches the history of media with the history of information. And it describes in capsule form "how information lost its body."[10]

The history of information, in a nutshell, recounts how communication came to separate messages from their material supports. Versions of this history are told by James Carey, Geoffrey Nunberg, James Gleick, John Durham Peters, and John Guillory, among others, all of whom point to nineteenth-century telecommunications media, from telegraphy to spiritualist mediums, as they unpick the stitching of medium and message.[11] N. Katherine Hayles and Gleick follow the story into twentieth-century cybernetics and information theory, which define information as a signal or a mathematical problem, independent of what it means or how materially transmitted. From there, it is a relatively short step from information packets to data, the transfer protocols of the internet, and the more recent atmospheric metaphor of the cloud. Of course, few of these scholars take that metamorphosis as a given, nor should we. Information always has material dimensions yet must seem to shed them to exist as such. We should ask, along with Hayles, "what had to be elided, suppressed, and forgotten to make information lose its body?"[12] What are the consequences of that erasure? How might we recover a sense of embodiment, digital materiality, or even the environmental dimensions of media? What does infrastructure reveal about networked media's claims of connectedness?

Researchers are addressing these questions from all sorts of disciplinary angles, including media history, critical infrastructure studies, history of the book, digital rhetoric, feminist computing history, and so on. These approaches can inspire methods in literary studies and, perhaps, benefit in turn from literary historical approaches, as this chapter will show. Information's disappearing act is not a property of communications technology. It is an effect of the discourse around communications technology in which journalistic writings and literary texts play vital roles. Literature, however you define it, does not stand outside media history, nor is literature merely conveyed through media like an inert substance. Rather, literature shapes the habits of mind and rhetorical frames by which technologies come to exist and function. The problems of disembodied information take their very shape amid nineteenth-century discourse about literary transmission and infrastructure. In fact, nineteenth-century literature is *still* shaping the ways we talk about new media, now in the form of the transoceanic internet.

This chapter locates an origin myth for the disembodiment of information in nineteenth-century reactions to landmark shifts in networked communications media, including the demise of the horse-drawn mail coach, its replacement by rail, the industrialization of print, and the transatlantic telegraph. If these technologies helped establish the sense of a modern information network, literary responses to those technologies built the frameworks for understanding them as such. Specifically, they establish the patterns of "disintermediation" in which information seems to lose material dimensions, in which the very conditions of communicating—agents, techniques, infrastructure, environments, global power—are erased. This, ultimately, is the poignant lesson of "internet train": the legacy of nineteenth-century media is not so much rapid networked communication as *erasure*. Or, at least, the shifts in attention away from the historical and material contingencies of media that continue to enable the virtualization of networks.

Interestingly, that does not happen simply by denying the body or ignoring the material. It paradoxically results from trying to understand telecommunications *through* the body—at least through normative bodies defined and delimited by the senses. What exceeds this framework becomes, as we shall see, "alien." Nineteenth-century discourse about physiology and transmission fails to apprehend materiality in nonhuman terms, producing the very ontological splits that much recent scholarship has endeavored to repair: between humans and things, agents and environments, media and ecology. Before those splits were fully accomplished, we see the dialectical stirrings of nineteenth-century media's self-awareness, as I show with examples from the periodical press—among the first domains of writing the teleculture transformed. On the cutting edge of change, nineteenth-century periodical media was caught between desires to celebrate its immediacy and to showcase its own transmission. It produced a dynamic of affective immediacy and bibliographic materiality—a nascent understanding of infrastructure that continues to inform how we study digitally networked media. Academic and popular negotiations of the internet as a cultural phenomenon have tried to balance claims of digital sublimation with critical studies of media infrastructure, understanding the emplacedness and asymmetrical consequences of a seemingly hyperconnected global village. Ultimately, I argue that discourse around nineteenth-century media offers an origin of the myth of disembodied information as well as an emerging counter discourse of what Peters calls "infrastructuralism."[13] Like the internet train arriving in the present, a mail coach carries us back to the past, arriving to discover surprisingly timely questions about how we understand new media as a phenomenon.

The Glory of Mediation

The information age, according to James Beniger, begins not with computers but with a crisis of "control" that followed the industrialization of communications and transport infrastructure in the early 1800s. Beniger's account of the "information society" is eccentric but useful in downplaying technological innovation in favor of the struggle to comprehend and socialize how technologies function.[14] Marvin makes a similar case: "The history of media is never more or less than the history of their uses [and] the social practices and conflicts they illuminate."[15] Those practices and conflicts come into sharp focus, Marvin argues, at moments when new communications technologies are introduced. This chapter considers a set of these "special historical occasions" as they provoke nineteenth-century writers to define, in their own terms, the significance of "new media."[16] As I will argue, they provide enduring conceptual frameworks that have been adopted to explain the internet.

The story begins with the mail coach. Or, rather, how the mail coach was reimagined after its functional replacement by the railway, bringing with it, as Beniger and Marvin would suggest, the disorientation of a new medium. As Ruth Livesey notes, writing about the antiquated stage coach became a trope during the railway's early decades, offering a way of pinpointing an otherwise massive cultural change: "nothing seemed to mark the division between the present and the past more than the coming of the railway and the passing of the stage coach."[17] As the stage coach carried mail as well as passengers, it also symbolized a concept of communication before networks.[18] Peters proposes that "technologies such as the telegraph and radio refitted the old term 'communication,' once used for any kind of physical transfer or transmission, into a new kind of quasi-physical connection across the obstacles of time and space."[19] The railway introduced similar conundrums, especially in how to understand its own "quasi-physical" experiences and its ever-reaching connections. In his pioneering study, Schivelbusch observes that "the railroad did not appear embedded in the space of the landscape the way coach and highway are, but seemed to strike its way through it."[20] As a result, the railway introduced "a kind of motion sickness," in Livesey's terms, disorienting people's relations to mobility, communication, and local and national belonging.[21] Seeking more stable ground on which to imagine that belonging, many writers returned to the mail coach.

The royal mail was an emblem of the horse-drawn stage coach system that carried the mail from 1784 to 1846, when the last coach route stopped, and mail service was entirely transferred to trains. As is well known, the 1840s in Britain were a decade of "railway mania": a financial bubble that saw the laying of thousands of miles of tracks, provoking obsessive coverage about the railway's transformative effects on British culture. Among the witnesses to those changes was Thomas De Quincey, who had earlier established fame as a Romantic-era writer, including his *Confessions of an English Opium-Eater* published in 1821. But almost thirty years later, he wrote a two-part essay for *Blackwood's Edinburgh Magazine* called "The English Mail-Coach, or the Glory of Motion" with its follow-up "The Vision of Sudden Death." Appearing in 1849, "The English Mail-Coach" takes a decidedly backward view to De Quincey's younger days, the political climate of the Napoleonic wars, and the mail coach system that had since ceded to steam-powered postal and passenger trains. Like other writers lamenting the stage coach, De Quincey is nostalgic not just for horse-drawn travel but for a whole way of life. In defiance of the railway's changes, the essay makes a reactionary argument about what connects people: to each other, to distant persons and news, and to national identity. De Quincey reimagines the mail coach as a spectacle of English power sent out to English subjects, or as a politicized communications medium.

Scholars like Mary Favret observe that De Quincey is "obsessed with channels of communication" at the very moment those channels were experiencing industrial-scale changes, switching to steam-powered and electric networks.[22] That's how I read the essay, too, but less as it reports on those changes than as it defines them. "The English Mail-Coach" works to reshape perceptions of communication at midcentury, helping to consolidate early ideas about networked information as such. De Quincey does so by complaining about the railway:

> The modern modes of travelling cannot compare with the mail-coach system in grandeur and power. They boast of more velocity, but not however as a consciousness, but as a fact of our lifeless knowledge, resting upon *alien* evidence: as, for instance, because somebody *says* that we have gone fifty miles in the hour, or upon the evidence of a result, as that actually we find ourselves in York four hours after leaving London.[23]

The modern modes of railway travel are "lifeless" and "alien." Their significance has to be explained rather than experienced. In later versions of his essay, De Quincey added language in case we missed the point: "we are far from feeling [railway travel] as a personal experience." This would come as news to actual passengers on the early Victorian railway, as they felt every violent bump on the iron road; they would know viscerally from the smoke, noise, and turbulence that it impacted the body. Victorian physicians would soon diagnose conditions like "railway spine" and neurasthenia that blamed the sensations of railway travel for physical maladies.[24] However, De Quincey reframes those intense physical experiences as alien and unintelligible. The railway conveys a physical experience that *does not communicate.*

As in this chapter's epigraph from "The Passing Railway Train," the modern passenger draws a blank during travel, as "the roaring speed benights / All sense and recognition for a while." Like the "unconscious" velocity that De Quincey describes in the "modern modes of travelling," the traveler loses their senses—and with them any intermediary experiences. Gone are their embodied relations to the carrier. By contrast, De Quincey celebrates the mail coach for its heart-pounding vitality:

> The vital experience of the glad animal sensibilities made doubts impossible on the question of our speed; we heard our speed, we saw it, we felt it as a thrilling; and this speed was not the product of blind insensate agencies, that had no sympathy to give, but was incarnated in the fiery eyeballs of an animal. (491)

The passage is saturated with feeling, the sensate, the incarnate. At every turn, the body resonates with the ride. The mail coach galvanizes feelings from grandeur to erotic encounter to deathly terror, which all become subsequent episodes in De Quincey's essay. Compared to the "alien evidence" of railway travel, De Quincey proves the "glory of motion" with the evidence of his affected body and the synesthesia of his prose.

As Marvin argues, the body furnished one the most significant arenas for negotiating the social impact of nineteenth-century communications technologies.[25] In the time since Marvin's book, scholars have expanded our understanding of the social life of bodies in terms of affect, describing the emotions, shared feelings, and the cultural and political work they do. Susan Zieger puts affect at the center of the nineteenth century's debates about its media and the communities it summons: "affect demarcates that friction . . . that results when a new mass medium repositions individuals in relation to the social."[26] Seen this way, De Quincey's essay is hardly old-fashioned, but entirely engaged with midcentury questions about the consequences of media shift, about the politics and character of Victorian connectivity. For De Quincey, affect resolves the problem of how things are connected. "The English Mail-Coach" celebrates the larger "mail-coach system," linking a passenger's consciousness of travel with "the conscious presence of a central intellect" invisibly orchestrating the unruly whole:

> To my own feeling, this Post-Office service recalled some mighty orchestra, where a thousand instruments, all disregarding each other, and so far in danger of discord, yet all obedient as slaves to the supreme baton of some great leader, terminate in a perfection of harmony like that of heart, veins, and arteries, in a healthy animal organisation. (485–86)

The feeling body, for De Quincey, is also the body politic. De Quincey's conservative political nostalgia attempts to bind humans to state power at the moment that emerging communication networks have unsettled their relations—the "danger of discord." And his chosen vehicle for doing so is affect. It elides his "own feeling" with healthy bodily harmony and supreme political control. It mediates between conductor and orchestra, between the system and any individual vehicle plying its route: "the intervening links that connected them . . . were the heart of man and its electric thrillings."[27]

Readers in 1849, increasingly familiar with the domestic telegraph, would spot the paradox of celebrating the antiquated mail coach for its "electric thrillings." Naturally, De Quincey is drawing from a Romantic-era discourse of organicism and electricity that also animated *Frankenstein*. As Jason Rudy explains, Victorians would increasingly translate these Romantic sensibilities into sensory analogies, including poets who hoped their texts would literally make readers feel. While this may have had "radical political implications," the physiological approach to communication also had negative consequences, including the erasure of communications infrastructure.[28] When De Quincey claims electricity as a function of human emotion, he evacuates the telegraph and the railway of any connection to the lifeworld. For De Quincey, a medium must not just connect, but affect its parties—which "the new system of travelling" conspicuously fails to do:

> iron tubes and boilers have disconnected man's heart from the ministers of his locomotion ... The galvanic cycle is broken up for ever; man's imperial nature no longer sends itself forward through the electric sensibility of the horse; the inter-agencies are gone in the mode of communication between the horse and his master. (492)

De Quincey defines any "mode of communication" by the "inter-agencies" it can or cannot generate. He defines those connections as an "electric sensibility" or the affective experience of the "galvanic cycle." As in the earlier quotation, De Quincey frames his imperial communications network as a set of "intervening links" that we can feel and invalidates the unfeeling materials of "iron tubes and boilers." The essay shows a pattern of infrastructural erasure that ironically recurs in celebrations of the very technologies De Quincey critiques.

Hardly a nostalgic look at the past, "The English Mail-Coach" exemplifies an increasingly Victorian understanding of media, in at least two senses. First, De Quincey seems to celebrate the organic body compared to the alien mechanisms of modern communication. But this move has the opposite effect. De Quincey recovers the body only as an organic machine, subordinate to what it feels or transmits. Just as for spiritualist mediums later in the century, the body instead becomes a passive conduit for the intangible, whether the spirit world or the realm of affect. Peters marks this as a turning point in the history of communication: when "the bodies of the communicants no longer hold the incontrovertible tokens of individuality or personality.... Communication has become disembodied."[29] For all of De Quincey's emphasis on feeling, he too describes the autonomous body as merely the medium for imperial affect. Second, De Quincey tries to reclaim electricity as something that can be felt and experienced; he tries to shift an understanding of communication to the scale of what humans perceive. But in doing so, De Quincey already stacks the deck. He abandons any attempt to understand the embodiment of communication in other terms—especially nonhuman terms. If the materiality of the medium can only be understood if we see, touch, taste it, we have introduced physiological and anthropocentric biases that make telecommunications media seem alien, other, "quasi-physical" or beyond bodies, like the creature whose eloquence we understand but whose monstrous form we shun. And that estrangement will only grow.

Feeling Machines

The rhetorical patterns of "The English Mail-Coach" can also be found in other notable responses to shifts in the nineteenth-century discourse network—even for writers who are as boosterish as De Quincey seems pessimistic. Consider a few signature announcements from *The Times* as it marked major changes in its infrastructure. As they industrialized, newspapers tried to distinguish themselves in a crowded field by celebrating their own technical accomplishments, whether in terms of printing speeds, copies printed, machines used, images made, or distances traveled. Yet even when showcasing their own production, newspapers mystified these processes for readers. An inaugural example appears in *The Times*'s editorial on Tuesday, November 29, 1814—the morning of its first printing on a steam-powered Koenig press. In aggrandizing style, *The Times* declared the steam press "the greatest improvement connected with printing, since the discovery of the art itself."[30] In claiming this epochal shift in printing, *The Times* weirdly celebrates its new "system of machinery almost organic." De Quincey, in his critique of mechanization, celebrates the vitalism of human and animal systems as well as their resonance with a distant intellect. Oddly, so does *The Times*, struggling through paradoxes to glorify an organic machine that seems driven by an "unconscious agent." *The Times* shifts the labor of printing and its organic agency from humans to the steam press. That mystification also covers the fact that, the previous night, *The Times* laid off dozens of its production staff whose jobs the steam press had taken.

The Times's biomechanical rhetoric follows a pattern in how the century's major developments in telecommunications infrastructure were celebrated. As Marvin suggests, people try to assimilate unfamiliar media using the scale of what they already intimately know. As a consequence, they *dis*embody what seems not to fit and conclude that new media happens in another realm. The transatlantic telegraph cable carried these freighted expectations during the 1860s, as writers try to understand new communications technologies through the body. *The Times*'s strange biomorphic fascination appears again in its coverage of the completed 1866 transatlantic cable. (The first cable laid in 1858 quickly failed.) What fascinates this journalist is "that so slight a thing should be pregnant with such results." Contrasting with the grandeur of engineering marvels, the transatlantic cable seems but a string in which "the life of the New and the Old World was pulsating to and fro." From this language of pregnancy and living pulsation, this writer builds a remarkable argument about the wonders of electricity:

> It appears a better imitation of the works of nature than men can generally produce. For a very great result we usually employ some stupendous machinery, whereas nature in the tiniest seed is pregnant with the largest tree, and a spark is sufficient to destroy an arsenal. The whole subject of electricity is an extraordinary revelation of this slight and yet gigantic agency. We are apt to think that the causes of what we see must be near at hand and tangible; but with the present subject before us we obtain a new idea of the infinite possibilities of natural influences. When we see a mirror wavering and flashing in a little room in Ireland, what imagination would ever have dreamt that the movement

was caused by a slight and silent operation on the shores of Newfoundland? You might lay bare that tiny wire and watch it, but you would see nothing and feel nothing.[31]

The telegraphic wire bridges not only previously divided continents but the ontological categories of the natural and engineered worlds, heard in the passage's antiphonies of exploding arsenals and silent wires, stupendous machinery and tiny seeds. With the submarine telegraph, we seem to be in a different realm, the domain of a "slight and yet gigantic agency." The writer then tries to look for this mysterious agency, hoping to present firsthand evidence of what exceeds our imagination and even our vocabulary. In an act of media vivisection, they propose to see for themselves. Yet "lay bare that tiny wire," and you would "see nothing and feel nothing" but wonder. The substance and causality of the telegraph disappears, as if "nothing" connects Ireland and Newfoundland, as if telegraphic messages travel without the friction of our sensory knowledge. The telegraph seems less a phenomenon of human infrastructure than an "imitation of the works of nature," an invisible thread dissolving in the waves.

This journalist plays the same sleight of hand as De Quincey. Again, De Quincey was pessimistic about modern modes of communication while *The Times* is positively aglow. But regardless of the technology or their attitudes, they both make the same rhetorical moves. They each create biomorphic hybrids; they idealize a connective technology; they naturalize its functions; and they make alien or unknowable those dimensions that exceed what we can see and feel. In each case, we're left with a fantasy about frictionless mediation, about the sublime transmission of messages. The legacy of the transatlantic cable does not celebrate the linking of Kerry, Ireland, to Trinity Bay, Newfoundland. It celebrates the connection of London and New York, annihilating the intermediary places, operators, machinery, and subaltern perspectives outside of this metropolitan ideal.

Illustrated newspapers played the same game. In the early nineteenth century, they made legion the inexpensive printed image, tantamount to what Patricia Anderson calls "the first medium of regular, ongoing, mass communication."[32] This transformation of images into a "mass" phenomenon depends in part on the industrial scale of printing, in part on the shared imaginary that critics like Benedict Anderson have credited to the newspaper.[33] That shared imaginary, in turn, depends on erasing as many mediating factors as possible between readers and contents. Listen to how the *Illustrated London News* (*ILN*) announced, in its very first issue, the significance of the "vast revolution" in industrial image making: "It has converted blocks into wisdom, and given wings and spirit to ponderous and senseless wood."[34] The *ILN* describes a particular reprographic process of end-grain woodblock engraving with the full force of dematerialization: from block to wisdom, from wood to winged spirit. The erasure of processes and materials allows the paper to metamorphose into new media, seen in the *ILN*'s grandest claim about what it delivers: "The public will have henceforth under their glance, and within their grasp, the very form and presence of events as they transpire, in all their substantial reality, and with evidence visible as well as circumstantial." As the mediating factors of wood, graver, ink, paper, and distribution disappear, the *ILN* substitutes its illustrated representations as having "form and presence," things you can see and grasp.

These scenes—from De Quincey, *The Times*, the *ILN*—all helped to stage the great disappearing act of the nineteenth century's new media, as it exchanged mediation for mimesis. Media studies scholars offer some useful keywords for this phenomenon. For Jay Bolter and Richard Grusin, any new medium strives for *immediacy*, less in the sense of "right now" than in the negation of mediacy, or the erasure of any intervening middle within a communications circuit. As they argue, that quest only ever produces its opposite, *hypermediacy*, in which the operations of a medium become visible, even quaint.[35] Other scholars have proposed the term *disintermediation* to focus on the cultural work required to effect that erasure. In other words, the actual newspapers from *The Times* or the *ILN* may not seem any more immediate than their precursors, but both papers work hard to promote that concept, drawing from a repertoire of representational and affective techniques. According to Liz Losh and others, the project of disintermediation has uneven consequences for social actors, privileging an understanding of agentless communication that not only erases human labor but denigrates the gendered labor of intermediation in other contexts, too.[36] Feminist studies of communication history have worked to recover these erased actors from nineteenth-century telephone and telegraph network operators to twentieth-century computing staff. Studies of infrastructure and logistics also attempt to restore the hidden dimensions of media's history, in part by moving beyond "subject-centered humanism" and toward "hybrid assemblages and technical networks."[37] But, in many cases, we hardly have to dig to find the material networks that disintermediation occludes. For a number of nineteenth-century newspaper writers, editors, and illustrators, the curious and sometimes spectacular details of mediation were their papers' biggest stories.

The Operational Aesthetic of the News

Perhaps no other engine of nineteenth-century media did as much as the newspaper to drive the myth of disembodied information as well as to showcase its own logistics and production. That performance played again and again as nineteenth-century periodicals celebrated their medial breakthroughs. The patterns of disintermediation are certainly legible in terms of Marxist critique, offering examples of how capital would obscure the conditions of its own production and fetishize information as a commodity on its own. However, newspapers created the commodity value of information by making a show of how they printed and distributed their goods. If newspapers obscured some aspects of their production in economic terms, they celebrated the materials, machines, and movement as part of what was new about news. Turning the newspaper into a commodity also meant showcasing to readers how it was made.

Four years before "The English Mail-Coach," the *Illustrated London News* published its ironic counterpart, "The Post Office Van," including a poem, statistics about its production costs, and a two-column illustration, all celebrating the *ILN* as a multifaceted spectacle of dis-

HOW THE INTERNET LOST (AND FOUND) ITS BODY   47

THE POST OFFICE VAN, CALLING AT THE OFFICE OF THE ILLUSTRATED LONDON NEWS.

FIGURE 1. "The Post Office Van, Calling at the Office of the *Illustrated London News.*" Source: *Illustrated London News,* January 18, 1845, p. 48.

tribution.[38] "The Post Office Van" was just part of the *ILN*'s continuing coverage of itself, from the brazen self-importance of its very first editorial to its regular illustrations and articles about its printing machines, illustration processes, and news gathering. Even while the *ILN* claims to transmute "senseless wood" into "wisdom," it cannot help showcasing to readers its own material processes for doing so. What looks like a contradiction shows the uncertainty of how "new media" in nineteenth-century Britain would be understood. The dialectic of new media had not resolved into the models that critics like Bolter and Grusin apply to digital change. Instead, the newspaper press shows the contest among discourses of mediation, or the blend of what now seem like incommensurate ideas. As Gitelman suggests, "dematerialization exists only in keeping with its opposite."[39] The newspaper press contributed simultaneously to the disembodiment myth and the spectacle of hypermediacy. Accepting its legacy only in terms of disembodiment, we miss the opportunity to reconsider the vital importance of the spectacle of hypermediacy, a missing history of embodied information that is crucial to understanding the digital age.

In its most materially self-conscious productions, the nineteenth-century newspaper press hosted a counterdiscourse to how information lost its body. Articles and illustrations about "press infrastructure" abounded, responding to and feeding "a fascination with how papers were made, how they travelled, and what they could do."[40] Alison Hedley sees these efforts as a distinct genre in the nineteenth-century periodical press, cultivating a reflexive media literacy by "equipping readers to view the magazine they were reading as an instantiation of the material history it documented."[41] In *Knowing Books*, Christina Lupton makes a similar argument about self-reflexive literature in the eighteenth century—texts that ironically referred to their own material status or contingencies of production and circulation.[42] But the expanding information networks of the nineteenth century made it harder to relate printed things to their complex origins. As Nicola Kirkby points out, industrialized textual media was "difficult to accommodate to existing literary and artistic forms," and the concept of "infrastructure" was yet undefined.[43] This very challenge would produce new forms of representing print. As among the first domains of communication it transformed, the periodical press was integral in defining the Victorians' "infrastructural imaginary."

That term comes from media scholar Lisa Parks, who argues that such representations offer "ways of thinking about what infrastructures are, where they are located, who controls them, and what they do."[44] Analyzing examples of such an imaginary can help encourage an "infrastructural disposition" in studies of media now, especially as such systems are moved out of sight or become difficult to perceive.[45] Parks's historical examples include two short films made in 1903 of mail sorting systems in a Washington, DC, postal center: "Throwing Mail Into Bags" and "Carriers at Work."[46] These films bring quotidian processes from behind the scenes right into the spotlight. In the nineteenth century, periodicals like the *ILN* were doing the same thing, making a spectacle of their own production processes and addressing their reader as what Parks calls "a citizen of infrastructure."[47] Like De Quincey's efforts to subordinate English subjects to the power of a central mail network, these productions bring the reader into their communications circuit, supplementing the difficulty of knowing the system with consumable representations of it. They offer what Lai-Tze Fan describes as a "literature of disembodiment," presenting a surrogate sensory encounter with the modern modes of industrially printed text and image.[48]

The example of the *ILN*'s "Post Office Van" shows the Victorian infrastructural imaginary at work, envisioning how a newspaper and reader interact. The illustration depicts a human chain as men heave immensely heavy bundles from the *ILN*'s Strand offices to a curbside carriage. Two horses, black and white, wait eagerly to depart while a small crowd watches the scene of the newspapers' delivery to the post office. The *ILN* would use such a composition again, as when depicting its own printing machines in action at the Great Exhibition with crowds watching behind.[49] Notably, these illustrations capture a live moment of their own production and distribution, supplementing the annihilation of a modern medium with action shots of its missing middle. A diagram of the printing press would hardly have the same effect. The *ILN* wants more than to elucidate its material processes: it wants those processes to carry an affective charge.

"The Post Office Van" depicts bundles of the *ILN* ready for distribution. Readers are invited to imagine their very paper as among those bundles. That January 18, 1845, issue contains the usual surfeit of domestic and foreign intelligence, coverage of winter assizes, and the issue's biggest story of "The Queen's Visit to the Duke of Buckingham, at Stowe," accompanied by an illustration of a triumphal yet still empty decorated archway, surrounded by crowds, waiting for the passing of a carriage. The royal carriage arrives on the next page with two illustrations of a decorated arch at the entrance to Buckingham. A few pages later, two more illustrations capture the Queen, still in her carriage, receiving a mace and then departing past waving crowds and an official bandstand. On the next page, the carriage steers through "The Grand Arch at Stowe" and then past the front of the Duke's mansion. The carriage's transit visually dominates the issue, page by page, from its anticipated arrival to its intermediary stops to its destination at Stowe. Yet on the issue's closing page, we find the *ILN*'s "Post Office Van" just above the newspaper's colophon with its office address. The Queen's carriage delivered her to Stowe, but the *ILN*'s "Post Office Van" brought the spectacle to even greater crowds. Seen this way, the postal carriage completes the same affective circuit as De Quincey's "English Mail-Coach," conveying national glory through the streets and making a show of its own vehicle. In this case, the vehicle is not the royal carriage so much as the newspaper itself.

Parading the news may have reached its peak with W. H. Smith & Sons. Famous for its string of railway bookstalls, W. H. Smith played an enormous role in the distribution of newspapers and their association with the railway network. Thomas Smits relays a story of how Smith's influence depended on the company's ability to put on a show. In January 1847, William Henry Smith Jr. planned a stunt to promote the company's reach and rapidity in delivering the news—specifically, about the Queen's speech to open the parliamentary year.[50] Smith saw an opportunity to connect news of national interest to the company's own pretensions as a distribution network, reaching from urban centers deep into English provinces. The newly incorporated Electric Telegraph Company—later the Press Association—would also coordinate coverage of a royal speech later that year. But Smith's success depended on the social factors of distribution as much as a technological backbone. Furthermore, Smith had to underscore the significance of its connectedness, turning its distribution of the Queen's speech into a media event.

Smith, along with eager newspaper editors, made the printing and delivery of the Queen's speech the day's major story. Newspaper articles detailed how "the whole apparatus, human and magnetic, set to work."[51] With fair copy of the Queen's speech in hand, Smith himself took to the rails, heading to Rugby as one of the trunk lines for telegraphs heading north. Upon his arrival, telegraph agents furiously transmitted the message to other regional newspaper offices for printing. Smith carried the printed papers farther north, riding along in an express train, and effectively racing the "normal delivery of London newspapers by the postal system."[52] Winning would glorify his own distribution network, which the company always worked hard to make conspicuous. As Graham Law explains, Smith "employed a fleet of distinctive red carts to ferry parcels of papers in time for early morning trains, hiring special locomotives if the occasion demanded."[53] And so the arrival of the Queen's speech by newspaper was fairly eclipsed by the spectacle of Smith's delivery. The *Bradford Observer* reported that "her Majesty's Speech was distributed from Land's End to John o'Groat's, anticipating by a considerable interval all the ordinary vehicles of information."[54] Riding the express, wheeling out the red carts, Smith called people's attention to the extraordinary vehicles of delivering the news. The Queen's speech, exciting as it may (or not) have been, was entirely eclipsed by the papers carrying its transcript. The *Morning Post* reported that people in Liverpool were "electrified, *not by the telegraph*, but by the *actual* arrival of the *Morning Post* shortly after ten o' clock."[55]

Smits uses the story of the Queen's speech to claim that national news was not merely a telegraphic or technological phenomenon, as scholars sometimes claim. In fact, the story emphasizes the opposite of telegraphic disembodiment: the papers, vehicles, and geographic traverse all reinforce readers' sense of broader connectedness. In the quotation above, the unlikely presence of the physical paper electrifies its readers. The *Morning Post*, like the W. H. Smith Company, like *The Times* and the *Illustrated London News*, all insisted that readers recognize the material history and delivery infrastructure that made them unique. Furthermore, like De Quincey, they hitched their vehicles to a sense of wonderment and just as often political glory. Even telegraphic information has a glorious body, as Smith was at pains to show. Yet ultimately the newspapers were victims of their own success. Smits claims that, within a decade, "the fast distribution of news was no longer news."[56] While self-reflexive stories about news infrastructure or materiality would not entirely disappear, they ceded to another lasting narrative about "an age of information" as such.[57]

So declared *The Times* in 1853, offering a choice quotation for information histories that accept the claim on its own terms, or that foreground ephemerality, mass distribution, and tit-bits of reprintable information as the hallmarks of the nineteenth-century press. But this argument already accepts a sublimation that had not—and still has not—occurred. As Marvin asserts, "There is no form of communication that does not require the body's engagement."[58] Yet the story of disembodiment is so powerful, so validating to a present perspective, as to sweep away the details of intermediation—even for scholars historically attuned. For instance, in a handbook to the nineteenth-century press, an otherwise superb discussion of periodical distribution succumbs to the myth of the informational sublime:

> The electric telegraph revolutionized the transmission of urgent intelligence, allowing newspapers to almost instantly report events occurring on the other side of the country, the continent, and finally the globe. For the first time, *long-distance communication could [travel] along paths independent of physical transportation* and at far great[er] speed, though land telegraph lines inevitably tended to follow railway tracks and submarine cables to track shipping lanes.[59]

Revolution and disintermediation make such compelling narratives as to make scholars hide or overlook what—even in this passage!—lies in plain sight: communication is never "independent of physical transportation" but depends on physical infrastructure and gets shaped by the geopolitical asymmetry of places otherwise subsumed by the "globe." The challenge for media history is to move beyond the frameworks for understanding communications that nineteenth-century writers largely defined. We need to develop the disposition to the infrastructures, materials, and environments the Victorians conspired to erase.

News Paper; or, The Mail Coach Is Not the Message

What might an essay like "The English Mail-Coach" look like with these perspectives in mind? Contrary to its own claims of disembodiment, how does the essay itself manifest materially? As a text about the channels of communication, how does it circulate through them in print? Materially minded studies of literature or critical bibliography might offer a bridge to the salutary research on infrastructure within media studies. Certainly critics of "The English Mail-Coach" have not lacked attention to the essay's ideas about mediation. John Plotz, Anne Frey, and Andrew Franta each find in the mail coach a metaphor for Victorian attitudes about crowds, national publics, imperial power, and publication—all dimensions of a changing discourse network at midcentury.[60] These critics argue that De Quincey wants to idealize a "system" and its administration more generally, which locates "The English Mail-Coach" within recent discussions of Victorian networks and "the effects of nineteenth-century connectivity," in Kate Thomas's phrase.[61] Yet in reading "The English Mail-Coach" for the media systems it imagines, such criticism may actually aid De Quincey's project to disembody Victorian media by overlooking its infrastructure. While "The English Mail-Coach" certainly delivers insights about Victorian systems and networks, in making those conclusions we should not perpetuate De Quincey's own story about the abstraction of information from a previously embodied state—a story we have inherited as the very language of new media. My claim is not that scholars have ignored materiality or embodiment, but that we need to insist on the materiality of *text* and the embodiment of the very medium—print periodicals—of De Quincey's major cultural transactions.

If De Quincey's essay seeps with nostalgia about a Romantic-era vehicle, that vehicle is not the mail coach but *Blackwood's Edinburgh Magazine*.[62] *Blackwood's* or "Maga" was among the most prominent titles that shaped periodical culture at the century's outset but was much diminished by the 1840s. As a writer, De Quincey was a magazinist and active participant in the periodical culture that so strongly defined early nineteenth-century intellectual life.[63] As such, he had a front-row seat for the drastic evolution of periodical media during the years

1820 to 1850, as monthlies like *Blackwood's* took over from the august quarterlies, which were themselves challenged by weeklies like *Chambers's Edinburgh Journal* and newspapers of even greater frequency and diverse, even multimodal, formats. Thomas Carlyle underscored the challenge for authors to adapt to this fragmenting publishing market, complaining in an 1832 letter that "One *has* no right vehicle: you must throw your ware into one of those dog's-meat carts, such as travel the public streets, and get it sold there."[64] "Vehicle" is an apt word here, implying message delivery and distribution technology. In essays like "Travelling in England in Old Days" as well as "The English Mail-Coach," De Quincey fantasizes about perfect communication while still needing to publish. Carlyle reminds us that vehicles of print, like those vehicles plying the macadam and iron roads, were undergoing considerable changes in kind.

As De Quincey writes about a vehicle to bridge "vast distances," communicate with distant parts of the country, and assert "the conscious presence of a central intellect," he is also writing about periodical media in transition, adapting to the geotemporal horizons of Victorian publishing (485). The essay not only appears within *Blackwood's Edinburgh Magazine*: De Quincey makes the mail coach into an analogy for the magazine itself. *Blackwood's* was inaugurated in 1817 as a resolutely Tory enterprise and maintained a reputation for holding the party line. The magazine's founder and first editor, William Blackwood, demanded political allegiance from his writers, and De Quincey was always eager to please, tailoring his opinions whenever necessary.[65] Writers were furthermore subsumed into the magazine as it did not openly credit its authors. Even after trends shifted in magazine publishing to use bylines, *Blackwood's* was among the holdouts for anonymity, effectively presenting its content as a singly named entity, governed by a strong editorial hand. Matched with the ambitious claims of its distribution—since its inception, *Blackwood's* claimed on its title pages to be "sold by all the booksellers in the United Kingdom"—it invites comparison to De Quincey's mail coach system for being centrally governed, politically conservative, widely distributed, and a corporate entity in which De Quincey becomes happily subsumed.

As Frey claims, "On the outside of the coach, [De Quincey] becomes not merely a passenger, but actually part of the medium that conveys information to the people along the coach's route."⁶⁶ But that medium is insistently textual, even when considering De Quincey's attempts to disavow the mediation of print—and newspapers in particular.⁶⁷ Near the end of the first installment, newspapers facilitate two of De Quincey's emotional encounters with grieving women. In the second, more extended one, he details the victorious battle in which an anxious mother's son was involved: "The sight of my newspaper it was that had drawn her attention upon myself" (499). Hoping she'll share in the revel of victory, he withholds the news that her son's regiment was decimated, leaving that tragedy for tomorrow's papers to divulge. In the other instance, De Quincey asks the coach's guard to throw a newspaper—the evening "*Courier*," most likely London's *Courier and Evening Gazette*—into a passing carriage, folded to emphasize the headline "GLORIOUS VICTORY" (499). Even while De Quincey sneers at the "blind insensate agencies" of steam-powered news transmission, he plays paperboy on a coach whose one-eyed driver would later fall asleep at the reins (491).⁶⁸ Time and again, De Quincey downplays printed news in favor of the "ensigns of triumph" and phantasmagoric sensations of the mail coach itself, but his role as "part of the medium that conveys information" (as Frey suggests) cannot be separated from its textual conveyances or their industrial metamorphoses.

De Quincey's disavowal of newspapers needs to be qualified: he had actually been the editor of one, serving between 1818 and 1819 as the idiosyncratic head of the *Westmoreland Gazette*. Intending to shape it into a "right vehicle" for publishing, De Quincey planned to revise its coverage so that court reports and news shared space with German philology, statistics, essays, and literature in translation.⁶⁹ Shortly after he was fired, De Quincey received an invitation from *Blackwood's* to become a contributor and strangely judged himself to be that suffering magazine's only hope, supposing he should write entire issues himself.⁷⁰ De Quincey wanted to make his newspaper more like *Blackwood's* and make *Blackwood's* more like a book, but he discovered in his itinerant writing career that neither was possible. In "The English Mail-Coach," he reconciles himself to (and draws income from) a vehicle that, approaching midcentury, looked to him like publishing's best hope. From this perspective, *Blackwood's*—not the mail coach—becomes the glorious Romantic-era stalwart to contrast with the soulless distribution of newspapers by the railway. Except, as with all the idealizations in "The English Mail-Coach," the story is more complicated.

For example, "The English Mail-Coach" originally traveled in a Scottish vehicle. *Blackwood's* aspired to national distribution and quickly opened an editorial office in London for industry contacts and attracting writers, but it was printed in Edinburgh, usually by the Blackwood's company itself. The magazine's not-so-glorious motion included travel in wheelbarrows from editorial to printing buildings to Blackwood's shop front, and also transport as freight on canal boats and coastal ships to warehouses, locked up until the scramble of "magazine day" and its coordinated release to booksellers and newsagents.[71] Ironically, for all of *Blackwood's* centralized control, it was also the first British periodical to be fully pirated by an American publisher, Leonard Scott of New York, who could undersell *Blackwood's* in America because of British import duties and the absence of international copyright agreements. In 1848, Scott caved to pressure and agreed to pay a licensing fee to become the authorized American edition. "The English Mail-Coach" and its companion "The Vision of Sudden Death" were De Quincey's last contributions to *Blackwood's*, appearing within the earliest issues affiliated with an American publisher.

"The English Mail-Coach" is about Victorian networks but also *of* those networks, especially those organs of print that were imperfectly managing early nineteenth-century changes in publication and broad distribution. Aileen Fyfe has suggested that our narratives of historical media change, especially when they borrow the language of modern information systems, need much closer attention to the professional and practical aspects of its development.[72] In attending to texts and their material histories, we can recover some of these infrastructural conditions, working against a widespread tendency to imagine modern media as beyond feeling. Exemplified by "The English Mail-Coach," this move would deepen the ontological split of media and material bodies, paradoxically disembodying information by attempting to understand it through the senses. Yet other Victorian texts showed off their dependencies, inviting readers to imagine the infrastructures that were retreating ever further from public view. This dynamic—between disintermediation and infrastructuralism—patterns much of Victorian writing about its new media. And it persists in attempts to know the transoceanic internet, still following many of the material routes and conceptual frameworks laid down in the nineteenth century.

"Alien Evidence" and the Location of the Internet
Where is the internet? What does it look like? How does it feel? What would it mean to understand the internet less in terms of the abstractions of its evolving metaphors—for example, a network of networks, an information superhighway, cyberspace, a global village, the cloud—and more in terms of its material reality, physical infrastructure, emplacedness, or environmental impact? These are the concerns of an emerging generation of media studies scholars, developing approaches like critical infrastructure studies, media archaeology, and cultural techniques, all of which attempt to resist the disembodiment of digital media and expose other dimensions of our networked life. To counter media's own dream of disintermediation, they realize the internet as a thing, a place, an ecological zone, or a highly capitalized system of manufacture and logistics. In chapter 5, I will apply a version of this critical approach to digitized nineteenth-century newspapers. Here, I want to relate the very impulses of such scholarship to mid-nineteenth-century struggles to apprehend a networked information system in its own time. The Victorians *did* produce a modern view of information in this sense: wrestling over the changing material dimensions of networked media in ways that still entangle with our own.

As in "the internet train," it gets cartoonish to talk about "the internet" as a singular noun or a coherent phenomenon. It is endlessly fractured by algorithmically tailored experiences, varied forms of access, dark webs, nationally firewalled networks, its cycle of obsolescence, and the radically different positions of those experiencing it.[73] The singular noun "the internet" suggests instead the rhetorical success of its promoters, from network engineers to cyberlibertarians to transnational media companies, all of whom celebrate (and often profit from) connectivity as a goal in itself. In *A Prehistory of the Cloud*, Tung-Hui Hu details how foundational metaphors of the internet—as a network of networks, seemingly built to withstand an attack on any central target—enshrine a decentered and disembodied vision of the internet that belies its actual infrastructure: often quite centralized, fragile, and deeply material. Yet a decentralized view still persists, now metamorphosed into the "cloud," which sublimates our data, its routes, material infrastructure, natural resource demands, and human labor costs in the interests of global capital. How and why these dimensions of the internet get concealed are complicated questions.

While Hu insists that "the cloud is both an idea and a physical and material object," he also offers several perspectives about its idealization.[74] Just as "information" defines itself by negating its materiality, a "network" also exists only by erasure. Liu proposes that we first understand networks as a "privative construct . . . something that subtracts the need to be conscious of the geography, physicality, temporality, and underlying history of the links between nodes."[75] By turning the network into a logical model, it becomes available to manipulate at various levels of abstraction. For Hu, the cloud is "the premier example of what computer scientists term virtualization—a technique for turning real things into logical objects."[76] Virtualization brackets out the messier details of networks. It compartmentalizes networks so that manufacturers, engineers, technicians, computer scientists, and users can concentrate on discrete yet interoperating aspects of the whole. These layers also allow for concentration on higher-order tasks—even emailing, to take a simple example—without needing to remain aware of all the cascading dependences of any single operation. From another view, this kind of attention blindness also "insulates" networks, in Nicole Starosielski's terms—offering protection in the service of strategic ignorance, commercial secrecy, and national defense.[77]

Network disembodiment has also been embraced as a seemingly radical politics. In an early statement of such cyberlibertarianism, dated 1996 and pointedly written in Switzerland, John Perry Barlow rebuked governments and their colonial interests in cyberspace. Instead, he argued, "cyberspace consists of transactions, relationships, and thought itself, arrayed like a standing wave in the web of our communications. Ours is a world that is both everywhere and nowhere, but it is not where bodies live." While he accepts as inevitable the sovereign "rule over our bodies," Barlow promises to spread freedom across cyberspace "so that no one can arrest our thoughts."[78] With an almost Carlylean flourish, Barlow projects "a civilization of the Mind in Cyberspace" which, in place of isolated bodies, thrives on communal thinking, heard throughout the manifesto in the pronoun "we." He beckons participants to transcend their bodies not merely to become information, but to join a network. The utopianism of the manifesto depends on making a political exchange: your body for your freedom, realized as an autonomous subject in cyberspace, which itself lacks any embodied infrastructure, at least in Barlow's picture. Yet as scholars of the politics of new media have argued, the seeming freedom of cyberspace remains subject to the "control society," in which sovereign or even disciplinary structures of power evolve into "a continuous set of cybernetic systems, financial incentives, and monitoring techniques molded to each individual subject."[79] In other words, networked disembodiment is a trap, baited with the promise of connectivity. Barlow's cyberlibertarianism is merely the flip side of militaristic fantasies of the distributed network as immune to attack from sovereign states, or the interests of capital to produce and manage "users" in global media networks. (The manifesto was written in Davos.)

That early manifesto also represents an achingly white masculinist fantasy, only in which it becomes possible to overlook differentiating conditions of lived experience. Worse, it perversely reimagines as "freedom" the unspeakable trauma of disembodied global circulation whose history extends well past digital networks to the transatlantic slave trade. As the inaugural routes of standing communication across the

Atlantic, the slave trade also effectively disembodied its cargo by dehumanizing African people as commodities, then by abstracting their value beyond things entirely. The first transatlantic network depended on the violent extraction of black bodies, their generalization into actuarial data, and abstraction into instruments of international finance.[80] The historian Jessica Johnson traces "the rise of the independent and objective statistical fact as an explanatory ideal party to the devastating thingification of black women, children, and men."[81] Perhaps the very concept of information, now collected and circulated as data, remains "in the wake" of that violence, in Sharpe's phrase. As Johnson argues, "bias is built into the architecture of digital technology," which can re-encode old prejudices and exploitative infrastructures in new media.[82] That architecture includes physical infrastructure, colonial ideologies, and racial epistemologies already built into the nineteenth-century transoceanic telegraph system, according to Dhanashree Thorat, which "has been inherited by the submarine fiber optic infrastructure of the Internet."[83]

Finding and redressing those biases means refusing to accept that computational abstractions, network virtualization, or network infrastructure happen in a cultural vacuum. For example, Tara McPherson argues that the fundamental features of UNIX permit "the infusion of racial organizing principles into the technological organization of knowledge."[84] Those features include the development of the "pipe" in the code, represented by the | symbol, which allows separate program modules to pass information without its entering the file system or needing the user's—or even the programmer's—awareness. Outputs get piped into inputs. Data flows across modules. The values they encode diffuse through systems, networks, and the social architecture to which they give rise—including, McPherson argues, the academic pursuits of digital humanities and digital media studies, which fall prey to the same biased partitioning. Importantly, McPherson cautions that recent turns in humanities discourse "to privilege networks over nodes . . . and to focus on globalization and its flows" may encode equally problematic forms of cultural logic. In critiquing hierarchy and rigid structures, they also accept an "unknowability" that is, according to both McPherson and Hu, the central cultural logic of the cloud.[85]

If the network necessarily subtracts knowledge of its intermediating contexts, feminist scholarship has done much to add it back in. As Losh explains, computer history has not only privileged the stories of white male innovators; it has privileged the very narrative of disintermediation as its progressive structure. This history accepts the erasure of persons, space, and systems as giant leaps forward in computing and communications. It extends earlier celebrations of the railway and telegraph annihilating space and time as obstacles to the idealized functioning of human intercourse. Losh and others would have us "acknowledge the material, embodied, affective, labor-intensive, and situated character of technology." Just as Marvin transformed communications history into social history, Losh wants to understand "computer networks as an aggregation of relationships" subject to power and historical erasure.[86] Like Losh, Mar Hicks, Lisa Nakamura, and Charlton McIlwain have all attempted to recover such occluded narratives of computer history.[87] Other researchers have tried to counter the pervasive myth of disintermediation differently: by going out and seeing the internet for themselves.

Before becoming an academic, Hu was a network engineer working at a major internet exchange in San Francisco—a bottleneck for global internet traffic, circulating through transoceanic fiber optic cables landing around the bay. Curious about just what was pulsing through all those servers, one night Hu apparently disconnected a network cable and peered into the end to watch its blinking red light. As he recounts, he was lucky not to choose a long-distance cable whose single-mode laser would have shredded his cornea.[88] The innocent anecdote launches Hu's sophisticated book-length meditation on what, exactly, the cloud is. It also recapitulates the story of *The Times*'s journalist in 1866 who, reporting on the completion of the Atlantic telegraph cable, wondered what, exactly, it was transmitting. Watching agog at the mirror galvanometer, twisting in a magnetic field in response to a signal, he ponders the electric source: "you might lay bare that tiny wire and watch it, but you would see nothing and feel nothing."[89] This chapter has suggested that the impulse to see and to feel in networked communications only further divorces information from its body, implying that the medium, even so nakedly encountered, carries "nothing." So disconnected from what he can sensuously experience, the modern network represents "alien knowledge," dividing the human world from an unknowable other. Yet scholars like Hu suggest that looking at the internet is possible—and necessary—in breaking down the problematic ontological divisions within communications history. Through their efforts, we revisit similar experiments from centuries past when many of these problems first obtained.

"Following a signal has long been a compelling way to represent a network," Starosielski writes in her own formidable exploration of oceanic cables.[90] In different guises, what Starosielski calls "transmission narratives" have also shaped earlier efforts to comprehend nonhuman infrastructure. The "it narratives" popularized during the eighteenth century, for example, imagined the secret life of things and their transmission through familiar systems of exchange, such as recounting the adventures of a coin, a doll, a letter, a shoe, or a bank note. As Leah Price explains, the protagonists of "it narratives" changed in the nineteenth century from things to "talking books"—especially bibles, religious tracts, and hymnals explaining how they've circulated. For Price, that change helps index the increasing "bibliographic materialism" of the Victorian era, its awareness of books as things subject to increasingly vast systems of circulation.[91] Arguably, "The English Mail-Coach" is an "it narrative," too. The protagonist-object is De Quincey: a passenger who is almost a parcel, a passive agent almost homologous with the newspapers he delivers. In a way, "The English Mail-Coach" may represent the turn from "it narrative" to "transmission narrative" in tracing not just a network but a *signal*. The essay does so right at the moment the "it-ness" or material status of that signal comes into question.

In 1996, Neal Stephenson made that investigation the focus of a long essay, "Mother Earth, Mother Board" in *Wired* magazine. While Barlow waved the banner of a cyberspace beyond bodies and nations, that same year Stephenson traveled bodily to multiple nations to follow a different FLAG—the Fiberoptic Link Around the Globe, at the time the longest oceanic cable ever laid. In seeking the newest instance of cyberspace infrastructure, Stephenson also travels explicitly to the past, noting the historical palimpsest of sites like a new internet exchange in Egypt "constructed virtually on top of the ruins of the Great Library of Alexandria," and editorializing that "everything that has occurred in Silicon Valley in the last couple of decades also occurred in the 1850s."[92] Stephenson spends a good deal of time in the long nineteenth century: he tells vivid stories about William Thomson, Lord Kelvin; lucidly describes the workings of historical equipment in the Museum of Submarine Telegraphy in Porthcurno, Cornwall; and explicates the relations of botanical gardens and colonial empire in the cultivation of insulating materials. More importantly for my story, the nineteenth century also refracts the essay's genre. What Stephenson explains as "hacker tourism: travel to exotic locations in search of sights and sensations" replays a mix of travel narratives and tropes of imperial romance that characterized Victorian encounters with the global periphery. Stephenson knows this, of course, and plays those genres against a decidedly unsexy topic—network infrastructure and the global telecom business, described in painstaking detail—to animate his essay. His sensationalism helps to dislodge perceptions of the "invisible, ineffable bits" of digital media as having instead material connections to laborers, local disagreements, heavy machinery, and lushly forested places. What results is a hybrid genre, something like steampunk creative nonfiction. "Mother Earth, Mother Board" encodes many of steampunk's signature tropes, as outlined by Rachel Bowser and Brian Croxall: it synthesizes technological realms, binds the Victorian past to the high-tech present, lavishes attention on old machines, and makes the "hacker" its hero.[93] The Victorian era offers its own generic resources for writers to interrogate its uncanny legacy in the globally networked present.

In a different way, the nineteenth century also haunts Andrew Blum's transmission narrative, *Tubes: A Journey to the Center of the Internet*. The subtitle signals the adventure to come, alluding to Jules

Verne's voyage extraordinaire, *Journey to the Center of the Earth*, with the added irony of pursuing the internet's decenteredness. Blum's title references a famous mischaracterization of the internet by Alaskan senator Ted Stevens as a "series of tubes" that turns out, on investigation, to be quite correct. The book is a classic transmission narrative through those tubes, following a signal from a home router through transcontinental cables and subterranean conduits to the basements of internet exchanges and data centers. Like Stephenson's essay, *Tubes* tries to counteract the network's disappearance: "it felt utterly disembodied, a featureless expanse: all ether, no net."[94] While Blum, like Stephenson, visits places associated with the physical network, *Tubes* also becomes a geographer's rumination on the idea of place after its seeming erasure. It becomes a romantic search for some original site of meaning, trying to reckon with the internet's lack of monuments or sensory evidence: "The networked systems are everywhere. . . . But all invisible. To see it you had to imagine it."[95] Like Stephenson's essay, *Tubes* also borrows structures of imagination from the nineteenth century.

Blum closes his introduction with a quotation from Henry David Thoreau: just as Walden pond has a "hard bottom," so the internet fundamentally exists somewhere, as a thing.[96] If Thoreau imbued Walden with deep significance for American Romanticism, Blum similarly tries to ennoble the otherwise underwhelming encounter with the things and places of the internet. To do so, Blum outfits his report into a quest of Romantic (self-)discovery. In starting out, Blum says "my map of the Internet was blank—as blank as the Ocean Sea was to Columbus."[97] But those blanks are hardly filled by the internet's physical architecture. Their transcendent reality derives from Blum's own imagination, as when he encounters a core exchange box: "an apparently unremarkable black box . . . this very machine was among the Internet's most important—the center of one of the biggest Internet exchanges—but it wore that significance discretely. Its meaning had to come from inside *me*."[98] Ironically, to generate that meaning, Blum looks not into himself but to an example from *The Education of Henry Adams* in which the protagonist gazes on an electrical dynamo as a "symbol of infinity." Elsewhere, struggling to convey the significance of what amounts to a room full of closets, Blum also invokes the sublime: "among the landscapes of the Internet, it was the confluence of mighty rivers, the entrance to a grand harbor."[99] Columbus has apparently arrived in the new world of new media. The significance of the internet comes less from Blum than from the literary tropes he imports, tropes that paradoxically render invisible the cultural infrastructure that a book like *Tubes* was supposed to reveal. Blum nowhere questions the cultural privilege of his perspective, the ease with which he finds access to protected spaces, or the baggage of his Romantic structures of feeling. My point is less to critique them than to gesture how easily those structures flow from the nineteenth century to the twenty-first. Remediation also works at the level of genre, in which something "new"—whether the internet or its attempted representation in prose—necessarily borrows the protocols of "old" structures to make its subject understandable. And moments of media shift set that conceptual transfer in motion.

There are now an increasing number of studies of the occluded histories of internet and computing infrastructure, revealing their colonial and racialized legacies with roots running deep into the past. Many of these studies would redress the damaging legacies of disintermediation, partly by rekindling the infrastructural imaginary that attends it. Resources for doing so are unevenly available from nineteenth-century precursors. The nineteenth century helped inaugurate damaging myths and provided durable tropes and genres used even now to perpetuate them. Yet it also shows examples of their contradiction. The new media moment—whenever it occurs—paradoxically co-generates disembodiment as well as infrastructuralist sensibilities. Nineteenth-century information culture offers both a troublesome genealogy and perhaps inspiration for how to redress what the Victorians made alien. As the next chapter explains, much depends, in looking to the past, on what appropriate or strategic uses we make.

TWO

DATA ETHICS FROM REALISM TO THE RIGHT TO BE FORGOTTEN

Such annoyances... become more intolerable as the years bring with them that increased facility of communication which makes the conjectures and inferences of local ignorance matter for current circulation throughout the Kingdom.... I only wish I could write something that would contribute to heighten men's reverence before the secrets of each other's souls, that there might be less assumption of entire knowingness, as a datum, from which inferences are to be drawn.
 —GEORGE ELIOT, letter to Charles Bray (1859)[1]

Forgetting used to be a failing, a waste, a sign of senility. Now it takes effort. It may be as important as remembering.
 —JAMES GLEICK, *The Information* (2011)[2]

MARIAN EVANS WAS DOXXED IN 1859. The early acclaim for *Scenes of Clerical Life* and *Adam Bede* had fueled much speculation about their pseudonymous author, which settled on the unlikely figure of Joseph Liggins before the secret of "George Eliot" finally came out. In a letter that year to her friend and mentor Charles Bray, Evans complained about a pair of annoyances related to her unmasking: first, "increased facility of communication" had turned local gossip into Kingdom-wide circulation; and second, why should anyone knowing her identity as a fact, "as a datum," feel satisfied with its primacy in understanding her work?

The two are related: communication networks stoke this push toward "entire knowingness" at the expense of reflective reverence for what we do not, or cannot, know. That same year, Eliot published her curious novella *The Lifted Veil*, which seems to thematize these problems in its gothic plot: the narrator Latimer, afflicted by a mix of prevision and clairvoyance, comes to know everything in the minds of others only to be thoroughly repelled. As critics have suggested, Latimer may represent the lifting of Eliot's pseudonymous veil.[3] Others propose *The Lifted Veil* as a turning point in Eliot's efforts to transform knowledge of others into the sympathetic understanding that grounds her ethical vision.[4] Paradoxically, knowing more about someone might mean sympathizing less.

Now, it isn't quite correct to say that Marian Evans was a victim of "doxxing." That term more properly refers to the targeted exposure of a pseudonymous internet persona or the online publication of identifying details about someone who would prefer privacy. In fact, George Eliot and George Lewes simply gave up the efforts to preserve the secret after the Liggins affair, letting Marian Evans's authorship be known personally to, and then disseminated by, select friends. In *George Eliot and Blackmail*, Alexander Welsh uses the episode to characterize identity in a culture that values information as a measure of its concealment or disclosure. Indeed, Welsh argues this dynamic brings "information" as such into existence—not as a unit of knowledge, or a packet of communication, or a kind of fact or figure, but as a symptom of much broader changes in the public sphere. Welsh attributes these only in part to communications technologies, pointing also to representative government, urbanization, and mobility, all of which heightened the contrast of public and private lives whose differences "information" seemed to define.[5] But I risk the anachronistic term "doxxing" to reframe the episode, along with Welsh's argument, as prefiguring early twenty-first century anxieties about information circulating through the internet. These relate not only to information scaled to the individual person, as Welsh defines, but to "data" surveilled, collected, and even algorithmically inferred about one's activities online or off, including relations, location, biometrics, hardware interactions, and more. In such a state, what happens to the knowledge of others, or what others can know about you? Who or what now defines the parameters of memory? What is the fate of sympathetic understanding in the digital age? What lies behind the veil we now know as a screen?

Welsh uses George Eliot to chart such sweeping changes during the nineteenth century's "information revolution" as it reshaped the boundaries of private and public life, personal histories and present personae, desire and ethics.[6] Neither Welsh's argument nor George Eliot's significance should be reduced to a technologized notion of informatics recognizable in the digital turn. Yet the framework is useful to compare what Welsh calls a "pathology of information" during Eliot's lifetime with the emergence of "information and computer ethics" as an interdisciplinary field.[7] Active since the mid-twentieth century, the field has only grown in urgency since "information and computers" have restructured global capital as well as permeated the intimacies and prejudices of everyday social networks. While these are subjects too vast to address in general terms, I do think they capture something like the condition Welsh describes: an unsettling of norms and boundaries for which "technology" furnished a background, but which manifest across other nineteenth-century contexts, including physiology, spiritualism, gender, and genre. The more recent discourse of information ethics helps to refocus their shared concerns for connection, sympathy, memory, and communications technologies. This chapter argues how this tangle of preoccupations—as illuminated by writers including George Eliot, George du Maurier, psychical researchers, journalists, and legal scholars—becomes the foundation for an emerging discourse of data ethics.

Like "doxxing," the word "data" is a useful anachronism.[8] It tethers "information" more closely to technical systems, to protocols of its usage, to problems of its preservation, and to communication between machines as much as between or about persons. "Data" compels attention to information captured, contrived, circulated, and sold in ways that exceed the political boundaries or even ontological dimensions of human ethics. It has provoked all sorts of new arguments as a result, ranging across sociological concerns, political critique, technical preservation, and international legislation, to name only the discussions touched on in this chapter.[9] These are each substantial fields, and I hope not to diminish their significance by bundling them under the sign of a Victorian discourse about data ethics. Yet they are "Victorian" in notable ways, including the ongoing reckoning with (and sometimes outright nostalgia for) nineteenth-century conceptions of liberalism, deep attention, and the right to privacy, as well as the fantasies and nightmares about digital memory that resurrect Victorian spiritualism. In turn, by reading data ethics into nineteenth-century works, I underscore the cautions and inspirations they offer to conversations about privacy, data surveillance, empathy, and the right to be forgotten. Ultimately, I find in Victorian exemplars a practice of socialized forgetting that might shape data ethics now.

This chapter begins with George Eliot and the paradox of omniscience and sympathy. Why does knowing more—even knowing everything about someone else—not result in sympathetic understanding? I suggest how this paradox was technologized in Eliot's time and how thoroughly it has recurred in arguments about a perceived "crisis of empathy" amid our own information overload and ubiquitous connectivity.[10] Eliot's own response seems to require limiting what we attempt to know, or accepting what we should ethically forget. I then turn to Eliot's connections with Charles Bray, who went on to publish psychical research on the omniscience of environments. If telepaths could know everything in another's mind, what if someone's surroundings were perpetually and perfectly capturing their presence? George du Maurier's novel *Peter Ibbetson*, a drama about telepathic intimacy and the "inner life," also dramatizes a shift toward *ambient* memory, or the continual capture of data by distributed recording technologies and surveillance environments. Concerns about that shift directly inform the legal discourse around the "right to privacy," first articulated in 1890, which now confronts the ubiquitous data capture of our era. In their own time, *The Lifted Veil* and *Peter Ibbetson* conjure a spectrum of perpetual memory and ethical forgetting whose polarity continues to structure opposing claims about the web, but which might offer a different model for how we use Victorian texts to imagine a sociable future in a world of data.

TMI, Teleparalysis, and Empathy

The Lifted Veil is conventionally seen as an outlier, a gothic experiment in the early development of Eliot's high realism. But, in its very weirdness, it also offers a useful counterpoint to the role and limits of sympathetic understanding in Eliot's fiction, as figured (or disfigured) by the protagonist's telepathy. The story concerns the second son of a wealthy English family, overshadowed by his lusty, successful older brother and subjected to a practical education when all he desires are poetry and the arts. Latimer, who also narrates the story, has an uncanny experience of déjà vu, a glimpse of the future that he calls "prevision." Not long after, Latimer begins to suffer from unwanted telepathy, as "the vagrant, frivolous ideas and emotions of some uninteresting acquaintance... would force themselves on my consciousness."[11] While he claims to have a "poet's sensibility," the interruption of other minds perversely fills Latimer's head with the mundane. In this respect, his telepathy reinforces his practical education: "I was very stupid about machines, so I was to be greatly occupied with them... I was hungry for human deeds and human emotions, so I was to be plentifully crammed with the mechanical powers... and the phenomena of electricity and magnetism" (6). Like the unwanted intrusions of others' psyches when all Latimer seeks is human sympathy, his education "crams" his head with electromechanical subjects against his wishes. Along with the frequent references to media technologies throughout the story, these beginnings suggest how thoroughly *The Lifted Veil* remains in conversation with, as Jill Galvan says, "the complexities of mediated communication itself."[12]

Scholars of nineteenth-century media have taken note, using *The Lifted Veil* to exemplify how the "ways of imagining the supernaturally occupied mind change with historical shifts in technologies of transmission of information."[13] *The Lifted Veil* dramatizes the boundary problems of nineteenth-century reprographic, electromechanical, and psychical mediums, sometimes explicitly referenced in the text, but everywhere inferred in Latimer's hypersensitive mediation. With his onset telepathy, Latimer's senses mutate, each seemingly calibrated to different frameworks of time. Latimer's knowledge of the future is visual, experiencing previsions as "the gradual breaking-in of the vision upon me, like the new images in a dissolving view" (10). Along with a reference to the magic lantern or phantasmagoria, Latimer's visions reflect early techniques of photography, as Menke has shown by comparing Latimer's inaugural prevision of Prague to William Henry Fox Talbot's 1858 picture "Bridge Over the River Moldau" and its circulation in print reproductions. Like the uncanny experience of early photography, Latimer's visions are "freed from time and space, stripped of any context, they are real but never realized."[14] Conversely, Latimer's experience of other minds in the present is aural: "my diseased anticipation in other people's consciousness . . . was like a preternaturally heightened sense of hearing, making audible to one a roar of sound where others find perfect stillness" (18). It would be some decades before the telephone would relay sounds into spaces where they otherwise did not reach, or when the technology to capture and replay sounds made the phonograph seem like the promise of human communication to come. Yet media's preternatural transformation of the sensorium was already operating in Latimer to experience other minds as the connection and transmission of noise.

Latimer is a passive receiver of these experiences. But as a narrator, he must actively construct his story from these impressions and his recollection. This activity, too, gets conspicuously technologized. His memory, his very efforts to write, become telegraphic, plagued by compression and the problems of encoding: "The recollections of the past become contracted in the rapidity of thought till they sometimes bear hardly a more distinct resemblance to the external reality than the forms of an oriental alphabet to the objects that suggested them" (33). The rapid contraction of discourse into unrecognizable alphabets seems to block Latimer's very function as a retrospective narrator. Later in the story he bemoans: "That course of our life which I have indicated in a few sentences filled the space of years. So much misery—so slow and hideous a growth of hatred and sin, may be compressed into a sentence! And men judge of each other's lives through this summary medium" (34). If the compression of language were not complaint enough, readers unjustly accept that "summary medium" as adequate for judging each other's lives. In Latimer's hands, those summary sentences are his own narrative, which turns fiction into merely a conduit for information. Menke suggests that Latimer reflects the problems of mediation at midcentury, comparable to "models of the era's new informatics" that, like photography or physiology, would stabilize the ephemeral and subjective into something like an objective, repeatable form.[15] Latimer's afflictions and misgivings show the consequences for fiction, the "dark suggestion that even as it amplifies our experience of the world and extends our contact with others, fiction may cast our most intimate knowledge—of places, of individuals, of embodied life—as information."[16]

I want to build on this scholarship by distorting its time frame, making Eliot's story its own fictional prevision of contemporary discourse about informatic intrusions. My approach starts not with the problem of information as such, but its new excesses, with strains on cognition and its consequences for sympathy. For Latimer, his telepathic impressions sound like a roar, overwhelming his senses and his abilities to relate to others. That we can know too much—or otherwise have to learn what to ignore or even forget—becomes a leitmotif in Eliot's writing. It manifests famously in the oft-quoted passage from *Middlemarch*:

> If we had a keen vision and feeling of all ordinary human life, it would be like hearing the grass grow and the squirrel's heart beat, and we should die of that roar which lies on the other side of silence. As it is, the quickest of us walk about well wadded with stupidity.[17]

In *The Lifted Veil*, Latimer gets stripped of that insulation, connected to the roar on the other side of a thinning veil. He does not die from it but suffers the symptoms of an extraordinary affliction. In Latimer's own words, "this strange new power" might "rather be a disease" (12). It manifests as the cognitive and emotional paralysis of information overload.

The concept of information overload or too much information (TMI) is both recent and a historical cliché. In *Too Much to Know*, Ann Blair documents that sense of crisis in earlier eras when a growing enthusiasm for collecting knowledge overwhelmed their own informational techniques. Blair points to the early modern reference systems and book designs that attempted to manage an explosion of printed knowledge.[18] As Maurice Lee has shown, the nineteenth century also makes a strong claim with its self-awareness about proliferating information and cognitive overload.[19] In their project *The Diseases of Modern Life*, Sally Shuttleworth and colleagues find "a qualitative and quantitative shift in the nature of such reflections in the second half of the nineteenth century," spurred on by the expansion of an international periodical print culture as well as by the very discourse of abundant knowledge, overload, and information management that the press capitalized on.[20] To many at the time, the shift seemed epochal. Addressing the Royal Society of Edinburgh in 1860, James Crichton-Browne warned that, "In the course of one brief month more impressions are conveyed to our brains than reached those of our ancestors in the course of years, and our mentalising machines are called upon for a greater amount of fabric than was required of our grandfathers in the course of a lifetime."[21] A similar condition seems at the root of Max Nordau's diagnosis in *Degeneration*, as "the vertigo and whirl of our frenzied life, the vastly increased number of sense impressions and organic reactions" lead to fatigue, exhaustion, and hysteria.[22]

In this context, Latimer seems like a case study of the psychic consequences of open channels and superabundance. He suffers life as what he calls a "dreary desert of knowledge" (18) and his symptoms of overload manifest as paralysis. Paralysis suffuses his story: Latimer's father dies of paralysis. Latimer's friend Charles Meunier seems "paralysed" at the story's conclusion, having seen what's behind the veil, as it were. And Latimer describes his gathering awareness of Bertha's mind in similar terms, longing for his earlier moments of ignorance like cherishing "the last pains in a paralysed limb." His "strange disease" turns his telepathy into teleparalysis; he is rendered completely ineffectual by the very phenomenon of being connected to others, flooded with impressions.

In contemporary definitions, information overload is less about superabundance than the mental response to it, "a problematic situation or state of mental stress arising" from "too much information."[23] The ratio between them is uncertain, making overload less a diagnosis than a warning about the unsettled relationship between information and emotional life. The very ambiguity of its definition—what is the threshold of too much? does it change? vary between people? depend on kinds of information?—suggests partly why so many other related ills have been proposed. These include "data overload, information anxiety, information pollution, technostress, data smog, and information fatigue syndrome," none necessarily more precise, and generally grouped as information overload.[24] They are all premised on a normative "conception of human information processing" that information somehow disrupts.[25] Yet this model may only contribute to the emotional stress it describes. The pathology of information overload may also include discomfort with this anemic approach to cognition, or resistance to the computational metaphor of the mind. From this view, Latimer is paralyzed not by the *fact* of too much information or too many impressions, but because he gets transformed into an information processor at the expense of other forms of sociality. (Remember, he wants to be a poet.) Information overload is less a useful diagnosis than a cultural symptom of something bigger: a dispute over the technologizing of communication. In *The Lifted Veil*, Eliot focuses this dispute as the conflict between connection and sympathy.

Laura Otis suggests that Eliot had greater hopes for the promise of the nineteenth-century's technologizing communications networks:

"In Eliot's eyes, one fostered sympathy through knowledge and experience of others, and England's new communications networks offered both."[26] Such knowledge and experience would lead, in turn, to an understanding of one's thoroughgoing connections across a social web. For Otis, *Middlemarch* represents the apotheosis of this networked ethical vision: "[*Middlemarch*] celebrates the flow of information for the potential it holds. The novel offers the communications web as an epistemological and moral model, suggesting that the securest knowledge and the finest life are those richest in connections."[27] Yet *The Lifted Veil* seems like the nightmare scenario for someone at the center of that connected web, wracked by every pulse along its strands, and retreating only further into self-regard. It's worth pointing out that Latimer does not suffer a roar of impressions from far-flung strangers, as if linked across the distances that telecommunications seemed to collapse. Rather, Latimer's suffering only worsens when attuned to the minds of those closest to him: "this superadded consciousness, wearying and annoying enough when it urged on me the trivial experience of indifferent people, became an intense pain and grief when it seemed to be opening to me the souls of those who were in a close relation to me" (14). Their crafted personae are torn away to reveal the seething frivolities and self-concern within. Here, the problem changes from information overload to the failure of intimacy he otherwise seeks. Latimer suffers less from "superadded" connections than from the supersession of a normal mind by a technologized hyperconsciousness. Latimer has a networked sensorium. And it produces the very opposite of sympathy.

Partly because Latimer is literally an omniscient narrator, aware of writing his own story and the minds of others within it, many scholars have read *The Lifted Veil* as metacommentary on Eliot's own project, a rumination on the darker side of the sympathy to which her fiction seems devoted. Rae Greiner writes that "Eliot has long been crowned the doyenne of Victorian sympathy, yet sympathy in her novels is surprisingly rare" and entirely absent from *The Lifted Veil*.[28] Greiner and others suggest that *The Lifted Veil* tries to distinguish sympathy from knowledge, casting doubt that the best way to become a moral agent or develop sympathetic understanding is to know other people intensely. If Latimer personifies omniscience, then the story shows "a growing distrust that omniscience was an ideal way to secure [sympathy]."²⁹ After Eliot's early successes, the story seems like an anxious pause; she seems uncertain about where her fiction will go. Perhaps Eliot uses Latimer as a "morbid authorial experiment," a nightmare about the incapacity of realist fiction to deliver sympathy at all.³⁰ Or perhaps, as Helen Small has proposed, *The Lifted Veil* casts doubt on the broader moral project of sympathy itself, in the story's implied critique of cosmopolitanism: "the belief or hope that a wider experience of the world will foster a more egalitarian allegiance to humanity beyond the proximate claims of family and nation."³¹ The "outlier" status of *The Lifted Veil* stems from its ethical perversity. If, as Nicholas Royle supposes, the very concept of telepathy emerges from Romantic notions of sympathy, Eliot sketches the opposite, as Victorian technologies make connecting to others ethically perverse.³²

But why shouldn't knowing more about people, gaining "insight into minds and hearts," generate more ethical understanding?³³ Why would Eliot, among other novelists of the period, seem so "dubious of the tie that binds sympathy to knowledge"?³⁴ Looking back at the difficulties Eliot faced in 1859 can offer some clarity. As Welsh and Bodenheimer point out, *The Lifted Veil* reflects the disillusionment of Eliot's difficult year: an anxiety that, once her pseudonym of George Eliot was fully exposed, and her controversial personal choices became linked with her authorship, her readers would only fixate on gossipy trivialities or be otherwise repelled.³⁵ Eliot worried about how she would even adapt: "The weight of my future life exerts an almost paralyzing effect."³⁶ Yet her letter to Charles Bray, quoted at the chapter's start, complains as much about *how* people know things as about what they discover. In it, Eliot points to a deeply problematic elision of communication networks with the assumption of entire knowingness. It might not matter what these networks did or did not spread, whether knowledge or experience or information or sympathy or gossip. Rather, the threat lies within the very ideology of networked communication: an assumption that such networks establish connections *at all*, or that they produce knowable things.[37] The problem is mediation itself as a way of knowing or relating to others. In *Thinking about Other People*, Adela Pinch has this very much in mind: the communication model of sociability "is often the least interesting, and least socially meaningful, way of thinking about thinking."[38] Perhaps *The Lifted Veil* ought not to be approached on its own terms, as a distortion of media technologies or a rumination on telepathy or omniscience or mediation, because these readings already accept a communications model that denatures thinking. Instead, *The Lifted Veil* is haunted by the transformation of sociality that attends technologized communication, imagining the consequences in terms we are now well equipped to recognize.

In her work on selfhood, socialization, and digital networks, the psychologist and technology researcher Sherry Turkle has arrived at a version of *The Lifted Veil*'s paradox: "We are increasingly connected to each other but oddly more alone."[39] The arc of Turkle's research bends from fascination with the virtual personae on the early internet to deep concern about the alienation provoked by social media and ubiquitous connectivity. Their effects compound to nothing less than "a crisis of empathy that has diminished us at home, at work, and in public life."[40] Turkle is certainly not alone in criticizing, even agonizing about the threats to cognition, empathy, and privacy heralded by an infoscape dominated by big tech. Indeed, there is a robust tradition of such reactions to any significant historical media shift—along with vibrant counterarguments and utopian claims.[41] Yet Turkle suggests how information overload mutates into a problem of empathy in terms that strongly resonate with nineteenth-century concerns about newly connected life. The problem of "information" is secondary to the eclipse of meaningful social ties by technologized connections, particularly those now orchestrated by mobile hardware, social media, and personal apps invested in our long-term commitment to their platforms, and capitalizing on the data they extract. Now "technology proposes itself as the architect of our intimacies," as Turkle suggests.[42] But those intimacies are poor substitutes, offering only "the efficiencies of mere connection" in place of healthier relationships that, in Turkle's view as a psychologist, are grounded in empathy.[43]

Turkle's rhetoric of "crisis" or even the "assault on empathy" has been taken up by other skeptics, too.[44] The writer Nicholas Carr concludes that Google—his synecdoche for searching, cursory reading, and informational efficiency—heralds "a slow erosion of our humanness and our humanity."[45] Like Turkle, Carr measures "humanness" in terms of the "moral sense" of empathy: "the more distracted we become, the less able we are to experience the subtlest, most distinctively human forms of empathy, compassion, and other emotions."[46] In a related critique, Sven Birkerts fears nothing less than "a millennial transformation of society" manifesting in the crisis of reading in an information age.[47] Unwittingly echoing nineteenth-century diagnoses of information overload, Birkerts writes that, "In less than a half century we have moved from a condition of essential isolation into one of intense and almost unbroken mediation."[48] The consequences of "the constant availability of data," the relentless streams of information, are uncannily familiar: in Birkerts's terms, a "cognitive and moral paralysis."[49] This discourse has fully reanimated the terms of Eliot's discontent in *The Lifted Veil*. I would even argue that such critiques verge on a gothic genre.[50] As media scholar danah boyd points out, anxieties about technology's "assault on empathy" are better evidence of a moral panic than anything else. Especially when it focuses on teenagers, such commentary can shade into fearful visions of alienated, repellent little monsters: "media coverage frequently portrays American youth in dark bedrooms with only the glow of the screen illuminating their faces, implying that there's a generation of zombified social media addicts who are unable to tear themselves away."[51] It is tempting to once again compare Latimer—in his frustrated youth, mediated telepathy, and moral paralysis—to such a vision. But the connections to Victorian discourse are also right on the surface of how, exactly, we should confront an empathic crisis.

In fact, contemporary arguments rehearse Victorian responses to this very problem, such as by advocating a return to an empathic social understanding taught by reading nineteenth-century novels, or to forms of apparently unalienated discourse within theories of Victorian liberalism. Turkle structures her entire program for "reclaiming conversation" on Henry David Thoreau. The lessons from *Walden* include his mindful attention to the needs for solitude, friendship, and wandering in the woods. Turkle's program also includes a return to "deep reading," citing research on how "literary fiction significantly improves empathic capacity," for which her primary example is Jane Austen.[52] Carr, too, uses the "two-hundred year old Victorian novel" as exemplary of the printed book and as counterpoint to the distracted reading of its digital counterparts.[53] As Nicholas Dames has pointed out, these arguments enshrine the Victorian novel as a bulwark of deep, attentive reading, at the center of a kind of "cognitive ethics" that has far more to do with contemporary debates than the novel itself.[54] Mid-nineteenth-century novel reading was already the domain of distracted consumption, aligning quite easily with a "liberal politics of autonomous subjects left alone to choose their own wants and needs."[55] That legacy, far more so than deep reading, fully endures in recent prescriptions for engaged, empathic life in the digital age. In his screed *The Dumbest Generation*, Mark Bauerlein invokes Carlyle's *French Revolution* and "classic Victorian novels," saving his deepest affection for John Stuart Mill, "the great Victorian liberal intellectual."[56] Bauerlein celebrates Mill's famous turn to Romantic poetry amid his own emotional crisis, in contrast with the endless, immediate self-concern of kids these days. But Mill is also present in Bauerlein's own nostalgia for a culture war, "a busy marketplace of ideas and politics" in which quality arguments will naturally win precedence.[57]

Bauerlein's solution to information overload is eminently Victorian: a neoliberal hope for self-organizing markets that also undergirds the claims of social media companies. As boyd explains, companies like Facebook promise themselves as "a tool for tolerance because technology enables people to see and participate in worlds beyond their own."[58] Google's short-lived experiment in its wearable platform Glass was actually touted as an "empathy machine," as if people would understand each other more deeply from literally seeing one another's recorded perspective.[59] (Glass famously did the opposite: repelling people who knew they were being recorded, and earning its wearers the title of "glassholes.") Facebook's pitch to provide internet service (and Facebook) globally claimed that "the more we connect, the better it gets."[60] It gets "better" because of our meaningful connections with others, our networked intimacies—as well as better for Facebook. When Mark Zuckerberg first demoed the "metaverse," he insisted that, in developing his company, "the dream was to feel present with the people we care about."[61] With its rhetoric of empathic connectivity, big tech claims a "new cosmopolitanism" that, as boyd argues, ignores all the structures of privilege and differential power that its networks, hardware, and marketplaces merely reproduce.[62] Yet even boyd characterizes American teenagers as "*digital flâneurs*," an odd phrase given her sensitivities to the exclusionary politics and asymmetrical spaces of online engagement.[63] Her point is that teens use online communication to experiment with their identities in relation to networked publics. We overestimate their moral paralysis and exposure to risk, but even for boyd the solution is "empathy."[64]

I highlight these debates to suggest just how thoroughly the Victorian pervades them, whether in explicit reference, metaphor, or structures of thought. Jade Davis claims that "technology carries affective biases and brings society not to the future but back to the past masquerading as the future."[65] In *The Other Side of Empathy*, Davis reveals the history of empathy as a strategy of affective colonization. From the "nineteenth-century gaze" at the racialized other to immersive technologies and social media, empathy substitutes white feeling for structural change. Instead, "technological empathy produces enlightened apathy."[66] Dames helps explain how Victorians produced this sensibility as a ready-made nostalgia. Established to confront a nineteenth-century experience of information overload, nostalgia now returns as the ironic solution to those problems today.[67] If, as Turkle argues, "technology... makes us forget what we know about life," discourses of new technology make us forget about their complex histories.[68] In promoting empathy, Turkle retreads Victorian nostalgia for a sense of connectedness it never actually felt, and extends its "empathic gaze" built on racial subjection.[69]

Eliot's work may suggest a different approach to technologized alienation, rooted in the tactics of remembrance and forgetfulness, knowledge and ignorance that Eliot, among others, would articulate as a kind of information ethics. Before discussing them further, I want to propose how those tactics get complicated when memory itself becomes technologized and distributed beyond the control, or even the cognizance, of the subject. Turkle and others fear that technology makes us forget now that the internet does all our remembering. The paradoxes of digital memory—either completely ephemeral or disturbingly permanent—also have their origins in the mnemotechnics of the nineteenth century, as well as the fantasies and anxieties they spawned.

Ambient and Digital Memory

Charles Bray would have been especially sensitive to Eliot's concerns about entire knowingness and telepathy. In 1866, Bray published *On Force, Its Mental and Moral Correlates; and On That Which Is Supposed to Underlie All Phenomena*, his entry to the burgeoning field of philosophical speculations on materialism, spiritualism, and the mind. Like many others at the time, Bray saw an evident connection between electricity and mental operations, arguing by analogy that the mind could thus be studied according to physical laws. Bray proposed a pervasive notion of "Force" that subsumed all material and spiritual phenomena—never so distinct—and that also obeyed laws like the conservation of motion, momentum, or matter. The conservation or "Persistence of Force" meant, by extension, that minds must also persist, transmuting beyond the conventional limits of the bounded individual. As a consequence, "Mind is in connection with all other mind."[70] Furthermore, as epiphenomena of an all-pervading Force, minds must also exchange with their environments: "We influence every one and every thing about us, and are influenced by them. We photograph our mental states on all the rooms we inhabit."[71] Our surroundings are capturing our presence, all the time, forever.

Bray offers a different entry point to the problems of connection and information, shifting the discussion from the "entire knowingness" of the subject to what objects or environments might know about us. Especially when those environments seem in constant connection with our passage, registering our presence, and transmitting it through networks and across time. For Bray and other spiritualists, this is a good thing, a promise of profound connections beyond the atomized self, or even proof of the immortality of the soul. But it has a very different valence now, returning with the rise of another seemingly transcendent medium for the constant interchange between minds, the capture of our movements and transactions, and passage through the georeferenced world. What Victorian spiritualists fantasized about the conservation and connection of souls through the ether, we now understand in a far more mundane, though almost equally mystified, context as data capture and surveillance, or what the Defense Advanced Research Projects Agency (DARPA) once menacingly called "Total Informational Awareness."[72] Beyond the omniscience of a single person, we now contend with the ambient capture of our digital contrails, processed in clandestine or corporate secrecy, otherwise masked within black boxes of algorithmic complexity, kept for who knows how long, by whom, or for what purposes. The extensive strangeness of it all manifests in the wildly disparate claims about its consequences, a contest between utopian and dystopian visions that strongly resembles what Pinch calls the "Victorian world crowded with extrapersonal thought-energy."[73] This section explains how the Victorians imagined such ambient awareness and how it anticipates surveillance cultures of data yet to come.

The idea that we leave psychical traces, unwittingly impressed on the world, was popular throughout the heyday of Victorian spiritualism. If Latimer represents a nightmare about other people's intimacies invading his brain, Bray sketches an inverse fantasy of the subject flowing into its environs: "Heat and electricity are constantly passing off from the body; so is mind."[74] Bray is preoccupied with the spiritualist's conundrum of connection, and, for all his emphasis on the "Persistence of Force," has very little to say about its persistence over time, or about memory, duration. That problem attracted other notable commentators, including Edgar Allan Poe. In a philosophical dialogue between spirits after the destruction of Earth, Poe hypothesized that "no thought can perish," as the "physical power of words" keeps them reverberating through the ether.[75] Poe likely borrowed the idea from Charles Babbage, whose *Ninth Bridgewater Treatise* dedicates a section to "the Permanent Impression of Our Words and Actions on the Globe We Inhabit." Babbage imagines the durability of sound waves inscribed on the air and potentially decodable by a supreme mathematical intelligence: "The air itself is one vast library, on whose pages are for ever written all that man has ever said or woman whispered." For Babbage, any natural medium permanently records our words and deeds: "the atmosphere . . . the waters, and the solid materials of the globe, bear equally enduring testimony of the acts we have committed."[76] Spiritualists would stretch Babbage's physics to explain less-tangible mediums. In their popular 1875 work *The Unseen Universe*, Balfour Stewart and Peter Guthrie Tait seize on a "principle of Continuity" to resolve the apparent schism between material and spiritual realms. They propose an "Ether" that connects them, but unlike Bray's Force, it has a memory: "a medium *plus* the invisible order of things."[77] Like the rooms Bray imagines imprinted with our photographs, the Ether conveys the memory of all it transmits. From this basis, Stewart and Tait argue that the immortality of the soul is assured, entirely congruent with physical reasoning. However we get to a future state, nothing will be lost, carried indelibly by the Ether that connects us all.

As Roger Luckhurst has documented, the efforts to theorize, even concretize such a medium as "force" or "ether" were widely shared between scientists and spiritualists at the time.[78] For some, recording media offered a useful metaphor. Bray turns to physics (heat and electricity) to model transmission but cites visual media (photography) to model recording, suggesting the entanglement of theories of memory with technologies of capture. That framework also appeared in the writings of William F. Barrett, member of the Society for Psychical Research, who reflected in his 1917 book *On the Threshold of the Unseen*:

> If our thoughts and characters are faithfully and indelibly being written on the unseen, we are, in fact, involuntarily and inexorably creating not only in our own soul, but possibly in the invisible world, an image of ourselves, a thought-projection, that embraces both our outer and innermost life.[79]

Like Bray's metaphor of the photograph, Barrett turns to the projection of images to explain this spiritual inscription, later comparing its records to "the rapid succession of instantaneous photographs seen in the cinematograph."[80] As Kittler and Gitelman have argued, late nineteenth-century recording technologies come to restructure ideas about memory, cognition, and expression.[81] In mixing with spiritualist (and later psychiatric) discourse, these technologies would take on dimensions of mind and memory. The resulting discourse of mnemotechnics inspired fantasies that have become tropes in science fiction, such as the uploading of all one's experiences and memories into an immortal life in the cloud, or the reanimation of deceased loved ones through AI, trained on the text, images, and video they leave behind. The origins of these fantasies, as well as the enduring confusion of data storage with memory, may themselves be lingering transmissions from the Victorian past.

Among the most vivid realizations of ambient memory appears in George du Maurier's novel *Peter Ibbetson* (1891).[82] The story is structured like a Victorian autobiography as the narrator recounts his life and revisits scenes—actually visits, thanks to psychic transport—from his youth. The narrator grows up in France (as Pierre Pasquier de la Marière, nicknamed "Gogo"), befriends a disabled girl, gets taken to England to grow up as a gentleman (becoming Peter Ibbetson), becomes an architect, then starts to "dream true" about meeting his young friend again, now in the guise of the unutterably beautiful Duchess of Towers, Mary Seraskier. For reasons that the novel poorly explains, Peter murders his uncle in an act of revenge and is committed to an asylum. There, in his enforced solitude, he lives a spiritualist's life apart, sharing a dreamworld with Mary, who teaches him further how to manipulate their vision. They start by revisiting all the scenes of their pasts, now accessible from the full spectrum of detail imprinted on their minds at the time, even though they paid little attention in waking life. As they hone their mnemonic sixth sense to traverse the fully documented past, they construct a house together, a palace of art with the wonders of European art and music and access to scenes and places beyond. Then, stretching deeper into ancestral memory, they start exploring their *genetic* pasts and even inhabiting other persons.[83] Every thought and act of every near relation or distant ancestor becomes exposed to their view, reaching back to Neanderthal witnesses of the great woolly mammoth. Years pass in the late nineteenth century, and Mary eventually dies, but she returns to Peter in dreams to describe a teeming universe of sound and light, the cosmos like "specks of spinal marrow" propagating itself through time and space (390). She brings back seven books written in cipher, and Peter starts to translate them, planning to include his own sketches of panhistorical tourism, whereupon he dies, ending the novel.

Peter Ibbetson is certainly part of an abiding late century psychophysiological interest in dream states and spiritual connections to people either distant or dead. In keeping with that discourse, the narrator relies extensively on analogies with recording media and attempts to hypothesize some material medium for the transcendental transmissions that establish dreamworlds and personal interconnections. He cites the optical telegraph (209), the "'camera-obscura' on Ramsgate pier" (216), and a participatory phantasmagoria that seems well on its way to imagining a Victorian virtual reality: beyond the "flat, silent little images" on a board or within his "dark chamber of the brain," he moves among the things and persons in his dream though it remains an "illusion" (217).[84] Peter even later asserts that, "It was no dream; it was a second life" (308)—a phrase that in 2002 became the name of the short-lived but widely popular community VR (virtual reality) platform. Acoustic media comes into play, too, as a way of explaining the ambient recording that now enriches their dreamworlds: "every word that had passed through Gogo's inattentive ears into his otherwise preoccupied little brain had been recorded there as in a phonograph, and was now repeated over and over again for Peter Ibbetson" (251). The capacity of photographs and cylinder recordings was, of course, hardly adequate for the fantasy of total recall that Peter explores, but recordable media shape his ideas about the mind: "Evidently our brain contains something akin both to a photographic plate and a phonographic cylinder, and many other things of the same kind not yet discovered" (277). If recording allows Peter complete access to his past, it seems also to hint at enhanced technologies of capture yet to come.

According Susan Zieger, du Maurier's novel itself is caught between two worlds of memory: "the rigorously organized, instrumentalized model of memory" in Victorian autobiographical fiction on the one hand, and the lavishly detailed "modernist version of aleatory memory" on the other.[85] Nor does *Peter Ibbetson* fully commit to the unconscious that psychoanalysis would probe below the waking mind. Rather, Zieger argues that the protagonist becomes a "media appendage," offering a consumerist fantasy of experience that could be played back anytime, anywhere.[86] In a similar vein, Galvan cites *Peter Ibbetson* as an example of the "phonographic unconscious" that allowed novelists, spiritualists, and psychiatrists to imagine different relationships to time.[87] Athena Vrettos uses the novel to show how "writers conceptualized memories, dreams, and the imagination as social, rather than solitary, mental functions, capable of making both telepathic and transhistorical connections with other minds."[88] I want to build on these arguments by shifting the focus from the remembering subjects to their relationship with recording environments. If *Peter Ibbetson* seems on the road to modernist "aleatory memory" or an impressionable unconscious, I argue it also forecasts a kind of *ambient memory* whose recording technologies did not yet exist. Zieger points to *Peter Ibbetson*'s legacy in speculative fiction about limitless uploadable brains, but *Peter Ibbetson* also suggests an uncanny reference point for thinking about data surveillance, digital storage, the technologizing of social memory, and virtual reanimation. Victorian spiritualism lives on in discourse about our digital doubles, the ghosts in the machine summoned by our unwitting passage through the data-collecting world.

Peter Ibbetson has to learn how to dream. Access to this "inner life" requires the paradoxical return to the details of his outer life he never thought to notice—but were captured nonetheless in his memory. As he explains, "Unconscious memory records them all, without our even heeding what goes on around us beyond the things that attract our immediate interest or attention" (227).[89] His dreamy return to these details resembles Barthes's photographic "punctum," whose strangeness resides not in the focused subject but in the curious capture of incidentals and background details the viewer might not otherwise have noticed.[90] But the discourse around information overload offers another useful framework for what Peter accomplishes: how to manage all the things in one's cognitive periphery: "everything you were aware of that didn't consume your attention, and that could be brought to the center of focus if necessary."[91] Malcolm McCullough, a professor of architecture, proposes that in an "age of unprecedented distraction," interface designers and users alike need strategies for accessing what remains *ambient*.[92] This includes what lies beyond our attention's periphery and reckoning with how thinking is embodied and environmentally extended, as in the growing field of research into extended cognition.[93] In learning how to dream, Peter has to reorient his memory to the penumbra of passing impressions and learn to access a memory that inheres in other persons, places, and things.

At first, Peter's dreamworld would seem circumscribed by the limits of his own lived experiences. He offers an analogy to the optical telegraph to explain these limits: for its visual signal to go farther, you'd need a line of sight to the next tower. But the novel plays a neat trick, making memory transferable from other people dreaming alongside. Like the character Neo in *The Matrix* who, facing his limits in the simulation, simply downloads into his brain some martial arts skills or the ability to pilot a helicopter, Peter need merely touch hands with Mary to infuse his memories with her own. What he calls "that strange sense of the transfusion of life" (292–93) or the "strange circuit" (301) or even "magical circuit" (303) connects them totally. It accords with visions of the complete sympathy enabled by telegraphic and even telepathic contact. But du Maurier adds a new dimension of shared memory. In the novel, this "transfusion of identity" affords them fantastical opportunities for shared exploration and world-building (359). At the same time, Peter cannot help notice that this "double dream, common to us both" (244) means unprecedented access to each other's minds: "Every thought she ever had from her childhood to her death has been revealed—every thought of mine!" (301). Latimer's real-time omniscience pales when compared to the total transfusion of mental history, the fire hose of someone's ambient experiences that even *they* might not consciously remember.

"Nothing is lost—nothing!" (391) exclaims the spirit Mary, having returned from the great beyond with a message of comfort that we, with all our memories and loves, will endure as surely as the ethereal soul hypothesized by Stewart and Tait in *The Unseen World*. But if this promise offers compensation after death, it serves a poignant warning in life, as every thought, every action, every dimension of your mental experience will join the ambient commons. Surveillance is total and forever. In *Self-Help* (1859), Samuel Smiles admiringly quotes Babbage's treatise, then explains the moral implications of such a durable past: "No man's acts die utterly. . . . It is in this momentous and solemn fact that the great peril and responsibility of human existence lies."[94] Becoming aware of this "peril and responsibility," Peter Ibbetson expresses relief that his own "self-restraint and self-respect . . . has kept me from thoughts and deeds that would have rendered me unworthy" to Mary who can now access his past. Not to mention the generational cascade of Peter's descendants who will all awaken to his psychically recorded life (302). Total memory implies moral judgment, and Peter asks us to "remember" in a didactic address:

> Reader, remember so to order your life on earth that the memory of you . . . may smell sweet and blossom in the dust—a memory pleasant to recall [. . . And] be tender to the failings of your forbears, who little guessed when alive that the secrets of their long buried hearts should one day be revealed to *you*! (361, original emphasis)

Peter Ibbetson urges readers to internalize the program of nostalgia that Dames finds in the Victorian autobiographical novel, but under stranger conditions, as nothing can ever be forgotten and all history seems to collapse into the eternally accessible moment of now. Again, spirit Mary finds this cause to celebrate, explaining to Peter the cosmic dimensions of immediacy: "there is no middle!—no end, no beginning, no middle! no middle, Gogo! think of that! it is the most inconceivable thing of all!!!" (401). Having returned from the far reaches of the etherverse, Mary presents the very dream of media—the erasure of its middle—as the alpha and omega of her spiritual realization.[95] This goes beyond theories of immediacy to a fantasy of universal storage, connected cognition, and lossless recall any time in the future. Memory is not only ambient, but permanent.

The fantasy of endlessly extensible, ever-enduring memory gets constructed in the late nineteenth century in the context of recording media, spiritualism, and emerging psychiatric discourse. This model of the mind extends through twentieth-century fantasies of total storage, many of which seized on the computer as a new mechanism to explain it.[96] And it has further evolved in reactions to the internet—especially in the social media era—which alternately fantasize and worry about the seeming perpetuity of digital memory. "The web means the end of forgetting," asserts law professor Jeffrey Rosen.[97] Or it promises "perfect remembering," according to Viktor Mayer-Schönberger.[98] For optimists, digital storage offloads the taxing mental activities of remembrance, often in keeping with a neoliberal ethos of optimization. Digital services allow for the "outsourced mind," according to David Brooks: "Memory? I have externalized it. . . . Personal information? I have externalized it."[99] Yet that sense of externalized, perfect remembering also creates a profound sense of unease about living in "a world where the Internet records everything and forgets nothing."[100] As individuals take on digital personhood, they confront a weird chronotopia in which "all moments of history are accessible via online search, all moments of time are equidistant."[101] Their ephemeral acts of conversation, performed identities, and transactions are seemingly stored somewhere for all time. According to Turkle, "everything you say online is kept forever."[102]

But, as with their spiritualist forebears, these hyperbolic claims are a fantasy, imagining a durable and intangible medium that does not exist. They confuse digital memory with the messy realities of storage and preservation.[103] And they hardly acknowledge other recent arguments that say exactly the opposite: that the web is forgetting *all the time*, that digital files are nightmarishly ephemeral. If Mayer-Schönberger claims that, in the web era, "forgetting has become the exception, and remembering the default," the International Federation of Library Associations and Institutions would beg to differ, having seen the concept of a "digital dark ages" introduced in 1997, in which we are, by default, not keeping but losing entire swaths of born-digital records.[104] The faith in perpetual digital memory actually produces its opposite: a lack of awareness, concern, and investment to curate precarious digital materials for even the near future. Like Brooks "outsourcing" his memory to "external cognitive servants," this perspective overlooks and devalues the infrastructures, care work, and globalized labor that support the fantasy of an autonomous consumer. Permanent digital memory is a political fantasy that preserves and deepens hierarchies of power. It also profoundly misunderstands how and why memory technologies work. As the computer scientist Jeff Rothenberg quipped, "digital documents last forever—or five years, whichever comes first."[105] The joke neatly collapses the paradoxical temporalities within discussions of digital memory, from eternity to evanescence. Between a whole historical era and the embarrassing lifespan of software, between lived experience and the picoseconds of arcane computational processes, between the horizons of death and permanent digital afterlives: the digital has warped the relationship of memory and time.

Digital memory blurs many of the same ontological boundaries that Victorian spiritualists and psychologists were attempting to theorize. As they proposed the "persistence" or "continuity" of force, ethereal order, spirit, and so on, data utopians likewise envision its continuity with the human mind, its perpetual reach into the future, and its bridge of the living and the dead.[106] Nothing will be lost. As Microsoft researcher Gordon Bell once promised about "e-memory," "You will have virtual immortality."[107] Some companies—like Re;memory—now promise your enduring connections to loved ones after death, reanimated in text, speech, image, video, and hologram by AI trained on your life's data.[108] In the cloud, our data becomes sublime. And it produces uncanniness of its own. As Grant Bollmer hauntingly suggests, "there is no real way to distinguish between the living and the dead online."[109] Like the ether, the "cloud" itself impossibly signifies both the unknown and everything that can be known.[110] It encourages supernatural fantasies. If *Peter Ibbetson* envisions a consumerist fantasy about endlessly consumable media, the cloud offers a fiction to information consumers untroubled by the intermediaries, material resources, invisible labor, and corporate extractivism it depends on.[111] We can dissolve into the cloud only if we learn how to dream. Peter Ibbetson learns with the aid of analogies to Victorian media, as they validate his psychic recording and actuate the "magic circuit" of his interchanges with his dream environment. Similarly, the grandest claims about digital memory depend on our embrace of computational models of mind and delusions of permanent information storage. But the fantasy that "there is no middle" remains just that. While Mary Seraskier beckons him to fully embrace the cosmic light, Peter Ibbetson remains uncomfortably tethered to the benighted earth, knowing that his actions, memories, and thoughts are apparently no longer his own. Like *The Lifted Veil*, the novel dramatizes the seductions and shortcomings for someone caught between worlds. In this sense, it also forecasts the uncanniness of life and death in an era of data surveillance.

Anxious claims about permanent digital memory have also emerged from the casualness and seeming ubiquity of data capture. Johanna Drucker has suggested renaming "data" as "capta," always captured within an epistemological framework with its own material dependencies and structures of power.[112] Data capture has become big business, with tech and media companies driving a new era of "surveillance capitalism."[113] As Blanchette and Johnson note, around the 1990s the discourse around data privacy shifted from concerns about discrete surveillance records of persons to the *transactional* data captured from different platforms.[114] What Meg Leta Jones calls "the web of trackability" now reaches far beyond the search habits of a Google user on a personal computer.[115] Newer digital traces get left with mobile devices, GPS units, credit cards, highway toll transponders, televisions, appliances, Internet of Things (IOT) devices, watches, security systems, frequent customer numbers, personal digital assistants, and smart speakers, in a room or a car, always listening. These transactions further cascade into data *about* the transactions, including information about devices, log times, location, and so on, all of which can be sold on data exchanges that most consumers have never heard of.[116] Commercial ventures also connect with state-sponsored data surveillance, brought infamously to light by the Edward Snowden leaks in 2013 about the NSA's programs to capture data from instant messages, cell phones, commercial communication providers, and immersive video games. These programs monitor for criminal activity and then try to *predict* it based on patterns within massive amounts of data. Prediction and inference are matters of great interest to big tech, too, from familiar instances like consumer recommendations to the creation of shadow accounts for people who have never signed up, but get nonetheless networked into a commercial ecology that profits from inferring their digital existence and selling it to others. Ultimately, captured data compasses the digital trails users leave as well as the proleptic activities they have yet to take. These days, we all have ghosts in the machine. And the machine not only seems to have unlimited memory, but prevision, too.

Privacy, Data, and the Right to Be Forgotten

As data capture infiltrates our environments and everyday transactions, we can reflect anew on the late nineteenth-century reckoning with mental life beyond the body, in which spiritualism and telecommunications pushed Victorians to imagine new models of the mind. As Jeffrey Sconce argued in *Haunted Media*, "many of our contemporary narratives concerning the 'powers' of electronic telecommunications have, if not their origin, then their first significant cultural synthesis in the doctrines of Spiritualism."[117] As this chapter proposes, that genealogy also extends to debates about digital memory: how much can the connected mind absorb and still ethically function? How much, or for how long, might an "externalized" memory retain information about us? And how can or should we respond to what seems like "the threat of digital memory"?[118] To this point, I have shown examples of how nineteenth-century literature modeled these questions in its own era, as well as some of the problematic ways that commentary about connectedness and digital memory have redeployed nineteenth-century tropes. These commentators are right to look to the past for inspiration, though wrong to normalize its politics, dreams of disintermediation, or salutary experiences of deep reading. Victorian literature can offer a genealogy of data privacy and ethics—but rooted instead in its ambivalences about what we can know and how to forget.

The previous section looked to *Peter Ibbetson* for du Maurier's awareness of the dialectics of endless memory and surveillance. The novel does not settle the case, as Peter dies in situ, caught between two worlds with his cosmic testaments untranscribed. Eliot's Latimer expires in a similar state: he dies at his writing desk having lost faith in language and short circuited the narrative with his pervasive omniscience. But elsewhere, Eliot's characters—perhaps like the author, post-1859—have to learn how to live through networked exposure, how to deal with the seductions and paralysis of "entire knowingness." If *The Lifted Veil* figures the moral paralysis of information overload, it also begins to suggest an ethics of forgetfulness developed more fully in some of Eliot's most famous protagonists, including Dorothea Brooke and Daniel Deronda. This ethic applies to individuals, such as tuning out the cacophony of the squirrel's raucous heartbeat. And it applies to an individual's place in history, so compellingly expressed in the last lines of *Middlemarch*: "the growing good of the world is partly dependent on unhistoric acts; and that things are not so ill with you and me as they might have been, is half owing to the number who lived faithfully a hidden life, and rest in unvisited tombs."[119] Starting with Eliot's wish in 1859 to cultivate "reverence before the secrets of each other's souls," she blends the recognition of social connectedness with an ethics of limited attention, not knowing, or what today gets called the right to be forgotten.[120]

Daniel Deronda was criticized for its attempt to compass too much. As Eliot wrote in a letter to Barbara Bodichon, "I meant everything in the book to be related to everything else."[121] But, as Dames explains, reviewers complained about *Daniel Deronda* for its own kind of overload, including its exhaustive "ambitions to totalizing interconnectedness."[122] Reviewers noted that such ambitions actually produced the opposite: fatigue and detachment.[123] And so *Daniel Deronda* is the exception that proves the rule: trying to compass everything, it ironically reveals our need to know less. The novel depicts that very process, as it works through the problems of omniscience and sympathy.[124] Mordecai possesses powerful forms of prophecy and mind connection, but Daniel seems to focus Eliot's skepticism from *The Lifted Veil*. The narrator notes that Daniel might even suffer from "a many-sided sympathy, which threatened to hinder any persistent course of action," resorting again to familiar language that his "too reflective and diffusive sympathy was in danger of paralyzing in him that indignation against wrong and that selectness of fellowship which are the conditions of moral force."[125] An overly capacious sympathy undermines his "moral force"; similarly, the indiscriminate pursuit of knowledge arrives at a "dead anatomy of culture which turns the universe into a mere ceaseless answer to queries."[126] As Pinch argues, the novel contradicts the premise that sympathy depends at all on "mental content or information transferred," a bias she finds throughout criticism on Eliot.[127] Instead, Pinch wants to consider sociality from a different angle. Sympathy assumes that we can know and feel with others, but Pinch startlingly turns this on its head: "thinking about another person starts being most social when it is least omniscient, and most wrong."[128] This does not mean cultivating ignorance about other people, but honoring, even revering, the value of limited social knowledge. Eliot's ethics might depend on what people ought not to know about each other.

Eliot and du Maurier together help outline concerns that are once again animating a discussion about mnemotechnics, exposure, and sociality, now under the aegis of the "right to be forgotten." This discourse has all kinds of contemporary international complexities and legal specifics but traces its own history to the late nineteenth century when Samuel Warren and Louis Brandeis published "The Right to Privacy" in 1890 in the *Harvard Law Review*. They argue that common law, based on property rights, no longer adequately protects the liberal subject in conditions of mass media. Now, "instantaneous photographs and newspaper enterprise" cross boundaries that cannot be defined as property, but as the province of "feelings."[129] Warren and Brandeis argue that feelings have a legal value but lack any legal protection, now made necessary as "numerous mechanical devices" seem to penetrate the "sacred precincts of private and domestic life."[130] They illustrate these "sacred precincts" with the specter of women's bodies and sexualities in public: "If you may not reproduce a woman's face photographically without her consent, how much less should be tolerated the reproduction of her face, her form, and her actions, by graphic descriptions colored to suit a gross and depraved imagination."[131] Ultimately, "The Right to Privacy" describes its legal framework within a classed, heteronormative reaction to the blurred erotic boundaries of Victorian telecommunications. As recording technologies became more ubiquitous and diffused across socioeconomic boundaries, Warren and Brandeis wanted a new legal framework to compensate for a lost social contract, or "trust." At the turn of the century, people seemed threatened by distributed forms of information capture beyond their control: "modern devices afford abundant opportunities for the perpetration of such wrongs without any participation by the injured party."[132]

Seeking some legal bulwark against the threats of socialized recording media, "The Right to Privacy" turns from property law to copyright within "the medium of writing or of the arts." Copyright, they argue, defends against unauthorized republication and "is merely an instance of the enforcement of the more general right of the individual to be let alone."[133] Notably, this argument depends not on the status of writing or the arts as intellectual property but as protected domains of feeling. Considering the importance of "The Right to Privacy" for so many contemporary legal discussions, it seems remarkable how firmly it enshrines the affective status of writing within the terms of the law: "The principle which protects personal writings and any other productions of the intellect or of the emotions, is the right to privacy."[134] Writing earns a privileged status as a container and conveyance of feeling, tantamount to the emotional privacy that Warren and Brandeis seek to defend against the assault of mediated exposure. In that sense, their argument has a long legacy in using literature to defend against networked media's assault on feeling, or its incursions into socially sacred spaces, as in Turkle, Carr, and others.

"The Right to Privacy" does not address some detachable concept of information. It protects an idea of feelings closely bound to literature and sexual propriety, developed by a privileged class in reaction to mass culture. But in responding to ubiquitous technological surveillance and the subject's loss of control, it establishes a throughline for privacy discourse in which information or data takes on a life of its own. In the landmark 1967 book *Privacy and Freedom*, law professor Alan Westin noted that developments in surveillance techniques had once again outpaced legal privacy protections established prior to World War II. Westin pointed to Cold War espionage, domestic surveillance by the FBI, the computerization of financial records (including by the nascent credit card industry), and psychological profiling with polygraphs and personality tests as hallmarks of a new era of surreptitious privacy invasion. Importantly, Westin recognized this was not just a by-product of "new recording and camera devices," but a larger shift toward the constant, machine-driven capture of quotidian experience, or what he calls "the *informal* arenas of conversation and action."[135] In contrast to "direct physical surveillance," Westin argues that privacy now must contend with "data surveillance—the maintenance of such detailed daily and cumulative records of each individual's personal transactions that computerized systems can reconstruct [. . . and use] for social control."[136] In addition to this prescient understanding of intrusive data systems, Westin also recognizes the individual's lack of control over this data or any legal recourse to challenge what it depicts. Privacy regulations must therefore also consider "how the individual will be able to challenge the data-file 'picture' of himself," left by daily traces and transactions, seemingly kept in perpetuity.[137]

Within the last few decades, mobile devices and the web have operationalized Westin's fears about a networked surveillance culture. They have also rekindled concerns at the heart of "The Right to Privacy" about publicity, reputation, and pornography. Just as Warren and Brandeis were responding to "recent inventions and business methods" in newspaper media, the legal discourse around internet privacy identifies media companies like Google as new agents of unwanted publicity.[138] Once again, no extant legal frameworks seem adequate for the boundary problems introduced by web searches, whose threats have been mostly litigated in the context of material damage to reputation. The legal landscape differs significantly by geographical and political context. Major cases in Europe eventually led to clarifications within the General Data Protection Regulation, instituted in 2018, which gives EU citizens the right to "delist" damaging information indexed by search engines.[139] However, just a year later, the European Court of Justice clarified that such privacy protections could not be legally enforced outside of the EU. That information might persist elsewhere, potentially still accessible through any number of connected channels. Similar appeals for individual privacy protection in the United States have failed to overcome courts' protections of free speech and commercial markets. But as Jones clarifies, "no country has a richly developed digital right to be forgotten."[140] As Turkle adds, "there is no place where you can 'fix' your double."[141]

Discussions of the right to be forgotten tend to highlight well-defined stories of people's exposure, embarrassment, or even trauma as a result of past or private information exposed in the networked present. For example, how outdated news reports of Mario Costeja González's debts prevented his making another attempt at a successful life.[142] How ill-judged photographs of Stacey the "drunken pirate" prevented her being hired as a teacher.[143] Or how two anonymous sisters are haunted by the forced pornography their abusive father captured of them as children, still lingering horrifically somewhere in the cloud.[144] The stories offer narrative structure with actors, transgressions, and a pursuit of forgiveness, redemption, or the peace of their story's erasure. They are narratives shaped by a "pathology of information" and the genres that have emerged to assess it. Faced with this condition, narrative tries to compensate for the otherwise unanswerable complexity and uncertainty of a social existence overshadowed by its own data. This patterns both Victorian spiritualism and its desacralized counterpart, the anxious discourse around digital memory.

Data privacy is uncannily contemporary and enduringly Victorian. Like that very anachronism, data privacy cannot resolve its own paradoxical temporality: what happens now is also forever. In an echo of *Peter Ibbetson*, Mayer-Schönberger claims the internet creates "a world of omnipresent history"—an oxymoron that compresses the stretch of history into any moment of omnipresent now.[145] Google's Eric Schmidt agrees: "It's very easy now to have a compendium of every word and deed," and users will have to get used to "living with a historical record," perhaps becoming more cautious about what they disclose.[146] Mayer-Schönberger calls this a "*temporal* panopticon" that prompts self-surveillance as well as anxiety about losing control of one's relation to history.[147] But this is "history" in its most anemic sense: the "history" of recent links in your web browser, rather than as a disciplined practice of researching, curating, and interpreting the past. As Jones explains, "the Internet is a lazy historian with no principled practices of preserving or protecting knowledge."[148] Yet that lazy historian seems to have remarkable influence, no accountability to the persons the data describes, and no institutional responsibility to preserve and share such data beyond a corporation's lifespan. As Bollmer points out, these contradictions come into sharp relief when corporations fail or when people die, yet their data endures, often beyond the control of family members appointed to execute any material legacy and memorialize a person's life. At these moments, "online information is revealed not only as separate from that of the user, but also as controlled and possessed by the network itself."[149] The digital subject is haunted by an omnipresent history when alive, superseded by a digital ghost after death.

Dispersed and exchanged and regenerated, data can escape the control of users and companies alike. The ambiguities of the digital subject are partly an effect of the business of data. In right-to-be-forgotten cases, companies like Google have contested take-down claims, arguing that they only index content that is actually hosted elsewhere. But many hosting companies hardly know what exists on their sites. Google Drive, Dropbox, and Amazon's cloud services have all been implicated in the sharing of illicit materials that darkly propagate across the web.[150] Further complicating things, users may have "doubles" constructed by algorithmic guesses about them, whether based on previously captured information or by inference from other users and their patterns. As Jones points out, "We are not only at the mercy of our own pasts; we are at the mercy of pasts of others who are like us."[151] Ironically, "personalization" technologies are largely based on predictions about *things you have not done*. The "network effect"—or mass consent to corporate data capture—allows such services perversely to become more personalized, based on your digital double they have inferred. Imagining how AI would allow Google to recommend things to a user, or remind them of their personal habits, even Schmidt conceded that "it's a little creepy sometimes."[152]

Users might try to scrupulously avoid services that capitalize on their data, but it can be difficult to "opt out" of the surveillance that mobile technologies and ambient signaling have enabled. Privacy advocate Cory Doctorow has highlighted how personal data leaks throughout the application ecosystem of mobile devices. Wi-Fi and Bluetooth sniffers installed in high-traffic public spaces can capture all sorts of demographic and geolocational data from passersby. This info can be sold to other data exchanges to follow users—or users like them—around the web. To opt out, Doctorow quips, "just stop ever leaving your house, never use the internet, and stop buying things."[153] State security apparatuses have likewise used an extensive network of surveillance cameras, CCTV, and computer vision techniques to transform public spaces into a zone of ubiquitous capture. One might recall Peter Ibbetson's dreamworld, reconstructed from the film of his ambient contacts: "We photograph our mental states on all the rooms we inhabit." We live this fantasy every day, ensnared by a network that captures while it connects.

The technology sector likes nothing better than to sell solutions to the problems it creates, including those this chapter has highlighted: surveillance and the loss of empathy. If users worry that their digital utterances are captured forever, just sell them "forgetting technologies" like Snapchat, which promise the rapid erasure of messages from a relatively closed circuit of communication.[154] Some scholars have similarly proposed technical solutions to the right to be forgotten, such as putting a time limit on personal information. But like Facebook's laughable pivot to "privacy," these technical modes of "forgetting" are still circumscribed by users' agreement to share their data, often superintended by commercial interests, and subject to manipulation. They do not fundamentally reimagine the rights of digital personhood.[155]

As with many technological problems, the more enduring solutions are likely to be social. They start by challenging the very vocabulary this chapter has used: who constitutes a "user," whether privacy is "personal," and if history or memory always need be remembered. The discourse around privacy, for example, emerged from an unquestioned faith in the rights of the autonomous liberal subject, largely consolidated during the nineteenth century and enshrined in Warren and Brandeis's patrician brief. But more recent approaches to digital privacy have measured its value differently. For instance, Julie Cohen reorients privacy in terms of an emergent, culturally situated notion of selfhood, arguing that privacy legislation must refocus from the individual to the conditions allowing subjects to variously establish their own engagements and boundaries.[156] Taking a similar approach, Ina Blom suggests that memory is a collective negotiation about a society's self-image, which has to be addressed in terms of a social ontology.[157] The perceived "crisis of memory" also results from certain cultural presumptions about archival control and the stability of messages. As an example, Rockwell and Berendt contrast the ethos of access and preservation within digital libraries with its inappropriateness for indigenous communities, for whom memory often cannot be separated from hierarchies of speakers and the forms and events of its retelling.[158] As Édouard Glissant insists, "opacities must be preserved."[159]

For many commentators, even those who fundamentally disagree about the threat of online exposure, empathy seems like a promising way forward. Turkle claims that "forgiveness follows from the experience of empathy."[160] danah boyd disagrees with Turkle about getting offline and disagrees with other commentators demanding technical solutions or strict internet regulations about privacy. Yet boyd's prescription is similar: "Fear is not the solution; empathy is."[161] It isn't that the internet disables empathy, but that discussions about digital privacy and data ethics could start with it—and with a notion of empathy that does not enshrine the white liberal ideal of "The Right to Privacy" but allows for difference, for subjects variously constituting their relations to others across the spectrum of cultural identification. Yet empathy may also fundamentally limit who is included in the conversation, or what structures of social relation are preserved or challenged.

The right to be forgotten might offer a different approach. Blanchette and Johnson recommend shifting the question from how privacy affects individuals to the social benefits of forgetting.[162] Jones agrees, pointing to a parallel discussion in criminal law about the ethics of restorative justice versus punishment. Jones wants to find forms of redemption, reinvention, and forgiveness suited to the digital age, but also acknowledges this is hard work.[163] In contrast with empathy, Davis suggests a framework of "mutual recognition": "accepting without understanding . . . recognizing that the Otherness is mutual."[164] Rather than seek connectedness, we might also accept and honor incommensurability, pursuing privacy, opacity, and forgetting as constitutive values in the socialized life of information.

Genealogies of these contrasting mindsets reach back through various traditions, but certainly include Victorian spiritualist discourse.

Its nascent sense of data ethics was clarified by fictions that imagine the consequences of ubiquitous connectivity and perpetual memory. They may help us understand and thrive within another historical era of mnemotechnical change. But not, as some commentators would have it, by restoring deep attentive reading and the empathic privilege of the literary. Imagined during another era of information overload and media surveillance, Victorian novels help us remember how to forget. Forgetting is not a solution to TMI but forms an ethics of sociality within these conditions. In looking to the past, we find a longer history of data ethics than what any new medium seems to dictate. We also find examples and cautions for how to sensibly use that history. Not as inspiration for rekindling forms of Victorian attention, but lessons in the complexity of responding socially to technological change.

THREE

HENRY JAMES, COUNTING WORDS, AND MACHINE READING

Her function was to sit there with two young men—the other telegraphist and the counter-clerk; to mind the "sounder," which was always going, to dole out stamps and postal-orders, weigh letters, answer stupid questions, give difficult change and, more than anything else, count words as numberless as the sands of the sea.
—HENRY JAMES, *In the Cage* (1898)[1]

The general methodological problem of the digital humanities can be bluntly stated: How do we get from numbers to meaning?
—RYAN HEUSER AND LONG LE KHAC, "A Quantitative Literary History of 2,958 Nineteenth-Century British Novels" (2012)[2]

HENRY JAMES BEGINS HIS 1898 novella *In the Cage* with an anonymous young woman who works in a London post office as a telegrapher. Consigned to work inside a dedicated "cage," the telegrapher is part of a rising tide of middle-class women working in late nineteenth-century telecommunications jobs, a source of significant Victorian anxiety about gender, class, labor, publicity, and privacy.[3] This telegrapher is engaged to marry a steady middle-class grocer, but she dreams of bigger things. In the course of her work, she becomes fascinated by the harried transactions of an attractive young aristocrat, Captain Everard, who is carrying on an affair with a certain Lady Bradeen. By surreptitiously memorizing their messages and deciphering the lovers' code, our telegrapher inserts herself into their relationship and, at a crucial juncture, solves a communications problem that might otherwise have exposed the aristocrats to scandal. However, at the moment of her triumph, when our telegrapher feels most closely linked to high society, her friend Mrs. Jordan reveals to her what really happened with the scandal—which, as happens in English stories, she learned from the butler.

On the surface, *In the Cage* is a story of aspiration and disillusionment. But thanks to its spotlight on the scene of telegraphy—"the most successful treatment of the telegraph in English literature"—*In the Cage* makes frequent appearances in scholarship on the literary and social history of late nineteenth-century communications.[4] As Menke suggests, *In the Cage* "represents telegraphy not just as a mode of communication but also as a social practice, a medium of discourse come to life, an information exchange rendered no longer transparent."[5] Scholars investigating the mediations of *In the Cage* have taught us lessons about telegraphic knowledge, gendered labor, surveillance, and the media ecology of the fin de siècle. But this chapter leaves telegraphy behind, shifting the scene to the media ecology of the near present. It argues that *In the Cage* offers a prescient glimpse of contemporary problems in humanities research: how to manage, read, and interpret texts at scale, specifically by counting words, or even by training machines to do so. The telegrapher's actual postal scale is just part of her quantitative labor; she deals in the quanta and counting of stamps, change, questions, and words. She also experiences texts in excess of measure: words "numberless as the sands of the sea." *In the Cage* thematizes the vast scale of textual proliferation that characterized the nineteenth century and dramatizes the telegrapher's search for meaning in those masses of words beyond counting—a problem also at the core of quantitative methods in digital humanities.

In this sense, *In the Cage* stages an early contest of "distant reading," a reckoning with how textual scale might require an unfamiliar form of hermeneutics. From one perspective, James seems far removed from the statistical analysis and exploratory data visualization that computationally minded scholars have used to explore digital collections of texts. Yet scholars including Natalia Cecire, Yohei Igarashi, and Benjamin Morgan have argued that the origins of "distant reading" appear well before even the mainframe punch card projects of the twentieth century in which DH conventionally finds its ancestry.[6] The interest in statistical analysis as literary interpretation develops in an earlier debate about the status of literature, reading, and criticism whose legacy shaped the profession of English. And James was right in the mix. As Dames explains, James has become a landmark for a theory of the novel—and an approach to literary criticism—that excluded more physiological or stylometric approaches to literary analysis active at that time.[7] That happened, as Cecire argues, by denying the possibility of other emergent forms of reading, including "machinic, outsourced, or otherwise cognitively displaced reading," which get gendered female and absorbed into technocratic regimes.[8] A hundred years later, "distant reading" has reignited those controversies and, in so doing, returned our attention to those formative turn-of-the-century moments to understand better our disciplinary legacy and its entanglements with reading machines.

In the Cage adds to these late nineteenth-century origin stories of distant reading, but it also moves that conversation from distant reading to questions about AI. While the telegraphist everywhere describes her labor as counting words, she succeeds in deciphering the aristocrats' coded messages because of her own quick intelligence. Critics have suggested the telegrapher breaks the social contract of telecommunications by showing how a transmission medium might still have memory—or what the telegrapher's boss calls an "underhanded game" (233). But there's another aspect of this game that the resurgence of interest in artificial intelligence has exposed: the self-training and predictive modeling of machine learning. In James's moment, such an approach to "learning" was already taking shape in psychometric approaches to education and pedagogies of speed reading. James wants to privilege the literary as a domain apart from mechanistic approaches to text.

But his own evolving composition practices, in dictating to recording secretaries increasingly attuned to his style, suggest that distinctions of authorial/artificial or human/machine or even close/distant were never so clear. I argue that these nineteenth-century contexts offer alternative genealogies of distant reading and machine learning without capitulating to their rhetoric. From telegraphers and speed-reading secretaries to gendered artificial intelligence agents and clickworkers, AI has relied on human labor it either marginalizes or renders invisible. Yet machine learning methods are entering DH practice; generative AI has prompted the next revolution in reading and writing. The analogy to a telegraph office might simplify the technology, but it reveals the complex negotiations of agency, authorship, and interpretation that AI would hide behind its curtain. To reckon with the future of automated reading and writing, we might return to the past, learning from late Victorian practices of counting words.

Counting Words

In the Cage is a crucial text for thinking about the relationship of late nineteenth-century literature and communications media. It concentrates the scene of transmission, its gendered labor, the varied expectations of class, the erotics of mediated contact, the limits of telegraphic knowledge, the unsettled boundaries of the psyche, the haptic dimensions of technology, the stylistics of telegraphic discourse—all of which have been treated in the extensive and excellent critical commentary on *In the Cage*.[9] I want to expand this careful historicism while once again shifting its time frame. James's story certainly enriches an understanding of fin-de-siècle telegraphic discourse in all its complexities, yet it also encodes latent messages about interpretation by the numbers that readers a hundred years later can uniquely understand. It signals the late Victorian origins of distant reading, as much a methodology as an argument about how interpretive reading can or should adapt to technological change. *In the Cage* characterizes telecommunication as people exchanging messages across different divides, including perhaps the divide of a century as we confront a similar shift in the mechanization of reading, the counting of words, and predictive intelligences for writing.

Throughout *In the Cage*, James describes late nineteenth-century telegraphy with an arithmetical lexicon; the telegrapher must "more than anything else, count words as numberless as the sands of the sea." Customers hand in slips inscribed with their messages; the telegrapher tallies the word count and the resulting charges, then passes the message to the person working the Morse key. She is constantly counting, figuring, adding, calculating for her appointed post office job. But she's also pursuing her own unlicensed interests, gathering impressions of a world beyond her cage. Circumscribed by the menial transactions of her job, she comes to speculate privately about what entities and relationships those counted words might reveal. Who are these people? What conversations and affiliations and secrets are they transacting? The messages lack context, are often indirect, and arrive in excess. She's absolutely awash in the quantity of persons and texts: "What *she* could handle freely, she said to herself, was combinations of men and women. The only weakness in her faculty came from the positive abundance of her contact with the human herd" (232). That herd is equally prolific with the most banal of correspondence, sent at an expense that shocks the telegrapher who grew up in harder circumstances: "she had often gasped at the sums people were willing to pay for the stuff they transmitted—the 'much love's, the 'awful' regrets, the compliments and wonderments and vain vague gestures that cost the price of a new pair of boots" (239). The flood of mundane correspondence distorts the very value of words, in their economic correspondence to goods as well as the "vague" signification of transmitted "stuff." Words have become commodities subject to conspicuous social consumption, flowing in such enormous quantities to wash away their semantic precision. When the telegrapher's friend Mrs. Jordan gently accuses her of having no sympathy for the telegraphing class, "The girl gave an ironic laugh, only retorting that nobody could have any who had to count all day all the words in the dictionary" (247).

In the Cage is a parable about alienated labor in the information age.

The telegrapher is not allowed to understand or interact with what she transmits. So she transgresses by imagining the significance of transmitted words *beyond* the dictionary, reconstructing the relations and subtexts they do not disclose or intentionally distort and transcending her station to join the "large and complicated game" of high-society intrigue (236). In a way, the telegrapher tries to labor like a novelist. We're meant to notice the parallel to James—as well as the privilege he claims as a novelist to know even more. As the narrator explains, "She had surrendered herself moreover, of late, to a certain expansion of her consciousness . . . there were more impressions to be gathered" from the traffic of telegraphs, which provides her "actual chance for a play of mind" (232). Compare this to the later preface to *In the Cage* that James wrote for the New York Edition of his collected works:

> The postal-telegraph office in general, and above all the small local office of one's immediate neighbourhood, scene of the transaction of so much of one's daily business . . . had ever had, to my sense, so much of London to give out, so much of its huge perpetual story to tell. . . . So had grown up, for speculation—prone as one's mind had ever been to that form of waste—the question of what it might "mean."[10]

If James's own visits to the postal-telegraph office inspired the story, the plot follows the search of its huge wastes of words for meaning. James the novelist speculates how its daily business might disclose the biggest possible story London could tell. "The question of what it might 'mean'" very much depends on scaling from the fragment to the bigger picture. "Any momentary wait" in the post office, James says, takes place in "the stiffest possible breeze of the human comedy" at large. And James celebrates widening the view: "The large intellectual appetite projects itself thus on many things, while the small . . . projects itself on few."[11] As he worked on such a grand scale for the New York Edition, James congratulates himself a little bit, elevating his collected works as a "human comedy" on the level of Balzac.[12] Yet, distinct from his other works, *In the Cage* uniquely transforms this general problem of interpreting "many things" into the language of counting words as a form of reading.

In the Cage shifts "the question of what it might 'mean'" into the language of quantitative inference, figured in the telegrapher's efforts to deduce patterns within the enormous volume of words she counts. As Otis puts it, "Bored by the task of breaking language into its component particles, she reconstructs it in her imagination even as she decomposes it in fact."[13] The story credits her with an "instinct for observation and detection," and the telegrapher turns her surveillance to account, coming up with "theories and interpretations" of what it all means (239). This plays out in her imaginative assembly of telegraphs and words as she tallies them at her desk, fixating on the relations of Captain Everard and Lady Bradeen: "in the thousands of other words she counted," she continually thinks of them (236). She supposes of Captain Everard that, "Nothing could equal the frequency and variety of his communications" (237). Increasingly fascinated by them, the telegrapher comes, in the language of the story, to "account him" as a new friend (237). She sifts their messages to attain a big-picture perspective, achieving what she calls "a prodigious view as the pressure heightened, a panorama fed with facts and figures" (239).

I share these examples to emphasize how numbers, counting words, and distant perspectives characterize the telegrapher's sense of her own power. She tells herself, "How much I know—how much I know!" (259). And yet she is humiliated to discover, by the end, that she knows very little: "[she] had, in the cage, sounded depths, but there was a suggestion here somehow of an abyss quite measureless" (300). Ultimately, her quantitative measures fall flat. Instead, "She caught only the uncovered gleams that peeped out of the blackness" (289). And: "she felt how much she had missed in the gaps and blanks and absent answers" (287). By disabusing the telegrapher of her supposed knowledge, James makes her a bad reader of these fractured texts and privileges the "gaps and blanks and absent answers" that inform his own narrative practice of encoding meaning between the lines, or within the "gleams" that peep out from his increasingly vague aesthetics.

In his later story "The Figure in the Carpet," James dramatizes the related failures of a literary critic to decipher the key to an author's greatness. Searching for the secret, at one point the critic wonders if it's simply a preference for the letter "P," decomposing the author's corpus to an elemental alphabetic fingerprint. The critic later travels to India, apparently having memorized the author's complete works, and at that distance—geographic and interpretive—he finally discovers the secret: "some day somewhere, when he wasn't thinking, they fell, in all their superb intricacy, into the one right combination. The figure in the carpet came out."[14] In his excitement, he telegraphs to his fiancée: "Eureka. Immense." But he later dies in a driving accident, leaving only a "heartbreaking scrap" of an explanation of his discovery.[15] Here again, James contrasts extreme scales of text and interpretation—fragments and complete figures, telegraphs and literary oeuvres—and the frustrated ambitions of someone trying to read between them. The critic might have discovered the secret, but, for James, he "wasn't thinking."

From a more contemporary perspective, these are stories about experimental reading methods in an era of unprecedented textual scale. They help show when quantitative modes of textual interpretation became possible, perhaps even necessary, and hotly contested.[16] Debates about the merits of distant reading are as old as the method, consolidating during the very late nineteenth century decades when James was formulating his literary criticism. As Igarashi argues, "As soon as one steps back from the fact of digitality, . . . one sees a longer history involving the application of statistical methods or nineteenth-century 'statistical thinking' to linguistic artifacts, including literary ones, long before the digital humanities or corpus linguistics."[17] Susan Hockey's "History of Humanities Computing" finds the mathematician Augustus Morgan ruminating in 1851 about a vocabulary-based quantitative study of Paul's Epistles, which the American linguist Thomas Corwin Mendenhall later performed on Shakespeare.[18] "The ancestors of modern stylometrics or computational stylistics" can be found in a robust turn-of-the-century discussion about literary stylistics, including linguists such as Mendenhall, L. A. Sherman, and Robert Moritz.[19]

Mendenhall's 1901 report, "A Mechanical Solution to a Literary Problem," published in *Popular Science Monthly*, reads like "a primal scene of distant reading, computer and all," according to Benjamin Morgan.[20] In 1887, Mendenhall had already published a study in *Science Magazine* about attributing the authorship of literary fiction based on counting word lengths alone. Mendenhall's guiding analogy is spectroscopy, or the physical analysis of materials by what spectrum of light they emit when heated. So Mendenhall proposes to find the "word-spectrum" of notable authors.[21] He argues that differences in specific works and periods of authorship will resolve into regular patterns *"in the long-run."*[22] Mendenhall and his assistants test books by Dickens, Thackeray, and John Stuart Mill as well as the political address of Edward Atkinson, opening them at random locations and counting words, the letters they contain, words of various lengths, and other features.

Mendenhall's study suggests both the long history of late nineteenth-century text analysis and its mutations into distinct disciplinary species, specifically into a social science that continues to trouble discussions of computational literary criticism. Mendenhall concludes by emphasizing the two "principal merits" of this method: first, it promises "a means of investigating and displaying the mere mechanism of composition, ... characteristics which a writer would make no attempt to conceal, being himself unaware of their existence."[23] Mendenhall notes how stylistic signatures can hinge on the smallest elements: the frequency of two-letter words distinguishes Mill from the other writers.[24] Second, this method is "purely mechanical in its operation ... independent of personal bias" in allowing comparisons among different writers and texts.[25] This mechanical and objective approach has its inheritors, too, in the stylometrics of authorship attribution studies, corpus linguistics, and the application of text analysis for certain projects in the sciences. For example, publishing in *Science* magazine in 2010, one such team claimed to invent a new field of "culturomics."[26] Like Mendenhall tracing the "characteristic curves" of authorship, they analyzed a digital corpus of over five million books to find "cultural trends" as graphed by Google Book's n-gram viewer (essentially, a tool for counting the frequencies of words or combinations of words over time). While Mendenhall used spectroscopy as his model, this team invoked genomics (rhyming "culturomics" with a long ō) and used its structural determinism to posit an evolving cultural genome expressed in 400 years of published books. Also like Mendenhall, they underscored how their "rigorous quantitative inquiry" offers a new approach to humanities and social science materials.[27] Ultimately, they claim that, "Culturomic results are a new type of evidence in the humanities. As with fossils of ancient creatures, the challenge of culturomics lies in the interpretation of this evidence."[28] Putting aside the problem that "fossils of ancient creatures" do not actually fall within the humanities' purview, the team's confidence raised hackles by claiming a method of text analysis—the "precise measurement of the underlying phenomena"—far afield from traditional humanistic interpretation.[29]

Mendenhall is not distant reading's only ancestor: other turn-of-the-century experiments showed how numbers, counting, and statistics could also accommodate more humanistic perspectives. Or, relatedly, how seemingly oppositional critical formations—distant and close reading, to take the obvious pairing—instead entangled quite closely. Lisa Marie Rhody has urged DH scholars "to create and to occupy many new critical distances" beyond that binary—and historical precursors might offer some salutary models.[30] Igarashi, for example, notes how I. A. Richards—among the founders of new critical close reading in literary studies—was interested in word lists, or Basic English, calculated by statistical commonality, as grounds for the paraphrase exercises his practical criticism required.[31] Underwood and Dames each point to Raymond Williams for his interests in sampling and critical experimentation in charting the *long durée* of cultural history.[32] Morgan considers the literary statistics of Vernon Lee—a "distant reader *avant la lettre*, lacking only the proper software"—who studied how units of language and sensory impressions could variously combine to produce empathy.[33] Yet distant reading suggests a philosophical difference that Lee did not herself observe. As Morgan suggests, Lee worked with "forms of interpretation that would not take for granted an opposition between a phenomenological account of reading and a statistical analysis of literary texts."[34] Computational criticism has underscored the differences between "forms of interpretation that are normally perceived as taking place at widely divergent scales," but experiments with literary stylistics between the 1890s and 1920s did not discriminate in quite the same way.[35]

This, too, has its more recent inheritance in DH discussions that either attempt to synthesize close and distant perspectives or else foreground the contingency that numbers and data always demand.[36] The surge of attention to "distant reading" during the 2000s tended to follow the arguments of its coiner, Franco Moretti, who emphasized the problems of scale in literary arguments.[37] Larger digital collections, more books, more data would seem to produce new assessments of literary history. In *Distant Horizons*, Underwood emphasizes the untold literary histories hidden by the "sheer scale" of what we cannot easily perceive and points to the possibilities of computational discovery from "thirty thousand feet."[38] But Underwood also notes that the rhetoric of distant reading has shifted away from scale. As the discussion around quantitative analysis or "computational literary studies" has progressed, its vocabulary has moved from counting words to the concept of modeling.[39] That concept tries to avoid the binary contrast between numbers and words, summoning instead a still-imaginative, still-contingent critical act of making an argument, though in a different way. As Andrew Piper explains, "Focusing on models... moves us away from this binary logic of size—where bigger is always better—toward one of representation."[40] Models are arguments about what data represents. And here is where digital humanities researchers come into their strengths: not in manipulating data, but thinking about the relationship of data to evidence—or, as James put it, "the question of what it might 'mean.'" In their pamphlet *A Quantitative Literary History of 2,958 Nineteenth-Century British Novels*, Ryan Heuser and Le-Khac Long put it this way: "The general methodological problem of the digital humanities can be bluntly stated: How do we get from numbers to meaning?"[41] Or how does counting words become reading them?

The genealogy of distant reading inheres as much in the hermeneutic challenge of interpreting counted words as in specific scholarly methods including concordances, statistical analysis of language use, and quantitative explorations of literary style, authorship, and genre. Furthermore, early experiments in distant reading—especially during the decades from 1890 to the 1920s—did not necessarily observe the disciplinary divides that now trouble its status in the humanities. Predigital debates about DH, so to speak, would concern the relation of counting words to the proper objects, method, and labor of literary criticism. James specifically helps show how text analysis gets constructed in opposition to idealized literary authorship and reading. As Morgan explains, James was a major figure in the rejection of "Victorian moral-aesthetic evaluative criticism" in favor of what became close reading as such.[42] Dames charts the Jamesian critical tradition emerging between "The Art of Fiction" in 1884 and Lukac's *Theory of the Novel* in 1920, displacing the interests in aesthetic physiology and mass reading culture that Dames has done much to recover.[43] *In the Cage* clarifies how this critical transformation occurred in reaction to more statistical interests in reading—as well as how those approaches became gendered and dismissed as unintellectual labor.

Social histories of technology have pointed to cultural factors in how mechanized reading was characterized and then denigrated. For example, Cecire finds an origin story in Gertrude Stein whose work was dismissed by critics like Edmund Wilson as "half-witted-sounding catalogues of numbers."[44] Cecire helps shift the question of distant reading to the devaluation of its gendered labor, whether in the form of late Victorian telecommunications workers or Stein's experimental poetics. At root was the "deeply gendered question of whose reading and writing counts as real work, which . . . always powerfully informs the history of digital reading."[45] Ultimately, Cecire argues that, "Distant reading is women's work"—by which she implicates the process of "female intellectual labor being naturalized, located in the body, and rendered as nonwork," from the turn of Stein's century to the digital present.[46] The erasure of women from the history of computing has likewise distorted histories of humanities computing. In "Roberto Busa's Female Punchcard Operatives," Melissa Terras recovers the numerous women computers who did the work of the "father of DH."[47] In a similar spirit, Buurma and Heffernan recommend that DH replace Busa with Josephine Miles in its historiography. In contrast to the managerial detachment of Busa, Miles worked much more closely with the data, valued imaginative programming, and "credited the woman typists and punch card operators she collaborated with." Yet because of this approach, because she "worked at a time in which the making of data sets was regarded as feminized and mechanical," her historical significance has largely been eclipsed.[48] As Lauren Klein argues, unless quantitative literary studies broadens its concepts of knowledge work, including editing and curation, it will render such labor invisible.[49]

These arguments all underscore why the anonymous telegrapher in *In the Cage*—"our young critic," James calls her at one point—cannot succeed in James's literary cosmos. Not simply because her interpretive strategies fail, or that James denigrates counting words compared to some higher aesthetic pursuit. Rather, her imaginative labor cannot be valued while men like James seek to claim literary critical authority. *In the Cage* forcibly teaches the telegrapher what real reading is supposed to look like. As Nicola Nixon demonstrates, *In the Cage* disabuses the telegrapher of her class presumptions and gendered credulity through the "metafictional" language of reading.[50] The telegraphist must learn to be a "critical reader" along the lines of the "critical heroism that James had detailed seven years earlier in 'The Science of Criticism.'"[51] If so, such criticism defines itself explicitly against the counting of innumerable words and the women who collect, quantify, and interpret them. Ironically, to resist the technologizing of reading, this discourse technologized women's bodies and work—a pattern that extends from Victorian telecommunications to recent representations of AI. But Victorian contexts also tell a different story about the mechanical re-imagination of reading. That history shifts the emphasis from scale to speed, from interpreting texts to predicting them, and from pedagogies of reading to machine learning.

Rapid Reading, Machine Reading

To this point, I have set *In the Cage* against debates in literary criticism, then and now, which are relatively easy to see given James's own declarations and his prominence in the disciplinary history of English. Here, I want to consider another contest that *In the Cage* subtly engages—and one whose relevance, like that of counting words, emerges more clearly in retrospect. *In the Cage* raises the "meaning question" of getting from massive amounts of words to social insight—and James seems to take sides. Skepticism about counting words has remained since the early objections to statistical literary analysis: Bode points to a 1922 handbook of methods in English studies that declares from the start that "statistics and charts" have no place in literary criticism.[52] Reactions to distant reading in its digital forms levy the same objections: Nan Z. Da argues that all computational literary studies devolve to "counting words," which, however elaborate the methods, has "no ability to capture literature's complexity."[53] Da echoes other critiques that argue how distant reading impoverishes the literary and cultural phenomena that remain unquantifiable, impossibly complex, and deeply subjective.[54] Yet these divides are less clear in a longer historical context; they also risk deepening the split between human/machine, close/distant that might deserve repair. Looking further back, we can see how the origins of distant reading entangle with major changes in the late nineteenth-century understanding of reading as itself a technical process. In this context, counting words shifts to a predictive intelligence that speeds up reading. Its legacy is a category of AI called machine learning; its lesson is resisting the problematic erasures by which AI pretends it is artificial.

What has become popularized as "artificial intelligence" offers more to marketers and the public imagination than it explains its computational process. Contemporary AI no longer tries to simulate a human brain or create consciousness in a computer, sometimes called artificial general intelligence. Machine learning, in contrast, is based on fuzzy statistical models and lots of human supervision to train them. Historically, the turn to statistical modeling occurs in the 1990s, as computer scientists moved away from logic trees of branching decisions (imagine a flowchart), and instead trained computing power on analyzing and then predicting relations among every possible variable within the data. A hundred years prior, such predictive modeling was also taking shape in the context of how to teach people to read—and to read faster and more efficiently than ever.

Amid turn-of-the-century developments in physiological studies of eye movement and speed reading pedagogies, we can see the stirrings of the predictive analytics that machine learning would formalize, and how it spurred sometimes anxious, sometimes utopian speculation about what it might facilitate. At the time, many readers were feeling the need for speed, given the overwhelming landscape of nineteenth-century print media. These days, defenders of a high-minded ethics of reflective reading like to hold up the Victorian novel as a contrast to the fractured reading of our digitally mediated experiences. But as Dames argues, the Victorians knew their novels differently:

> the novel of the nineteenth century trained a reader able to consume texts at an ever faster rate, with rhythmic alternation of heightened attention and distracted inattention locking onto ever smaller units of comprehension ... the Victorian novel was a training ground for industrialized consciousness, not a refuge from it.[55]

Dames understands the novel less as a negative example than as part of a broader interest in the "physiology" of reading, as he calls it, which explored the connections between reading, cognition, and the mind: "Physiology was the metalanguage of nineteenth-century novel theory."[56] Toward the end of the century, developments in ocular physiology "fundamentally altered reading as an object of knowledge," exchanging questions about aesthetics and understanding for studies of eye movement and speeds of comprehension.[57] With that change, Victorian anxieties about rapid reading shifted toward utopian aspirations for speed reading and, ultimately, "telegraphic" methods of mental communication.[58] As we shall see, the physiological approach to reading opens a historical path from training efficient readers to training intelligent machines.

The French ophthalmologist Louis Émile Javal was among the first to track eye movements as a way of studying how people read. He realized eye movements were "discontinuous and fragmented" as they passed over text, "indicating for the first time that the way the human mind responded to language was less lineal than structural."[59] The American educational psychologist Edmund Huey did Javal one better, attaching to subjects' very eyeballs (!) a plaster-of-Paris cup that would move a tracing arm as they read. In another effort to quantify response speeds, James McKeen Cattell had subjects "place a telegraph key between their lips, which, when dropped, would break an electrical current and provide a record of split-second timing."[60] Cattell would later adapt this device to measure subjects' reading speeds. But the mechanization of ocular physiology found its killer app in the "tachistoscope," a device that vertically mounted text or symbols or other visual information, with a small window allowing only a small section to appear at one time. To test reading speeds, operators could move that window downward at varying rates. If ocular physiology shifted reading studies from epistemology to cognitive mechanisms, the tachistoscope shifts reading from "the page to the screen," establishing a design rationality that extends into twentieth-century instructional technology and the development of computer display hardware.[61]

Setting *In the Cage* against these backgrounds reveals a different aspect of the telegrapher's work. First, the telegrapher's cage morphs into a tachistoscope: the cage is a "frail structure of wood and wire" whose walls are a "transparent screen," and the numberless "words of the telegrams [are] thrust, from morning to night, through the gap left in the high lattice." The small window regulates the exchange of words; the cage itself becomes a space of controlled symbol processing, the site of James's fictional experiment about how much the telegrapher can read and comprehend. The telegraphist's cage turns into her classroom. During these same decades, 1890–1920, experiments with the tachistoscope shifted from physiology to pedagogy. If reading speeds could be observed, quantified, and statistically rationalized, then other readers could be taught based on those principles. Furthermore, typography, page layout, and prose style could be optimized based on what ocular physiologists had deduced about eye-to-brain cognition. Together, these principles established an emerging pedagogy of hyperefficient reading that persisted well into the twentieth century. For instance, Charles Acland shares a 1966 advertisement for a tachistoscope marketed to schools: "Thousands of Schools are Teaching MORE with LESS EFFORT by using the Keystone Tachistoscope."[62] The ad's descriptive text starts to clarify how this works: "Perceptual reading skills are quickly developed by tachistoscopic training."

At the turn of the century, such "training" was informed by observations about how readers wanted to find information from a text, about how they learned. Sue Currell suggests that "attempts to measure reaction time had a huge impact on ideas about the transmission of language and meaning through printed media."[63] As in the advertisement, the discourse shifted from speed reading to efficient learning. The tachistoscope and related devices showed that speed was also a function of what readers could successfully *predict* about a text. Experimental physiologists noticed proactive as much as reactive tendencies in measuring reader responses to machine tests. In his 1908 *Psychology and Pedagogy of Reading*, Huey reflects that "the most striking thing observed in the experiments" with the tachistoscope was readers' desires—when shown only parts of texts—to extrapolate missing information. They variously described this desire as a "forward push," "forward tendency," or "tendency to fill out."[64] And the more prolepsis readers brought to the text, the faster they could go, the more they could intuit and understand. As Currell explains, "Huey's tests showed that anticipation and association made reading faster . . . rationalized reading was not in fact a speeding up the reading of individual words but training the mind to anticipate the structures of language and make associative connections more quickly."[65] Other scientists concurred: Adelaide Abell in 1894 proposed that "any attempt to improve reading ability must include the effort to increase the rapidity of association by repeating and multiplying associations and by intensifying interest and attention."[66]

From association to anticipation, from training to predictive understanding. Here too, we see the underappreciated talents of James's telegraphist. She embodies an approach to learning characterized by sifting data, finding patterns, and inferring particulars. When seen in the context of tachistoscopic reading, the telegrapher helps make the connection between counting words and what would become machine learning—as well as how both become contentious for literary criticism. Stuck in her cage with words flooding through the small gap, the telegrapher has to rely on both her instincts and her notable capacity for recognition. According to the narrator, "Her eye for types amounted nevertheless to genius" (239). As she processes messages, she establishes "combinations of men and women" in the regularity of their contacts (232). These combinations become the template for her imaginative embellishment: "She found her ladies, in short, almost always in communication with her gentlemen, and her gentlemen with her ladies, and she read into the immensity of their intercourse stories and meanings without end" (241). James's language of reading—she will "read into" messages and find scenes to "beat every novel in the shop" (256)—tends to overdetermine what we think the telegraphist aspires to do: rewrite her own life as a florid romance novel. Presented with "an unintelligible enumeration of numbers, colours, days, hours" in the telegrams she sorts, the telegraphist would reconstruct them into stories (245). To make such enumeration intelligible again, she has to supply missing information, which, she knows, is not always accurate: "Sometimes she put in too much—too much of her own sense; sometimes she put in too little" (234). At these moments, the telegraphist remains aware of her own intervention and makes adjustments: as "she lived more and more into the world of whiffs and glimpses, she found her divinations work faster and stretch further" (239).

The telegraphist seems to improve her ability to extrapolate stories from scraps, like James speculating on London's grand story outside his post office. But James characterizes her "divinations" as a very different sort, emerging from a statistical as much as a romantic approach to social discovery. As she comes to fixate on the case study that really interests her—Lady Bradeen and Captain Everard—the telegraphist turns counting words into a basis for text prediction. Her excitement rises through several scenes of self-training: "Every time he handed in a telegram it was an addition to her knowledge" (253). The telegraphist works with more than the usual interest for Lady Bradeen too, as when she "pushed in three bescribbled forms which the girl's hand was quick to appropriate" (233). The word "appropriate" does a lot of work here, as the telegraphist physically collects the paper, absorbs the logic of the encoded messages, and learns the "hand" in terms of handwriting as well as the agency of composition. Indeed, "She would know the hand again any time" (235). The more examples she trains on, the better she gets at decoding and ultimately predicting their exchanges:

> He was sometimes Everard, as he had been at the Hôtel Brighton, and he was sometimes Captain Everard. He was sometimes Philip with his surname and sometimes Philip without it. In some directions he was merely Phil, in others he was merely Captain. There were relations in which he was none of these things, but a quite different person—"the Count." There were several friends for whom he was William. There were several for whom, in allusion perhaps to his complexion, he was "the Pink 'Un." (238)

In this passage, the telegraphist tracks word correlations as a way of indexing this man's masked relations. To put it differently, the telegraphist builds a model. She uses whatever untruths or nicknames or indirect references she receives and infers their network. "Words" matter less than the unarticulated logic of their relations. In fact, the telegraphist delights in all that remains *unsaid* between her and Everard. When the telegraphist conspires to talk to him, their conversations are an absurdity, based on the evacuated words characteristic of his class, but still demonstrating her knowledge of the relationships they nonetheless constitute: "Everything, so far as they chose to consider it so, might mean almost anything" (253). Of course, with this paradox, James satirizes the banality of their spoken exchanges. But the question of what things "might mean" looks a little different than just counting words. Now, the meaning question has become a social agreement, an acknowledgment that the telegraphist understands the rules of the game.

The telegraphist enters that game as a player at two uncanny moments in the story. In the first, she finds an error in one of Lady Bradeen's encoded telegrams: it mistakes which false name corresponds to which place. But the telegraphist knows: "for Miss Dolman it was always to be 'Cooper's.'" Discretely, she suggests the correction much to the shock of Lady Bradeen. "Oh, you know—?" Lady Bradeen stammers, with that dash marking the links she thought were invisible. The telegraphist knows the linkages: whether or not those amount to "knowledge" is very much James's point. But the telegraphist has at least learned the hidden pattern: "her grasp was, half the time, just of what was *not* on the face" (259) thanks to "her own grand memory" (260) or what's later described as "her recollection of previous arrangements, fitted into a particular setting" (285). To make the correction, the telegraphist suggests "I'll do it" and "put out a competent hand" to rewrite the message. Having appropriated that hand already, she can write for Lady Bradeen, a telegraphist turned into an autocorrect algorithm. The second intervention comes later in the story and is more obscure. This time, a harried Everard rushes to her cage to track whether or not a previous message was sent to the right recipient. At risk of exposure to scandal, he is incredibly relieved to discover that the telegram had been sent to a wrong number. That revelation happens when the telegraphist improbably retrieves from memory the number to which he sent the message. Once again, she intervenes by completing his phrase: he starts "Seven, nine, four—" and she finishes "'Nine, six, one'—she obligingly completed the number" (290). Again, the em dashes mark the links she understands, here articulated only as numbers, collected along with the thousands of words she's counted.

The telegraphist's story could have ended there, after torturing the aristocrats with her bravura performance of a blasé customer service agent and, afterward, telling her boss it was all "none of his business." Mic drop. But James must make a point that the telegraphist's triumph is actually tragedy. She may have learned patterns, but she apparently does not understand the truth of the matter. The last paragraph of *In the Cage* returns the telegraphist to ignorance, descending into a London fog as a metaphor of confusion: "she was full of her thoughts. They were too numerous to find a place just here" (302). Just as she began, awash in a countless sea of words, she returns to the obscurity of superabundance. The telegraphist's experimental reading methods, her theories, her suppositions of social drama are discarded in favor of the vagueness, even unknowability that largely defines James's work. In this sense, *In the Cage* offers a metafiction about James's own literary trajectory—but it also suggests a counter story in which reading machines remain very much involved.

Megan Ward argues that James's fiction "depends upon a belief in the opacity of human consciousness—that fiction can only capture consciousness by showing how it seems to defy another's complete understanding."[67] This obscurantism becomes James's preferred formal strategy for representing psychological depth and interiority, setting the terms for a literary critical tradition that represents consciousness as a blank.[68] But James doth protest too much against machinic reading. In a wonderful reversal, Ward claims that "James's narrative techniques have become definitive of depth psychology not necessarily because they portray a more realistic version of the human, but because they portray a naturalized version of a machine."[69] To substantiate this, Ward finds "artificial algorithm-like predictors" operating within James's free indirect discourse, as well as a strategy that presents characters as "blanks to be interpreted."[70] She perversely likens James's portrayal of human consciousness to its seeming opposite: "a particular kind of artificial mind" that AI research would formalize in the 1960s.[71] While James would loathe such a comparison, Ward wants to recover the generative possibilities of thinking about humans through their machines for simulating or augmenting the mind.

For much of the nineteenth century, technology already provided metaphors for understanding the brain. As Otis has documented, Victorian neurophysiology and communication machines were theorized in tandem, largely in terms of electrical signaling and network architecture.[72] But this pervasive metaphorical framework of structures and signals had given way at the century's turn, part of "the recognition of transmission's expansion into realms in which proximity or touch are not necessary to its workings," according to Thurschwell.[73] With science "severing the links between materiality, visibility and transmission," a different framework arose for thinking about communication and the brain. Thurschwell calls this the "telepathic imaginary" and relates it to the emergence of psychoanalysis, though it also effectively restructured discourse about the pedagogy of reading.[74] Edmund Huey—the optical physiologist par excellence—concluded his research into speed reading and efficient learning with predictions that "telegraphic" methods would ultimately outpace reading entirely, allowing an author to "talk his thought directly into some sort of graphaphone-film book which will render it again to listeners."[75] From tachistoscopes to the ambiguous hybrid object for which Huey still lacks a name, mediating technologies brought new functions of memory and transmission into the discourse network of 1900, as Kittler would have it. Huey's telegraphic fantasy, like Kittler's media theory, privileges technology as the determining factor of how people would read differently. But that change also depended on a different metaphor of the brain. By century's end came a turn toward psychoanalysis as well as the seemingly dematerialized processes of computation. Such an "information processing psychology" would shape the twentieth-century landscape of artificial intelligence research and define lasting computational understandings of cognition.[76]

Amid the late Victorian changes in theories of minds and communication machines, writers like Hardy and James were exploring the consequences for literary character. According to Ward, their strategies to represent the human suggest different ways that literary authors could naturalize the artificial—strategies that would also take shape as contrasting models of artificial intelligence in the 1960s. Ward likens James's representation of literary character to a processual model of AI then called a physical symbol system: it does not imitate the brain as a network but as a logical model working abstractly.[77] I would extend this to more recent developments in AI research that only strengthen Ward's point. Starting in the 1990s, these processual models evolved into statistical modeling, in which large numbers of variables and little bits of training came to determine the logical relations within the system, from the ground up. This shift was variously referred to as "machine learning, pattern recognition, knowledge discovery, data mining."[78] These terms all have different valences and particularities, but they share a lineage that reaches back a great deal further than AI's recent hype. In his study of machine learning as a data-based epistemology, Adrian Mackenzie suggests that "many machine learning techniques have long statistical lineages (running back to the 1900s in the case of Karl Pearson's development of the still-heavily used Principal Component Analysis)."[79] But defining machine learning in terms of logic or statistical techniques already accepts its erasures. Mackenzie points out that "machine learners" should be "understood always as human-machine ensembles."[80] Looking back to those earlier decades can help restore the human—and her labor—to a history of machine learning's development.

Critics of *In the Cage* have seen the telegrapher as part of the "human-machine ensemble" of late nineteenth-century media. For instance, Clayton calls the telegraphist "an early version of Donna Haraway's cyborg, a woman wired into the information network, the interface between a vast technological network and a human system."[81] But I want to grant her a different role. Behind the screen, the telegraphist is also an *operator* within that system, developing her own techniques for interpreting its signals. If she is a cyborg, she is also an early version of a "machine learner." If the telegraphist is a distant reader avant la lettre, she also represents an early version of a machine reader that the fin de siècle knew by other names. The telegraphist learns by counting words at scale, then by exercising the predictive pedagogy that speed reading was concurrently formalizing. She observes the statistical regularities of messages, infers patterns of association from them, and makes predictive statements with varying levels of accuracy. These ensembles of techniques are now recognizable in the statistical modeling that currently characterizes AI. In the nineteenth century, they were realized in the development of stenography, telegraphic codes, and speed reading in which women featured prominently as operators.[82] "Machine learning" evolves from activities in which the human and her labor were very much involved. Crediting the telegraphist as an early machine reader should not diminish her status compared to being a "reader of realism—one who might even appreciate James."[83] Rather, it might restore some of the nonliterary, even nonhuman dimensions of "reading" that James (among others) worked so hard to devalue. James helps consolidate the very ontological opposition between machine intelligence and human knowledge whose legacy is the erasure of women from the history of computing, figured as the never-named telegraphist disappearing into the cloud, as it were. But recovering the telegraphist as a machine reader may ironically help restore the human dimensions of AI, and even present an alternative approach to computational creativity.

Nameless Operators, Automatic Writers
The initial section of this chapter emphasized how counting words locates the telegraphist within early debates about distant reading. Following that, I sketched how the telegraphist selectively learns in parallel to theories of speed reading. Taken together, those may suggest an alternative genealogy for machine learning, especially as it was embodied in gendered readers and information workers whose historical presence machine learning has consistently erased. I understand this might draw too stark a connection between different eras and occupations. Call it an overcorrection, though, as the erasure of such connections is part of how machine learning came to constitute itself as such. *In the Cage* blames romance novels and naivete as the telegraphist's greatest influences as a reader, linking her to a tradition of endangered and dangerous women readers as long as the novel itself. But projecting

the telegraphist's reading strategies forward suggests a different genealogy in which the danger of women readers was resolved by excluding them entirely from the machinic intelligence they powered.

The telegraphist explains to her coworkers simply "I remembered" (290). Her boss disapproves: the telegraphist is not supposed to have a memory. As the story ends, she exits toward a fog and, eventually, a marriage that will remove her from the workforce. Each helps to expunge the gendered threats of memory and erotic, cross-class intimacy that such information workers raised. In the absence of an automatic system for sending messages, nineteenth-century telecommunication networks instead attempted to control their operators: "what was needed as a mediating agent who was not an agent at all."[84] Marvin demonstrates how social class would partly police that role, as a telegraph or telephone operator was understood to be "only a servant, not truly a member of the class to whose secrets she had access."[85] As Katherine Stubbs points out, management saw in women operators the promise of lower wages, political quiescence, and humility enough to become "an inert element of the communication apparatus."[86] These gendered logics extended to typewriters as well: women operators were assumed to be rapid transceivers of dictation, subordinate to a speaker, and detached from the touch-typed messages they didn't have to see.[87] As is well known, these workers shared a name with the devices they operated: they were called "typewriters" and, later, "computers."[88]

Various scholars have argued against that narrative of women's erasure from nineteenth-century media history, showing their persistent agency in what they mediated. That erasure also patterns the twentieth-century development of communications media and computing, in which women were omnipresent, yet excluded from management positions and later expunged from technical ones, like programming, once that work rose in prestige.[89] Furthermore, given the global networks and outsourcing of more contemporary information practices, especially in machine learning, these critiques also need to become intersectional.[90] While the fuller story is beyond the scope of this book, I would point to a few important stops along the way, as gender gets erased and reconstructed in media fantasies of machine learning. These examples link James to the uncanny return of automatized agents and predictive writing technologies. If nineteenth-century contexts offer a corrective, they also help us articulate some dimensions of AI's sociotechnical problems otherwise difficult to describe. Ultimately, the underappreciated roles of James's telegraphers and secretaries might suggest different approaches to the return of automatic writing in our own time.

The presence of such labor has been consistently denigrated and caricatured in media fantasies about automating knowledge work. For instance, Vannevar Bush's famous 1945 essay "As We May Think" gets frequently referenced as anticipating the networked structure of the World Wide Web. Yet the essay also resounds with a weird confluence of what Bush calls "race knowledge," eroticized labor, and artificial intelligence.[91] Bush imagines a new machine in a lineage of other information processing systems—all characterized by the presence of "girls."[92] "As We May Think" presents a series of eroticized secretarial demonstrations, including a Voder machine at the World's Fair: "A girl stroked its keys and it emitted recognizable speech." Imagining a demo of a stenotype machine, Bush writes: "A girl strokes its keys languidly and looks about the room and sometimes at the speaker with a disquieting gaze." The machines speak or write; the girls—and they are always girls—languidly touch and silently gaze and answer the mechanical desires of computers. Later, Bush explains of the Memex that, "Such machines will have enormous appetites. One of them will take instructions and data from a whole roomful of girls."[93] The power of the Memex is measured not by the data it requires, but by the "roomful of girls" who feed its appetites. At the same time, like other male visionaries of communication futures, Bush ultimately hopes to eliminate mechanical interfaces entirely: the Memex will capture and transmit its associative findings directly to and from men's thoughts, seemingly without any girl-supplied instructions.

The silent girls of the Memex would become the gendered speaking voices of popular AI assistants including Apple's Siri, Google's

Cortana, Amazon's Alexa, and others. The demonstration girl would morph into the machine itself, a black box that, even lacking the girl's eroticized body, still elicits gendered assumptions about their subservience.[94] Voice assistants were almost immediately interpellated within heteronormative desire on their release: for instance, web pages proliferated around "The Funniest Questions to Ask Siri," which included entire sections on "Flirting" or "Dating." Questions include: "What are you doing later?" "Do you have a boyfriend?" "Can I kiss you?"[95] The user community Macworld includes a set of warm-up questions for "Getting To Know Siri" before transitioning to "Flirting with Siri."[96] That section begins by quipping, "Let's move on from small talk and get down to business," suggesting the short leap from tech bro humor to sex robots. As Leopolda Fortunati argues, "reproductive immaterial labor" including care work, sex, communication, and emotional support has increasingly moved into the realm of "intellective machines."[97] Jennifer Rhee sees the consolidation of that labor as the very history of AI: "Artificial intelligence and care labor, a feminized and routinely undervalued form of labor, have been entangled since AI's earliest days."[98] That genealogy reaches back through twentieth-century fantasies to the perturbations around late nineteenth-century telecommunications workers. Turning her own labor squarely toward care work, James's telegraphist decides to aid and protect Everard in his own little scandal, remaining at her job solely for that purpose. Even off the clock, she seeks him out to reassure him: sitting together on a park bench one night, she promises that, "I'd do anything for you. I'd do anything for you" (268). On your iPhone, try asking what Siri dreams about: "I only dream of helping you."

According to online sources, it's also apparently funny to ask Siri how much she earns: the voice assistant replies, "The work is my reward." The joke of a robot not needing a salary belies how the human voice behind Siri—the voice actor Susan Bennett—did not know how her recordings would be used. Her voice was recorded to capture all the phonemes and intonations necessary to reconstruct those sounds into natural language. That work *was* her reward, as Bennett was never paid royalties from the uncountable interactions Apple's voice avatar has since serviced.[99] In general, artificial intelligence has consistently masked the degree to which it depends on human labor—and labor made increasingly piecemeal and globally outsourced.[100] Powering a particular kind of AI called "deep learning" is a largely invisible workforce. In deep learning, a computer is taught to perform tasks based on a set of positive or negative examples, or else a set of labeled training data. Based on these initial conditions, the process can then run on its own, with humans further correcting its errors or refining its results in a feedback loop. Creating these sets of training data requires lots of arduous, repetitive work, sometimes supplied by crowd-sourcing platforms like Amazon's "Mechanical Turk," offering micropayments per task, or else by dedicated employees of data labeling companies. "We are the construction workers of the digital world," one such spokesperson told the *New York Times* about China's growing industry of cheap digital laborers.[101] Even that optimistic phrase hides the boredom, alienation, and even emotional harm of much of this labor, including content moderation for social media sites and large language models.[102] Updated for the twenty-first century, *In the Cage* might recount the story of an invisible microlaborer stuck in a data farm, perhaps even confined to the *actual human cage* for which Amazon received a US patent: "a metal cage intended for the worker, equipped with different cybernetic add-ons, that can be moved through a warehouse by the same motorized system that shifts shelves filled with merchandise."[103]

In the Cage polices the new intimacies of late Victorian telecommunication, disciplining its ambitious young worker and seeming to valorize James's authorial versus mechanical labor. But he lived a different story as a working writer. James had his own voice assistant during the composition and revision of his later works, employing a series of secretaries to transcribe from dictation, starting from February 1897, after sustaining wrist pain. Notably, *In the Cage* was among the first compositions he made aloud and had transcribed. James declared this a freer mode of writing, and the impact of dictation and typewriting on James's work is interesting to consider.[104] It also introduced a new intimacy with a stranger who, as an employee somewhat like the telegraphist, ostensibly served as a frictionless operator rather than an agent of composition. However, contrary to desiring an "inert element" to transform his speech into text, James wanted something more.[105] James had preferences about how his secretaries related to his work. Reviewing his sequence of employees—William McAlpine, Mary Weld, and ultimately Theodora Bosanquet—James would complain that McAlpine and Weld seemed too detached, with "their apparent lack of comprehension of what I was driving at."[106] By contrast, Bosanquet learned to appreciate his ideas and aims: she was not simply a typewriter, but capable of anticipating what would or should come next. While "Mary seems only to count words," Theodora strives for "access to James's mind and machinery."[107] Bosanquet would go on to vigorously promote James's work, including by defending his oral revisions of earlier publications into his difficult late style. Bosanquet never fully disappears into the medium, even while her agency gets limited by the tricky power dynamics of their relationship. As Thurschwell puts it, she represents the blurring of "mind and machinery" in the composition process. Bosanquet embodies the technologized conditions of labor, the mechanical aids to memory, and the abiding sympathy that drives her abilities to understand and even appropriate James's writing. Including after death.

Bosanquet would write several books of her own and was among James's most ardent supporters in the early twentieth century. She was also deeply curious about spiritualism, the work of the Society for Psychical Research (SPR), and automatic writing.[108] Like many at the time, including James's brother William, Bosanquet maintained curiosity alongside critical skepticism, though she also experimented with the practice. William loaned her the SPR's reports about the medium "Mrs. Holland," whose automatic writing Bosanquet found so "wonderfully interesting and suggestive" as to even try it herself.[109] Later, she would adapt automatic writing into her continuing work of channeling Henry James's voice. At one sitting with a medium who specialized in contacting deceased literary figures, James's spirit, relaying his message via

Ouija board, addressed Bosanquet directly: "I will draw her attention to the similarity between the past and the present. In the past she acted to a great extent as a mouthpiece for me. . . . A lending of the mind to follow mine, or should I say a willing perception of my work and intention."[110] Like the blurring of "mouthpiece" and "mind" in James's purported message, Bosanquet and the woman coordinating the Ouija board each blend communication technology with the gendered body as medium for the author. According to Thurschwell, Bosanquet developed a "psychic secretarihood" in continuing to receive and transcribe James's messages from the beyond.[111] Bosanquet's "willing perception of my work and intention" defined her success in each realm.

In life and after James's death, Bosanquet became an inextricable part of James's ability to create. Bosanquet is more than an occluded presence in a communications circuit, but a predictive intelligence trained on the corpus of James's fiction. Like the best speed readers, like the autocorrecting telegraphist, Bosanquet anticipates the writer's language before he speaks—or long after he ceases to. If these figures anticipate machine learning, they remind us of all the labor AI erases. Bosanquet herself was long erased from Henry James scholarship: reviewing the field's history, Daniel Mark Fogel points to the disappearance of "important responses to James by women who were not academics."[112] Recovering her contributions is a good first step, but I would also underscore what someone like Bosanquet teaches us about the hybridity of composition—especially as automatic writing returns in a newer and still-suspicious technologized context. With the advent of language models and generative transformers, trained to predict what words should follow an initial prompt, we are again wrestling with complicated questions of occluded labor, the veracity of output, and computational creativity. Who is the author of a text partly generated by a machine? Can we accept machine-generated language as knowledge? Whose words and work has it absorbed, and how are its outputs valued?

While synthetic text and computationally assisted writing has a longer history, the rush in the early 2020s to release transformer-based language models sparked broad public and academic discussion about their consequences. These debates all implicitly addressed what Leah Henrickson calls the "hermeneutic contract" of how words make meaning—which AI seems dramatically to unsettle.[113] That contract changes with different rhetorical situations and genres of writing, but AI demands its terms be renegotiated. Opinions range wildly. Prominent critics of AI have pointed to its ideology of disruption, its ingrained cultural biases, and its harmful consequences, suggesting that text should be grounded in "communicative intent."[114] Others describe AI output as "hallucinations" with dangerous capacities to deceive. The specific applications of AI yield other problems, including plagiarism for writers, the exploitation of creatives whose work gets resold without credit, and the consequences of using chatbots for education, marketing, therapy, or even, in the guise of "thanabots," to reconnect with the dead.[115] In many ways, this discourse revives reactions to spiritualist and surrealist automatic writing from a hundred years earlier, ranging from skepticism about the veracity and authenticity of such mediated output, to the ethics of such practices for human expression and emotional contact.

Setting contemporary AI alongside nineteenth-century contexts brings the phenomenon of automatic writing into a different light. For one, it restores some necessary attention to gendered, outsourced, and erased human labor. As Sarah Allison notes in "Authorship after AI," we need to "account for the full history of how a text takes shape and the reality that more than one hand is often at work."[116] Yet it might also help us recover this labor without reinscribing the binaries of human versus artificial, or subordinating a medium to authorial intent. If scholars have suggested how to recover Bosanquet's agency and contributions to scholarship, we probably also need to reckon with the spiritualist automatic writing that likewise shaped her life. As Sconce suggests, late Victorian spiritualism let women "imagine social and political possibilities beyond the immediate material restrictions placed on their bodies." But, as Sconce also asks, was spiritualism just a means to that end? Did these women believe it? Did they think they were deceiving others? Did those others really believe it?[117] In the context of Bosanquet, did James really speak to her from beyond the grave? Personally, I find that hard to credit. Yet as the philosopher of death Patrick Stokes suggests, "when it comes to things supernatural, once you stop asking 'is it real?', a number of other questions, perhaps more interesting and certainly more productive, come into view."[118] Not believing means discrediting the work Bosanquet pursued in good faith, dismissing again her automatic writing and mediumship in ways that perpetuate her erasure. We should not dismiss her spiritualism to only celebrate Bosanquet's work on James's novels or her published scholarship. As an automatic writer, Bosanquet embodied a mind-machine hybrid whose complexities touch on spiritualism as well as machine learning. Bosanquet's example may challenge us to take a more capacious approach to AI, open to synthetic combinations that do not lose sight of whose labor is involved or whose perspectives are excluded, but which remains aware of its power differentials and sensitive to the unresolved questions of meaning that are still culturally, rather than technologically, determined.

As of this writing—which, I promise, was not automatized by AI—these debates are ongoing, rapidly changing, and unsettled. A historical contrast does offer some stability in trying to find footing on such shifting ground. In the long view, *In the Cage* reveals a trajectory of telecommunications work as reproductive immaterial labor that extends to the literal dehumanization of artificial intelligence. Late nineteenth-century preoccupations (and occupations) about reading, information work, and gender continue to be our own. Yet the generative anachronisms of nineteenth-century contexts also allow us to see the present differently. In this chapter, they offer a model of quantitative reading that does not alienate close from distant. They emphasize the human origins of predictive intelligence that persists in AI. They urge us not to dismiss its varied agents or overlook their marginalized status within automatic writing. They may even challenge us to imagine hybrid forms of computational creativity beyond the binaries that stubbornly render AI as humans versus machines. However, if they offer some inspiration for more critical and creative thinking about AI, Victorians also produced the conceptual oppositions that continue to harden in our own reactions to technological change. The conflict between Jamesian literary criticism and technologized modes of reading, for example, has again flared in debates about digital humanities as an institution. As the next chapter will show, those debates do more than extend Victorian contexts, but have adapted the tropes and genres in which Victorians reckoned with threats to literary professionals long ago.

FOUR

JEKYLL, HYDE, AND THE DARK SIDE OF DIGITAL HUMANITIES

Some among these degenerates in literature, music, and painting have in recent years come into extraordinary prominence, and are revered by numerous admirers as creators of a new art, and heralds of the coming centuries.
   —MAX NORDAU, *Degeneration* (1892)[1]

The digital humanities is the dark side.... The dark side, after all, is the side of passion.... This dark side also entails taking on our fears and biases.
   —WENDY HUI KYONG CHUN, "The Dark Side of the Digital Humanities" (2014)[2]

AT THE DRAMATIC CLIMAX OF *The Strange Case of Dr Jekyll and Mr Hyde*, the lawyer Mr. Utterson and Jekyll's butler Poole finally break down the door of Jekyll's inner sanctum.[3] They find Hyde dead on the floor, clues variously scattered, and a set of documents that Utterson takes home to read in quiet, including the narratives of Drs. Lanyon and Jekyll that ultimately close the case. The mystery also briefly alights on two other notable books: a "pious work" in which Hyde has added blasphemous marginalia, and, earlier, an "ordinary version book" in which Jekyll tracked his transformations with a series of dates and notes: the list runs to hundreds of entries (67, 71). As Stephen Arata has pointed out, *Jekyll and Hyde* is littered with scenes of writing—wills, letters, checks, narratives, annotations—along with contests over the legitimacy of that writing. In his classic analysis, Arata links this to a crisis in middle-class masculinity, the professionalizing of literary authorship, and fin-de-siècle anxieties about "degeneration" as articulated by figures including Cesare Lombroso and Max Nordau.[4] From a more contemporary vantage, we can see a different driver of this Victorian crisis, as its professional authors and interpreters of text reckon with the seemingly blasphemous mutations of books into data.

The contests over writing in *Jekyll and Hyde*, as Arata makes clear, dramatize late Victorian contests over the status of literary authorship, including its seeming decline (according to some) into rank professionalism. In the background were an array of emerging, popular, and mass media formats that were alternatively seductive and repellent to authors like Stevenson who depended on acclaim yet postured against the literary marketplace. The transformations in *Jekyll and Hyde*, I suggest, not only resonate with a crisis in literary professions but register a deep unease about the media shifts that so frequently drive them. For most of the story, what makes Jekyll and Hyde's case "strange" is their unreasonable social linkage, which consistently, stubbornly manifests in their handwriting. Jekyll's will, Hyde's signature: what is "unquestionably the doctor's hand" is also "a murderer's autograph" (63, 54). The handwriting-as-identity paradox draws from the forensic interests of its day and helps to generate the story's dramatic irony. But it also raises a question about literary transformation: when does a transformed medium change the message? What happens to the integrity of writing when moved across mediums, into new domains of reading and interpretation that experts no longer control? Into multimedia spaces that blur the professional boundaries of who produces and interprets literary texts?

This chapter recasts *The Strange Case of Dr Jekyll and Mr Hyde* as a nightmare allegory of late nineteenth-century media shift. Holographs, writing, books, and reading all offer Stevenson a proxy language for the media theory he cannot yet articulate: specifically, a theory of media transformation or remediation. As Menke helps us see, Victorian debates about writing and print offered a "vernacular media theory" whose fuller articulation would only come later.[5] *Jekyll and Hyde* sketched such a theory for its day and, in so doing, became itself a prototype for transforming text into other mediums. This manifests historically in the novel's immediate adaptation to the stage as well as to phonographs: *Jekyll and Hyde* was one of the first "talking books" (audiobooks) ever recorded. It also compelled several film adaptations on its way to becoming a Broadway mega-musical. But I think *Jekyll and Hyde* has another legacy too, as a record of professional convulsions in a shifting media landscape, and even as a template for how professionals continue to represent a perceived crisis in literary studies and even the humanities writ large.

The novel's contests and anxieties have reappeared in a newer scene of media shift, one that has unwittingly adapted *Jekyll and Hyde*'s gothic framework to explain its own transformation. Scholars are haunted once again by the anxieties of Victorian literary professionals, now as the shadow of digital humanities. Sometimes latent, sometimes surfaced in critiques of the "dark side of the digital humanities," the widespread unease with DH replays late Victorian concerns about the professional and philosophical consequences of media shift, including the authority of text, primacy of narrative, aesthetic reproducibility, erosion of professional elites, and violation of disciplinary boundaries and humanistic values. Furthermore, the "dark side" critique has reanimated Victorian gothic tropes to tell a story of monstrous disciplinary change. I do not mean that *Jekyll and Hyde* offers some bald analogy to a conflict between upstanding literary scholar and impetuous, benighted DHer. Rather, I want to suggest how Stevenson consolidated a latent awareness of late nineteenth-century media shift into an enduring characterological template, continuing to influence the way we argue now. *Jekyll and Hyde*'s latest adaptation shows on the stage of our profession's debates, implicitly shaping the dark consequences of digital media shift in humanities work.

Handwriting on the Wall

Jekyll and Hyde is part of a broad reckoning in the late nineteenth century with the fate of writing amid shifts in mass media. As scholars have noted, many of the century's signature technologies had been figured in terms of writing, "as a something-graph that made something-grams, as the newest *-graphy*."[6] But Stevenson works in a different milieu, in which writing is no longer the default paradigm for understanding new media. Menke claims that, "What's modern about media in the late nineteenth century isn't simply the arrival of particular new technologies but the fact that all forms of media, old and new, now enter a world in which they will converge, contrast, ally with, or distinguish themselves from others."[7] That world, as both Menke and John Guillory suggest, lacked a conceptual vocabulary to describe these complex interrelations. Guillory finds "the genesis of the media concept" in the struggle to explain new representational technologies and understand shifts between them: "The proliferation of remediation by the later nineteenth century demanded nothing less than a new philosophical framework for understanding media."[8]

Guillory uses the term "remediation" to mean something transposed from one medium into another. This simplified definition offers a useful starting point for considering the medial preoccupations within *Jekyll and Hyde*. Consider when Dr. Henry Jekyll describes the eureka moment of his research:

> I began to perceive more deeply than it has ever yet been stated, the trembling immateriality, the mistlike transience, of this seemingly so solid body in which we walk attired. Certain agents I found to have the power to shake and pluck back that fleshly vestment, even as a wind might toss the curtains of a pavilion. (77)

In this passage, Stevenson joins a late nineteenth-century discourse that mixed spiritualism with interests in the materials and "agents" of embodied life. What connects these domains? What gauzy veil keeps them separate? Spiritualism offered Victorians a "new philosophical framework" for theorizing mediums and mediation. However, *Jekyll and Hyde* explores the supernatural in a different way. Jekyll does not communicate with distant worlds; rather, he materially transforms his own consciousness from one embodiment into another. Moreover, Jekyll's goals align with the stricter definition of remediation from Bolter and Grusin. Remediation is not simply a state change from one medium to another: it describes media's pursuit of direct experience (immediacy) and the production of its opposite, an awareness of the obstructing body of any new medium (hypermediacy).[9] So Mr. Hyde offers a new body for the immediate pursuit of Jekyll's desires, yet Hyde unsettles the novel's other characters with the hypervisible yet undefinable aberration of that body.

The novel's onlookers are continually repulsed by Hyde without ever being able to explain quite why. As Enfield says to Utterson: "He must be deformed somewhere; he gives a strong feeling of deformity, although I couldn't specify the point. He's an extraordinary looking man, and yet I really can name nothing out of the way" (39). This unnamable problem recurs when Utterson actually meets Hyde: "he gave an impression of deformity without any nameable malformation" (41). These passages support familiar critical readings of the novel's prejudices in terms of Hyde's class identity, racialization, and nonnormative body. As Arata argues, the novel's professional men also experience the uncanny recognition of Hyde as their own dark tendencies in several domains: as mutable biological species, as representatives of a normative code of Victorian masculinity, and as members of an upstanding professional class.[10] The novel's anxieties about degenerative "malformation" in these areas also track its attention to media, sensitive to the uncanny significance of media change without quite being able to name it.

To my mind, one of the weirdest moments in *Jekyll and Hyde* appears during an encounter in Jekyll's private room in the laboratory when Utterson and Poole finally break down the door. Hyde is dead on the floor, draped in the clothes of a larger man. Nearby is a full-length mirror on a pivot called a cheval glass:

The searchers came to the cheval-glass, into whose depths they looked with an involuntary horror. But it was so turned as to show them nothing but the rosy glow playing on the roof, the fire sparkling in a hundred repetitions along the glazed front of the presses, and their own pale and fearful countenances stooping to look in.

"This glass has seen some strange things, sir," whispered Poole.

"And surely none stranger than itself," echoed the lawyer in the same tones. (67–68)

Remember: this mirror has witnessed a human forcing his entire physical form to change into a different body. Yet apparently stranger still, for Mr. Utterson, is the mirror seeing itself. What does that even mean? Mirrors placed opposite each other (seeing themselves?) create a diminishing tunnel ad infinitum. Similarly, images multiply in this passage with the "hundred repetitions" of the reflected firelight. The lawyer "echoed" the butler in the same whisper or tone, but it is not really an echo, as Utterson says something quite different from Poole. The passage everywhere signals the problem of distorted replication that the novel cannot name. As Menke argues of *Dracula*, "The uncanny emerges from the margins of mediation itself," becoming gothicized in the gaps of intermediation.[11] Like its characters who cannot define Hyde's strangeness, the novel lacks a vocabulary for its own incipient awareness of media propagation.

Jekyll and Hyde also wrestles with this problem in the form of handwriting. Time and again throughout the story, handwriting or a handwritten document indexes a connection between Dr. Jekyll and Mr. Hyde that other characters would prefer not to exist. When Mr. Enfield relates the story of Hyde trampling a girl, he explains that Hyde returned with a signed check for restitution "drawn payable to bearer and signed with a name that I can't mention" (36). Likewise, Utterson is repulsed by Jekyll's legal bequest to Hyde: "the will was holograph" and thus beyond dispute (38). As a result, "this document had long been the lawyer's eyesore" (39). The signature or holograph grants each document its unwelcome authority, seemingly from Jekyll. When Jekyll passes along a letter from Edward Hyde, the novel scrutinizes its handwriting very closely. Utterson calls in expert help from his clerk Mr. Guest, "a great student and critic of handwriting," to analyze the inscription. And whereas Utterson presents the document as "a murderer's autograph," Guest compares it to a letter from Jekyll and finds "a rather singular resemblance; the two hands are in many points identical" (54). Readers pick up the clue. However, while here identical, the novel elsewhere spotlights those "two hands" to show their shocking difference. Jekyll, in his final statement explaining his case, wakes in horror to discover his involuntary transformation written, as it were, on his hand:

> My eye fell upon my hand. Now the hand of Henry Jekyll (as you have often remarked) was professional in shape and size: it was large, firm, white, and comely. But the hand which I now saw, clearly enough, in the yellow light of a mid-London morning, lying half shut on the bed clothes, was lean, corded, knuckly, of a dusky pallor and thickly shaded with a swart growth of hair. It was the hand of Edward Hyde. (84)

Critics have read the contrasts of the white, comely versus dusky, hairy hand as signature examples of the novel's prejudices and preoccupations. But the stark differences between these "hands" are elsewhere blurry, as the connotation of hand slips between writing instrument and style. On the one hand, so to speak, Jekyll and Hyde share an identical script; on the other; they possess radically different embodiments. How can this warped mechanism produce the same writing? The paradox of hands in *Jekyll and Hyde* underscores its larger question: can two dramatically different mediums generate a consistent message?

In historical context, *Jekyll and Hyde* aligns itself with the uses of identificatory marks in criminal forensics, biometrics, and psychology. These decades saw the emergence of fingerprinting, the handwriting analysis of graphology, and eugenics photography, among a whole range of evidentiary discourses premised on the measurable body and its readable signs. Many of these biometric discourses were committed to proving the racial, criminal, and atavistic difference of nonnormative bodies like Hyde's.[12] They also sought, as Carlo Ginzburg has argued, to establish measures of identity as a response to individuals' retreat into the crowds of urban modernity, mass culture, and technological reproducibility.[13] Historical media scholars have made similar arguments about the increasingly anonymous agents and uncertain semiotics of late nineteenth-century media cultures. When new communications technologies were named as forms of writing (e.g., telegraphy, photography, phonography), their yet-unfamiliar media was granted writing's accepted terms of symbolic inscription. This reinforced an ideological continuity between writing and authorship, or between hand and hand, that new media actually destabilized. For example, technologies like the typewriter unsettled the "seamless continuity between eye, hand, and paper" that writing seemed to guarantee—an uncertainty that prompted Sherlock Holmes, in "A Case of Identity" (1891), to trace a typewritten text back to one specific machine. By the 1880s, even handwriting absorbs some of the uncertainties of mediation then in the air. Forensic handwriting analysis would measure a clear connection between hand and hand, or style and mechanism, message and medium. Yet its very premise is the uncertainty of that linkage, unsettled by communications technologies that, like "all new media . . . inspire conflicted cultural moments of self-consciousness about the making of meaning."[14]

As Victorian new media unsettled the terms of writing, text, and meaning-making, *Jekyll and Hyde* tries recasting the conflict instead as an issue among professionals. In this context, Hyde's identical writing *is* radically different: if visually indistinguishable from Jekyll's style, it nonetheless inscribes an epistemic violence on what his profession holds sacred. Among the examples of Hyde's writing, the novel refers twice to Hyde defacing a book. In the first, Utterson discovers "several books on a shelf; one lay beside the tea things open, and Utterson was amazed to find it a copy of a pious work, for which Jekyll had several times expressed a great esteem, annotated, in his own hand with startling blasphemies" (67). In his own account of this episode, Jekyll explains Hyde's monstrous marginalia as a tantrum against paternal authority: "Hence the ape-like tricks that he would play me, scrawling in my own hand blasphemies on the pages of my books, burning the letters and destroying the portrait of my father" (90). These two passages contrast Jekyll's "own hand" with Hyde's impious writing and the destruction of authoritative documents. Jekyll here strains to distinguish "me" and "he" as separate entities, but in his own guise the doctor had long since broken faith with the sanctities of his profession.

According to his former friend Dr. Lanyon, Jekyll became a monster years before his physical transformations began, having violated the norms of their science. In many ways, Dr. Lanyon is the portrait of Jekyll's disciplinary father that Hyde destroys. As Lanyon explains to Utterson, "it is more than ten years since Henry Jekyll became too fanciful for me. He began to go wrong, wrong in mind.... Such unscientific balderdash" (38). Hyde blasphemes a "pious work," but Jekyll had already committed what Lanyon calls "scientific heresies" (46). Jekyll, in telling his side of the story, twice insults Lanyon as a "hide-bound pedant" before tossing in "ignorant, blatant pedant" for good measure (46). The two doctors characterize opposing positions in their field: Lanyon remains "bound to the most narrow and material views," which Jekyll sneeringly surpasses with his "transcendental medicine" (74). Stevenson elevates this disagreement into a philosophical contrast of materiality versus transcendence, but their conflict also inheres in disciplinary practices of writing. Here, it is not Hyde's writing that seems monstrous, but Jekyll's.

In the novel, Lanyon's narrative is delivered as a sealed letter that itself begins with the story of a formally registered letter: "I received by the evening delivery a registered envelope, addressed in the hand of my colleague and old school companion, Henry Jekyll" (69). In it, Jekyll requests that Lanyon visit his private cabinet, obtain a specific drawer therein, and bring it home to await a visitor. The drawer's contents include Jekyll's bespoke chemistry set and a "paper book" that Lanyon describes: "The book was an ordinary version book and contained little but a series of dates" covering several years, running to "several hundred entries," and coming to include cryptic annotations such as "double" and "total failure!!!" (71). ("Total failure" implies that the note was, by default, also written by Hyde.) The book collects Jekyll's extensive data and shows his preoccupations as much with scientific replication as with human transformation. His scientific heresy, I suggest, has as much to do with contested methodologies as with any grand philosophical debate. Like the "pious work" that Hyde vandalizes, Jekyll's scrappy "version book" offends the genteel epistolary communications and formally registered narratives exchanged between the novel's "old school" professional men.

Stevenson cannot yet name or resolve his media problem, so he shifts it to another domain: the contests over professional forms of writing and reading that preoccupied Stevenson (and many others) in the 1880s. As Arata argues, Stevenson was "intensely engaged at the time with the question of what it meant to be a professional author," and encodes *Jekyll and Hyde* as a "displaced critique" of literary authorship as it becomes professionalized.[15] Arata points to the establishment of the Society of Authors and debates between Walter Besant, Henry James, and Stevenson himself. These debates centered on whether or not literary fiction is "governed by certain laws, methods, and rules" that are a young writer's "first business to learn," as Besant explained.[16] With his controversial remarks on "The Art of Fiction," Besant pushed literary authorship toward a rule-governed business, while still straining to distinguish fiction writing from the "mere mechanical arts."[17] Nonetheless, Arata argues that Besant's proposal for fiction was "wedded to the twin gods of positivism and empiricism," which looked like absolute heresy to some, "forming a risible do-it-yourself manual."[18] James's rebuttal in this debate insists on the beautiful vagueness, irreducible complexities, and ineffability of experience that can neither be reduced to repeatable patterns nor critically prescribed for literary fiction: "the measure of reality is very difficult to fix."[19]

These contests over authorship focus on the business of writing at the moment fiction writing was becoming more like a business, as popular print media put increasing pressure on the literary marketplace as such. Gissing's *New Grub Street*—a novel deeply self-conscious about "the state of print in a nascent media age," according to Menke—exemplifies these changes in its variously struggling and successful characters.[20] Success meant adapting to a popular market, regardless of taste or literary principles, partly by reenvisioning the medium of print. Gissing's extreme example is the barely fictional magazine *Chit-Chat*—a stand-in for George Newnes's hugely popular *Tit-Bits*—with its cascade of short consumable units of text on the page.[21] For many, these magazines represented the mechanization of authorship—and practically its automation. At one point, the character Marian Yule sees an advertisement for an efficient reading chair called "The Literary Machine" and initially misrecognizes it as an "automaton" for writing books and articles, soon to replace authors entirely.[22]

Arata reads the suspected forgeries and irregular documents in *Jekyll and Hyde* as evidence of Stevenson's own ambivalence about this change—indeed, as his fraudulent sense of being implicated in fiction's commercialization.[23] The novel casts its professional contest nominally between doctors—though we never really see their medical practice. Instead, *Jekyll and Hyde* consistently stages the unlikely drama of reading. Time and again, the novel presents scenes of textual blasphemy and professionally authenticated forms of reading. While this strategy creates narrative suspense, it also resolves the threats of a blasphemous textual practice premised on quantification, experiment, and replication.

Utterson is the quintessential professional reader in this story: managing documents, sequencing their disclosure, and reading them intensely at the appropriate time. We know what we know only because of Utterson's combination of curiosity and discretion, dramatized as his reading—and often not-reading—of the story's collection of documents. For example, when Utterson receives the deceased Lanyon's letter:

> Written by the hand of Lanyon, what should it mean? A great curiosity came on the trustee, to disregard the prohibition and

dive at once to the bottom of these mysteries; but professional honour and faith to his dead friend were stringent obligations; and the packet slept in the inmost corner of his private safe. (56)

As Arata argues, these men safeguard the very category of Victorian gentleman through their tactical ignorance and committed silence.[24] So much of that work occurs by managing and reading documents in a professionally legitimated way. The novel's dramatic climax—when eye witnesses bust into Jekyll's laboratory—quickly turns into the anticlimax of Utterson flatly demanding to go home and read. With Poole's help, Utterson breaks down the door, surveys the mysterious scene, gathers some letters, and declares that "I must go home and read these documents in quiet" (69). What follows are the narratives of Drs. Lanyon and Jekyll, which close the case. As Jodey Castricano puts it, "the scene of the crime is uncannily the scene of reading."[25]

So conspicuously does *Jekyll and Hyde* build its plot around such textual disclosure that it was immediately satirized in *Punch*. In the short "The Strange Case of Dr. T and Mr. H. / Or Two Single Gentlemen rolled into one," a "Mr Stutterson" gets mocked for his "button-holding propensities"—including his control of the reader. Near the start of the parody, "he suddenly disappeared into a house that did not belong to him, and gave the crowd a cheque with a name upon it that cannot be divulged until the very last chapter of this interesting narrative."[26] *Punch* declares Stutterson "a bore." But his abilities to focus and defer attention are crucial. Through Utterson, as Castricano says, "the text compels us to participate in the novel's quasi-epistolary dynamics."[27] Sometimes unwillingly, held by our buttons, as *Punch* would have it. But Utterson's discipline makes our participation a matter of reading professionally. According to Arata, the very status of professional men in novels depends on "close reading" and the authoritative interpretation of documents.[28] While Arata does not follow up on that term, nor did "close reading" yet signify in the 1880s, it suggests how *Jekyll and Hyde*'s anxieties about literary professionalization might reside in appropriate methods of reading—methods that, then as now, seemed unsettled by shifts in media. Stevenson writes a story fascinated with monstrous remediation and its potential consequences for writing, then resolves that story in Utterson's safe retreat to his reader's chair, leaving behind the mutated body and violated books to peruse a set of prose narratives from "old school companions."

Transforming Jekyll and Hyde

The bodily transformation from Jekyll to Hyde serves as a metaphorical warning about the commercialization of writing by a multimodal mass media at the fin de siècle. Recall that Jekyll worries that Hyde is just one possible self among a "polity of multifarious, incongruous and independent denizens" within him. Jekyll experiences this subjective fracture as a "perennial war among my members," which doubles as the late nineteenth-century media landscape with its multifarious, incongruous, and technologizing mediums competing for a popular market (76). With its retreat to close textual attention, the plot would seem to resist this change. Yet ironically enough, *Jekyll and Hyde* was almost irresistible as a text to further transform. Arguably, the novel's implicit drama of remediation compelled its own adaptation time and again, from theatrical stagings to early phonographic recordings and audiobooks and films. Stevenson's story gives these adaptations a self-reflexive charge, becoming popular any time its questions about media transformation emerge anew. These moments show the enduring appeal of *Jekyll and Hyde* and its gothic tropes as a framework for media shift and its challenges to cultural authority.

Jekyll and Hyde was published in 1886, became a runaway bestseller, and was adapted for the stage within a year. The first stage adaptation, by Richard Mansfield and Thomas Russell Sullivan, appeared in New York in 1887 and in London in 1888. There, it ran for ten weeks until rumors appeared in the press that its producer and lead actor, Richard Mansfield, was a possible suspect in the Jack the Ripper case. On stage, Mansfield famously shocked audiences with his uncanny transformations from Jekyll to Hyde, "so fierce . . . that both women and men fainted and people couldn't sleep after seeing the show."[29]

Sharon Aronofsky Weltman reads that transformation as theater's unique claim to what readers of the novella could never themselves see—in fact, what the novella actively hides. In the text, Jekyll/Hyde's transformations all occur off stage except once: when Hyde announces "Behold!" and transforms in front of Lanyon, which in turn prompts Lanyon's melodramatic reaction and eventual death. Yet even here, Hyde commands him to "remember your vows: what follows is under the seal of our profession" (74). The text flirts with exposing the transformation, and then retreats to professional nondisclosure. The "seal of our profession" may allude to medicine, but it manifests as Lanyon and Jekyll's sealed envelopes containing their narratives, opened and read according to Utterson's own "professional honor." In contrast, the stage play makes the transformation scene into a visual spectacle and thus violates the novel's commitments to text, to the integrity of careful reading. Where Stevenson sends Utterson home to read in private, the stage play ends with Utterson and Poole busting through the laboratory door and discovering the body in the spotlight. The adaptation breaks with the text, yet it keeps faith with the mediated multiplicity at the heart of *Jekyll and Hyde*.

Weltman follows the trajectory of the stage play through Victorian melodrama to twentieth-century cinema to a Broadway megamusical. She claims that *Jekyll and Hyde* is "limitlessly performable," as each adaptation actually underscores the proliferating uncertainty about selfhood that the story invites. These adaptations do more than depict doubleness and transformation: *as* adaptations, they actively fracture and transform the text, manifesting the instability at the heart of the story and the performativity of the subject.[30] Each adaptation is a different monstrous indulgence of the story itself. In a related way, each adaptation indulges the pleasures of remediation that Hyde embodies. As I have argued, Hyde stands in for Stevenson's dawning awareness of the pleasures and repulsions of media shift, specifically by representing how the pursuit of direct experience through new media always produces its opposite: hypermediacy, or an awareness of the opacity and mediating conditions of a given communications technology. As

Bolter and Grusin point out, hypermediacy is not necessarily a problem to solve; rather, it sets the terms of our engagement, even becoming a source of pleasure unto itself.[31] Adaptations of *Jekyll and Hyde* tend to appear at moments and in contexts where these medial relationships are in transition.

For example, Manfield's performance refocused audience attention from the stage adaptation's plot—widely acknowledged as weak—to the mechanics and motivations of the actor. The review in the *Daily Telegraph* noted how the play and its melodramatic transformation scenes would seem ridiculous but for "the extenuating circumstance of the actor's power . . . it foreshadows great gifts in the future which may be of immense assistance to the stage."[32] This is less praise for Mansfield than fascination with his performance, seemingly done by a single actor without trickery, yet using "state-of-the-art special effects," including stage makeup and contrasting banks of lights for each role.[33] The performance lets reviewers praise "the actor's power," so immediate as to frighten audiences and raise suspicions that Mansfield was the elusive Jack the Ripper: how could an actor accomplish this unless he were the real thing?[34] Simultaneously, audiences and the press knowingly entertained the fabrication, prompting speculations about how it was done, as in the *Pall Mall Gazette*'s "The Transformation in 'Dr Jekyll and Mr Hyde.' How It Is Done by One Who Knows."[35] In this light, reviewers and audiences adapt *Jekyll and Hyde*'s dynamics of remediation for another medium in transition: the theater. Danahay and Chisholm identify Mansfield as "a transitional figure between the more modern and conversational form of acting and the older, declamatory style."[36] Beyond stage effects and acting techniques, this transition also concerned changes to the economic and organizational structures of the theater business. Mansfield's career, as Danahay and Chisolm argue, "bridged the transition from the traditional preindustrial forms of organization, to the commodification of 'mass culture' in the twentieth century."[37] Stevenson's *Jekyll and Hyde* follows the same trajectory, reanimated any time another medium appeared to negotiate those relationships anew.

FIGURE 2. "Mr. Richard Mansfield as Dr Jekyl and Mr Hyde." Source: Billy Rose Theatre Division, The New York Public Library. New York Public Library Digital Collections.

Jekyll and Hyde's narrative helps to stabilize the uncertainties of a new medium. A promotional photograph for Mansfield's play (figure 2), produced by Henry Van der Weyde in a New York studio in 1887, is a veritable picture of this process. The double exposure captures Mansfield posing in each guise, layering his upright, inquisitive Jekyll against his signature version of Hyde: hunched, grimacing, threatening with distorted hands. The photograph plays with the irony of its own mediation, claiming representational fidelity (the actor in his double role) while simultaneously showing its own visual distortions (the double exposure that Mansfield could never effect). The image shares some of the thrills of spirit photography, itself a kind of "transcendental" practice, as it stabilizes immateriality and summons the co-presence of people's spiritual attachés. Yet the Jekyll/Hyde image does not invoke a philosophical debate about spirituality so much as it indulges the paradoxes and pleasures of photography, drawing easily on the dualities and transformations of Stevenson's novel.[38] The photograph uses the Jekyll/Hyde transformation to play with its own medial possibilities. As Daniel Novak suggests, "it showcases the complicated temporality and ontology of photography in the Victorian imagination."[39] *Jekyll and Hyde*'s enduring popularity derives from this built-in self-reflexivity about mediation, reactivated at various historical moments of media change. As a text about transformation, it provided a useful case to consider whether and how new forms of mass media and communications might distort the experiences they would convey.

A 1910 advertisement from the American Telephone & Telegraph Company (AT&T / Bell System) invokes "Dr. Jekyll and Mr. Hyde At the Telephone" to illustrate a problem of mediation it could not yet (and perhaps could never) solve: that some telephone users turned into assholes when talking to central operators, impatient at any delay or interference with their connection.[40] As the ad explained, "Perfect service depends on the perfect co-ordinate action of all three factors": the two "anxious and probably impatient" communicants plus the operator—who, try as they might, the company has not been able to mechanize: "All attempts to entirely eliminate the personal factor at the central office, to make it a machine, have been unsuccessful." As Galvan points out about telephony as well as spiritualism, the fantasy of direct mediation "required asserting the medium's automatism."[41] More often than not, this meant reimagining women's bodies as the ideal passive conduit, or subordinating them as part of the machine. While they remained on the line, operators were taught "*civil* listening," as Michèle Martin puts it, to hear directives without listening to conversations.[42] In this ad, the telephone company tries to teach its customers a related lesson. Ma Bell warns against "discourtesy" to switchboard operators,

FIGURE 3. "Dr Jekyll and Mr Hyde at the Telephone." Source: *National Geographic Magazine*, vol. 21, 1910.

giving its customers a stern parental lecture as much as an explanation: "*It will cease when they talk over the telephone as they would talk face to face*" (original italics).

Besides its title and image, the ad nowhere else refers to Jekyll or Hyde, relying perhaps on the memory that Hyde stomps innocent girls (like operators) in his way, or that even the most courteous gentleman conceals a monster within. Here, that monstrous transformation is effected by the telephone. Simple enough, but I would underscore how the advertisement invokes the framework of *Jekyll and Hyde* at a moment when the telephonic medium is still taking shape, yet to "eliminate the personal factor" that both connects and obstructs. *Jekyll and Hyde* tends to appear at intervals when a technological mass medium has not yet been fully mechanized, when its protocols and representational claims are still being negotiated. It appears when a communications technology is *itself* transforming into a medium, including the transformation of women's labor into mechanized forms. At these moments, *Jekyll and Hyde* becomes doubly useful: one, as a narrative framework for stabilizing the curiosities and uncertainties about a new medium; and two, as a moralizing framework for qualifying the right behavior, social norms, and professional boundaries that medium seems to unsettle.

The transformation scene made an appearance in another modality in its early changes into a mass entertainment medium. In 1904, the American character actor Len Spencer recorded "The Transformation Scene" for Columbia Records, distributed on a 10-inch phonographic disc the following year.[43] The performance lasts about two and a half minutes, constrained by the record's capacity of three minutes per side. Spencer performs an excerpt from an 1897 Philadelphia stage adaptation, rather than reading from Stevenson's text. Such early recordings did not yet imagine themselves as books read aloud, but offered "scraps, gems, portions, and pieces" more closely allied with anthologies and recitation albums, as Jason Camlot argues.[44] In 1904, Columbia offered a catalog of such excerpts, ranging from vocal performances like Spencer's to orchestral marches, imitations of battle scenes, vaudeville sketches, historical speeches, acoustic novelties, and miscellaneous "tone pictures." Jonathan Sterne has called this fugitive recording genre the "descriptive specialty," whose goal was "not to get as close to reality as possible, but to . . . present a distinct aesthetic experience."[45] Like the early cinema of attractions, as defined by Tom Gunning, these audio recordings indulged the fascination with what a new medium could do.[46] They experimented with the representations and pleasures of recorded audio itself, rather than necessarily aiming to convey an aural experience with ever more immediacy. Descriptive specialties taught listeners how to understand the recording and reproduction of sound, especially at this crucial moment of its "plasticity" and "mutability."[47] This was the scene of the technology's transformation into a medium.

Like the Mansfield photograph, Spencer's "Transformation Scene" plays on its medial self-awareness. Though excerpted from a staged version of *Jekyll and Hyde*, Spencer's recording does not try to capture a snippet from a live performance, as if offered to listeners who couldn't attend the show. Rather, Spencer was showcasing his own talents "as a master mimic and performer of multiple voices"—a performer specifically for the recording machine.[48] Spencer left an extensive catalog of such performances, including many with ethnic caricatures, various dialects, and minstrel sketches—a matrix of racialized audio entertainment in which Jekyll's transformation to Hyde also uncomfortably fits. Ironically, Spencer's vocal distortions would testify to the phonograph's claims to high-fidelity representation. In 1906, Spencer was hired by the Edison company for a promotional recording called "I am the Edison Phonograph" distributed on a wax cylinder only to dealers to help promote their new product. As Camlot describes, in this recording Spencer "speaks from the point of view of the phonograph and claims he can perform all levels of entertainment, all voices, all languages, with absolute naturalness."[49] I would argue that Spencer also speaks for the phonograph in "the transformation scene," which thematizes the dynamics of media in transition as well as the aesthetics of the descriptive specialty.

Spencer plays a series of voices—the announcer, Dr. Jekyll, Mr. Hyde, and (briefly) Utterson. In the scene, Jekyll composes his final note, hears knocks at the door, transforms into Hyde, dies, and gets discovered. The recording overlays sound effects and organ music onto Spencer's voice acting. And when Hyde emerges, the first thing he does is break the fourth wall:

> Jekyll: . . . [Organ music.] Ah, I must pray—Pray God to keep away the demons. Ah, God, look into my heart and forgive my sins. You were right. I was wrong. Ah, ah the fiend is coming. Yes. Hyde is here!
> Hyde: [Shrill throaty noises.] Stop that damned organ! The noise offends me ears! [Cackling laughter.] [Knocking.][50]

The Philadelphia stage adaptation includes the same gag, as Hyde seemingly erupts into co-presence with the audience ("Hyde is here!"), shouts at the theater organist, and cackles at his own joke. The scene offers what Camlot calls the "oscillation between immediacy and hypermediacy" for stage and sound alike.[51] In Spencer's recording, Hyde shouts at the background organ recording while offering his own signature sound effects ("Shrill throaty noises," "Cackling laughter") and rough accent. Listeners are cued to marvel at Spencer's performance as well as the new experience the recording machine makes possible. As Sterne points out, these early recordings delivered not only such a self-reflective audio aesthetic, they also compartmentalized and commodified the human soundscape, "rendering experience mobile and available for repeated consumption."[52] Stevenson anticipated only too well that his shilling shocker would be hugely marketable, perfectly suited for the adaptive transformations of new mediums into mass entertainments.

Early film adaptations also show how *Jekyll and Hyde* opens a metadiscourse of medial transformations and their relations to the market. A 1908 film of *Dr. Jekyll and Mr. Hyde* has not survived but was adapted closely from the Philadelphia text—perhaps including the "Stop that damned organ" line that the audience, watching a silent film, could have only read.[53] Making a bigger impact was the 1920 silent film *Dr. Jekyll and Mr. Hyde* starring John Barrymore in the lead roles. A brief review in *Variety* pans the story as "ridiculous" but praises the film's "value as a medium for Mr. Barrymore."[54] Just as Richard Mansfield became the focus of his play's London debut, shifting attention from the play to the actor-as-medium, Barrymore preoccupied many of the film's critical responses. According to Frederick James Smith, writing in *Motion Picture Classic*, Barrymore makes the film into the "stuff of nightmares" with "the most ghastly make-up we ever recall seeing in the films."[55] As with early audio recording, *Jekyll and Hyde* lets film test its own production capacities, encouraging its audiences to evaluate the story in terms of its medium's successes or shortcomings. The *film* is shocking; the story is beside the point. Burns Mantle, in a review in

Photoplay, complains he cannot see past the film's disturbing artifice; the medium overwhelms its message: "I am so very conscious of the actor's acting that I become much more interested in the facility with which he achieves his effects than in the effects themselves."[56] This same review warns against letting children or pregnant women watch the film for the corrupting influence it might exert on the next generation. The threat derives less from the story than from its adaptation into a mass cultural product beyond the control of male critics. The film itself threatens to transform its audiences.

While the 1920 silent film experimented with visual effects, it was also adopted for demonstrations of theatrical organ music. Musical accompaniments appeared throughout the "silent film" era, but Barrymore's *Dr. Jekyll and Mr. Hyde* arrived as films were increasingly given their own musical scores. In 1922, Hugo Riesenfeld and Frank S. Adams collaborated on a dedicated score for the film, performed that same year as part of "Music Demonstration Week." Described in a report from the *American Organist*, the event included a lecture by John Hammond, president of the New York–based Society of Theatre Organists, on the "ideal accompaniment of pictures."[57] According to Hammond, composers and organists need not follow the action of the plot, but should seek to "intensify the story" by emphasizing its moods.[58] Frank Adams then played the score of *Jekyll and Hyde*, without a concurrent showing of the film, for its run time of one-and-a-half hours. He received a "thunderous outburst of applause" as the audience realized, according to this article, they had witnessed "a masterpiece of picture interpretation."[59] The words are well chosen, as the *American Organist* joins a larger debate about the cultural status of music vis-à-vis theater performance and film accompaniment. While organists could increasingly find professional opportunities to accompany motion pictures, some commentators lamented abandoning the classical organ repertory for cinematic entertainment. Similar debates took shape about the proper kind of music for film accompaniment. George Beynon, a practicing accompanist and author of an instructional book *Musical Presentations of Motion Pictures* (1921), decried the use of popular or "cheap" music, especially by organists, as "the prostitution of their art."⁶⁰ In this context, it is especially ironic (or appropriate) that *Dr. Jekyll and Mr. Hyde* would facilitate an early "masterpiece" of feature-film-length musical scoring.

Notably, *Jekyll and Hyde* was also among the first full-length audiobooks ever recorded, chosen by the Royal National Institute for the Blind (RNIB) as part of its initial catalog of "talking books" in 1935. As Matthew Rubery explains, the RNIB intended that this catalog should include 75 percent works of "permanent value" and 25 percent for "popular taste," all based on recommendations from committee members, correspondents, and published lists.⁶¹ Appearing among six book-length works of fiction, Stevenson's *Jekyll and Hyde* had potentially attained classic status alongside Thackeray's *Henry Esmond* and Conrad's *Typhoon*. Though not articulated by the selection committee, *Jekyll and Hyde* is also an entirely appropriate choice for sharing the capacities of a "talking book." Here, too, the technology occasioned familiar debates about the status of the audio medium, about popular and permanent literary value, and about the legitimacy of listening as a form of literary experience. From the moment that phonographic books were first imagined, commentators warned about the consequences, including the death of print and the degeneration of reading: "book-making and reading will fall into disuse," opined the *New York Times*.⁶² As Rubery points out, this late Victorian discourse about "the end of books"—as in an eponymous 1894 essay by Octave Uzanne and Albert Robida—more precisely concerned their remediation into other forms.⁶³ Media death, degeneration, and obsolescence are the proxy language for other arguments about what a new medium seems to challenge. The talking book again provoked contests over "the legitimacy of alternative forms of literacy, rivalries between print media and new media, and definitions of self-sufficiency."⁶⁴ In this context, too, *Jekyll and Hyde* was an ideal work to showcase.

Objections to a medium are usually proxy arguments about the socioeconomic and cultural systems that it seems to reconfigure. Talking books were envisioned as the transformation of reading into passive consumption and of books into entertainment commodities.⁶⁵ In fact,

Edison marketed the phonographic book in just this way, so that the "average reader" could enjoy the product of a professional elocutionist, or that "the lady or gentleman whose eyes and hands may be otherwise employed" could find "great profit and amusement" in listening.[66] At the same time, talking books were conceived and developed as aids to blind readers—including by Edison. As Rubery suggests, "disability has always been a driving force behind the technology for recorded books."[67] Kittler goes even further, identifying the history of media as a history of disability.[68] Thus, a strong current of ableism runs through negative reactions to new media, including talking books. To claim (as many have) that "listening is not reading" is to stigmatize blind people, which continues to pattern even contemporary arguments about audio literacies.[69] But it is the wrong question to ask whether reading or listening amounts to the same experience of a text. That framing already elides the social, economic, and institutional conditions that establish reading or listening as interpretive acts. It matters more *who* is reading and in what conditions of authority.

Even among advocates for books for the blind, criticism of the "talking book" reveals the normative values it seemed to unsettle. In a controversial lead editorial in 1937 for a magazine about the blind called *The Beacon*, Arthur Copland argued that the talking book was overhyped, too expensive, and likely to serve only the already privileged. It provided only an "artificial facility" in contrast to printed books using "punctiform systems of reading and writing" like Braille.[70] Furthermore, Copland objects to the third party of the reader as an obstructing intermediary: "Being read to, however perfectly the reading may be done, necessarily involves the intrusion of a third personality between the author and his public." Note the starkly gendered terms: the pronoun "his" defines a direct line of communication in contrast with, in Copland's following example, hearing a newspaper read aloud by "the lady who ... always translated the English into Scots."[71] Like the Bell telephone ad that cannot erase the gendered labor at its system's heart, Copland complains about the intrusion of a "lady" intermediary, aligned with the degeneration of English to Scots, literature to newspapers, and authors to near-mechanized readers. The argument is not about the medium but its intermediaries and their seeming challenge to the established norms of textual interpretation.

Prejudices against talking books have been reanimated with the popularity of digital audiobooks. Here too, complaints about the debasement of print-based immersive reading into passive, distracted audio consumption encode other sets of values. For instance, Birkerts, in *The Gutenberg Elegies*, "accused audiobooks of posing a threat to concentrated attention or what he calls 'deep reading,' the unhurried, meditative immersion in the language of the printed page."[72] Notably, Birkerts rounds up audiobooks within a broader complaint about the "triumph of the digital" in which fractured attention, shallow engagement, and moral relativism now prevail.[73] I am less interested in the substance of critiques like Birkerts's than the forms and metaphors they often employ. What we find is a familiar fiction of displacement, disfigurement, and degeneration inherited from the nineteenth century. Notably, Birkerts quotes Antonio Gramsci, excerpting from the *Prison Notebooks*: "The crisis consists precisely in the fact that the old is dying and the new cannot be born; in this interregnum a great variety of morbid symptoms appears."[74] Birkerts lifts Gramsci from any 1930s political context to characterize the effects of 1990s-era media change, a transitional state with "morbid symptoms."[75] He may as well have quoted Max Nordau in blaming "steam and electricity" for upending fin-de-siècle life, especially the psychosis brought by the newspaper, as readers suffer the frenzied desire to simultaneously and continuously absorb "the thousand events which take place in all parts of the globe."[76] Just as Nordau diagnoses the degeneracy of readers and authors in the context of 1890s information culture, Birkerts sees "morbid symptoms" resulting from the emergence of the web and digital consumer media. In the following decades, that critique—as well as the morbid characterization of illegitimate reading practices—would surface again with the seeming transformation of literary criticism by digitized materials and methods.

The Dark Side of Digital Humanities

Whether adapted directly or lurking in the shadows, *Jekyll and Hyde* uncannily appears at moments of media shift, especially those that unsettle the cultural authority of legacy media and its credentialed interpreters. As a novel obsessed with textuality, monstrous transformation, professional anxieties, and popular entertainment, it has latent thematic appeals that get reactivated any time new mediums rewire those relationships. I wager this explains the punctual appearance of *Jekyll and Hyde*'s adaptations along a time line of media history. It may likewise help explain a more recent reanimation of its gothic framework within the popular and critical discourse surrounding digital humanities. If less visibly present, *Jekyll and Hyde* helps us recognize a Victorian gothicized template adapted once again for the professional reconfigurations of new media. I do not want to insist that Stevenson's novella establishes some master pattern; rather, *Jekyll and Hyde* cues us to look for novelistic adaptations in moments when new media unsettles professional norms. Reading the digital humanities into *Jekyll and Hyde* may help, in turn, to read the characterological and emplotted tropes within digital humanities discourse.

As Sarah Allison explains, it matters "how we think about character in digital humanities work," not fictional characters, but DH's own field characterizations as they figure "the clash between close and distant reading, between threatened humanities and privileged STEM fields."[77] On this point, Allison cites Amanda Anderson's *The Way We Argue Now*, whose introduction urges attention to "the 'character' of various theories" or how they "get imagined in distinctly characterological terms."[78] Anderson wants to challenge how recent decades of theory have established—falsely, in her view—a "framing opposition between rationality and ethos."[79] Those oppositions arise, in part, from the very narrative frameworks in which theorists structure their discourse, or what Anderson intriguingly calls "the novelistic imagination of particular theories."[80] Matt Erlin has taken a similar narratological approach to recent histories of and commentaries on digital humanities, suggesting how they "*emplot* the rise of digital humanities in order to render it intelligible within a range of intellectual, institutional, and societal contexts."[81] That allows Erlin to identify and analyze a set of "masterplots" in DH historiography. But some of DH's "masterplots" were drafted well before its contemporary dramas. Looking back to nineteenth-century precursors helps identify what narrative and characterological models have shaped the metadiscourse of technologizing humanities labor. In this longer view, we can see that DH has a novelistic imagination of its own, formed across at least a century of engagements between literature and new media.

There are latent resonances in *Jekyll and Hyde* with certain facets of DH. For all Jekyll's talk about transcendental medicine, his day-to-day practices involve the recording and tabulation of data in his version book. Hyde works, in the same study, to annotate the texts in Jekyll's library. As I have suggested, both represent blasphemies in context of disciplinary norms of reading. Additionally, beyond his unruly methods and monstrous transformations, Jekyll's real problem is replicating his results. The version book captures data as well as mounting despair about the experiment's predictability, which the plot eventually blames on an "unknown impurity" in Jekyll's initial supply of salts (89). The experiments produce Hyde, but the replication crisis leads to Jekyll's death. In a way, the novel makes monstrous the idea of experimental replication, which aligns with contemporary skepticism about an empirical approach to the literary arts. Henry James says, pace Besant, that there is no "recipe for calling . . . into being" a sense of reality that novels must convey.[82] The audacity of Jekyll's experiment comes in trying to devise quantitative recipes for transcendental subjects. It is with similar audacity that Andrew Piper and Matt Erlin propose the quantitative studies of culture: "the most important, discipline-changing, research-altering concepts for the future of the humanities." Yet that epistemological framework brings forward a new problem: if empirical hypotheses can be tested, they can theoretically be tested again and verified. As Piper and Erlin observe, "the humanities have a replication crisis of monumental proportions," which hypothesis testing and quantitative studies purport to solve.[83]

Jekyll and Hyde solves this crisis by killing its characters and subordinating Jekyll's epistemological and methodological blasphemies to authenticated forms of writing and "close reading," invested in the novel's professionals.[84] Similarly, in the art of fiction debates, Besant lays out certain rules for writing novels, as a guide for practical replication. But James mounts a different defense, celebrating the ineffable qualities of the *novelist* who remains one of a kind. Arguably, James does not contest Besant's prescriptions for writing so much as he enshrines the standing of an author, above and beyond mere membership in a professional society. In a related way, debates about digital humanities are ultimately less about contested hypotheses or methodologies than a changing landscape of academic work. As Mark Cooper and John Marx have argued, "'digital humanities' more aptly names a new division of labor than it does a reaction to a technological revolution that has already swept us all up."[85] If the digital humanities emerged with claims about its technological distinctiveness, debates about DH reckon as much with its consequences for institutionalized humanities labor. As Stevenson does in his novella, these debates displace professional anxieties into contests over reading, the legitimacy of interpretive methodologies, and the institutional status of its practitioners. Furthermore, they also adapt thematic and characterological tropes that place DH on what Kirschenbaum calls "monstrous institutional terrain," gothicizing its consequences as the "dark side" of the humanities.[86]

As this book has endeavored to suggest, the history of digital humanities reaches back well before the coinage of that phrase. Arguments about DH also have a longer history, emerging when episodes of media shift provoke concerns about shifting academic labor practices. As Cooper and Marx demonstrate, the "humanities" itself gets perennially constructed in relation to "the coeval development of mass media" across the twentieth century.[87] For instance, faced with the emergence of film, the "humanities" defined itself largely in reaction, perceiving a crisis both for the public mind and the fate of an elite education that aimed to shape culture in its own image.[88] Chad Wellmon offers an earlier example, looking to "big humanities" projects in late nineteenth-century Germany like Theodor Mommsen's textual archive of classical Latin texts from the Roman Empire (the Corpus Inscriptionum Latinarum). The assembly, collation, and tabulation of these texts by large groups of scholars represented a different kind of labor than hermeneutic interpretation by a single reader. Mommsen's project was critiqued as a form of scholarly positivism or even industrial work, including by Nietzsche. As Wellmon argues, these figures "struggled to understand and adapt to what they considered to be a new era in knowledge, one defined by an explosion of cultural objects; intellectual specialization; the division of labor; and the estrangement of the scholar from his traditions, his scholarship, and meaning."[89] Redefining work in such a "new era" also means confronting the appearance of new workers and their claims on intellectual labor. In this context, definitions of reading and interpretation collide with the history of information work and institutional prestige.

As in these earlier contexts, the naming of "digital humanities" as such in the 2000s brought heightened attention to the shifting terrain of professionalized humanities labor. The newfound publicity of DH took shape with some familiar tropes of crisis. When Pannapacker announced DH as "the next big thing" in 2009, a grim year for the postrecession academic job market, he emphasized its potential to revitalize humanities studies and rescue its declining fortunes from communications and computer science. Yet the "current transformation" that DH represents, he continued, would have to face an internal struggle between traditionalism and innovation.[90] Many other commentators have entered the fray to define, critique, defend, and redefine digital humanities. But Pannapacker's frequently cited piece shows some of the patterns this discourse followed: DH is a new, risky, but necessary experiment in a field facing decline. The "transformation" of DH includes a shift in professional capital and prestige that attends the uses of novel technologies. And the struggle will occur between traditionalist versus experimentalist attitudes in the field. These familiar characterizations all make DH a matter of stark oppositions. As Amy Earhart suggests, when the historiography of DH constructs the field as a cohesive whole, it produces the disputes along which proponents and detractors must grudgingly align.[91] The narrative framework for these debates has already been set.

While Pannapacker wrote as an early DH enthusiast, other notable commentators figured their pessimism in similar ways. "The old order changeth," wrote Stanley Fish in 2011 of another MLA Convention, threatened by an "alien invader" and a "new insurgency." Fish worried that DH seeks nothing less than to change "everything," ironically producing "the death of the whole shebang" by its very efforts to revitalize the humanities.[92] However, the scope of Fish's critique belies his specific concerns about the fates of text and reading. Fish's follow-up piece, "The Digital Humanities and the Transcending of Mortality," grandly identifies a theological aspiration in DH "to liberate us from the confines [... of] partial and situated" knowledge, and deliver us to a "full and immediate" awareness of the digital mediascape. Notably, the former condition is represented by the literary text: "a hitherto linear experience—a lone reader facing a stable text provided by an author who dictates the shape of reading." But, as Fish argues, "the effect of these technologies is to transform" that experience, fracturing it into "a multi-directional experience in which voices (and images) enter, interact and proliferate in ways that decenter the authority of the author who becomes just another participant."[93] It doesn't take much to twist Fish's story into a paranoid resemblance of *Jekyll and Hyde*: DH risks a transcendental method for achieving immediacy but ends up splitting its subjective coherence into a polity of voices beyond its control, ultimately leading to its own demise. While tempted, I do not really mean to match these stories point for point, but to show more generally how Stevenson framed monstrosity in a context of debates about media and a transforming professional literary sphere, and, in turn, to illustrate how debates about DH adapt that gothic template to represent the consequences of media shift for humanities labor.

A frequent target in DH criticism is Franco Moretti. He earns more than a fair share of citations, especially in the context of the overlooked work of many other scholars—especially women—who continue to develop these methods.[94] Particularly in light of sexual assault allegations raised against him, Moretti's case resonates with a narrative about atavistic professionals and predators. His overrepresentation in DH's early press coverage also suggests how DH debates can default to arguments about literary studies, in which reading methods become metonyms for the humanities. As Cooper and Marx document, the "paradigm for setting literature in opposition to 'mass communications'" structures a history of twentieth-century articulations of the humanities, and continues in many critiques of digital humanities, which use arguments about textual interpretation to define DH in opposition to the proper work of humanities scholarship.[95] Additionally, Moretti himself invites the oppositional ways these positions are often characterized. As Jonathan Arac points out, Moretti's version of distant reading is a "deliberately scandalous agenda."[96] The jacket copy of Moretti's book *Graphs, Maps, and Trees* twice uses the word "heretical" to describe itself.[97] In Moretti's earliest piece promoting distant reading, he sounds not unlike Stanley Fish later critiquing it. Here's Moretti: "At bottom, it's a theological exercise—[a] very solemn treatment of very few texts taken very seriously—whereas what we really need is a little pact with the devil: we know how to read texts, now let's learn how *not* to read them."[98] Note two things: the deliberate scandal of premising literary studies on "not reading" and its characterization as a theological violation, or a "pact with the devil." Similarly, Allison illustrates the quantitative methodology of her book *Reductive Reading* with another Manichaean metaphor: "Reductionism is the evil twin of simplicity." In choosing what textual features to analyze at a distance, she explains, the analyst risks "exaggerating a single trait to monstrous proportions."[99] The devil's dealings, evil twins, exaggerated personality traits: the darker characterizations of DH do not just come from its critics.

The gothic characterization of DH emerged most starkly in the "The Dark Side of the Digital Humanities" panel at the 2013 MLA Convention, later to become a special 2014 issue of the journal *differences* on "In the Shadows of the Digital Humanities." The primary allusion was to *Star Wars*: the MLA panelists played "The Imperial March" as their opening soundtrack. Yet there's a familiar pattern in its oppositional framing and the characterizations of DH as a dark pathway to corruption, strengthening an empire hostile to traditional forms of humanities methods and labor. As the organizer, Richard Grusin, explained: "it is no coincidence that the digital humanities has emerged as 'the next big thing' at the very same moment in the first decades of the twenty-first century that the neoliberalization and corporatization of higher education has intensified."[100] Notably, Grusin develops this argument based on his own sense of a "structure of academic feeling": specifically, the "incommensurate affective moods" of academic crisis, on the one hand, and excited prospects of DH, on the other.[101] To this affective structure, Grusin then welds a narrative structure of enlightened scholars battling the "dark side of information capitalism."[102] While Grusin observes that "there is a stark contrast, and I believe a growing divide" between DH and "mainstream humanities," his discourse also helps produce that divide, defining its oppositions in characterological terms that we have collectively learned.[103]

As Kirschenbaum would argue in response, these critics are less concerned with specific incarnations of digital practice than with DH as a "discursive construction" that helps to focus larger, and often worrying, transformations of the humanities as a whole.[104] Constructing that discourse—by DHers as well as skeptics—has also meant producing the differences that preoccupy it. The nagging question "what *is* DH?" creates the structures of difference that become characterological frames. In his 2009 reflection on "Digital Humanities and Academic Change," Alan Liu claims that "digital technology is on the threshold of making a fundamental difference in the humanities because it indeed serves as the vector that imports alien paradigms of knowledge."[105] Liu admires this alienation as an opportunity for intellectual defamiliarization; others decry its appearance as a "retrograde transformation" that is fundamentally alien to the proper work of humanities study—and presages the "death of a discipline."[106] Both sides use alienation to define the field. For this reason, Jamie Skye Bianco has criticized the very phrase "the digital humanities," drawing from traditions in feminist, Lacanian, and queer theory to suggest how the act of naming both creates and subordinates the other.[107] Establishing the name, a definition, participation within, or the boundaries for digital humanities may help establish what it is or does, but it also invariably produces what is outside, other, or even abject. Glossing Judith Butler's work on the subject, Diana Fuss explains that defining boundaries "has everything to do with the structures of alienation, splitting, and identification which together produce a self and an other."[108]

Such characterizations may be just as influential as the conceptual apparatus of a discourse. They may also be adapted from predigital precursors. Rita Raley, another participant on the "Dark Side" panel, aptly explained the consequences of drawing DH's boundaries: "the argumentative stakes in the debate over 'what is' are ineluctably economic, affective, and psychic. Its locus is twofold: who are *we*? and who are *they*?"[109] At the panel and afterward, many DHers complained that they did not recognize themselves in the grim characterizations of their work. But those characterizations, along with the divisions of us/them we/they, do not necessarily come from careful analysis of digital scholarly practice. They emerge from preexisting plots that give them shape and which have consistently proved useful in framing the professional repercussions of media shift. They adapt narratives of decline, an "invasion of barbarians," dark impulses, and the essential doubleness of an institutional crisis.[110] The Manichaean contrasts and "twofold" dimension of DH come to shape, as Raley demonstrates, the way critics explain its "economic, affective, and psychic" consequences. In the editorial head note to their special issue of *differences*, Ellen Rooney and Elizabeth Weed take pains to claim that it "refuses any single origin story" or a "single version of the present or . . . future" of DH.[111] They explain that choosing an origin story will cast varying shadows, depending on what point of origin or story one selects. Yet "In the Shadows," "The Dark Side," and early DH discourse all reveal the attraction to stories in a gothic mode.

Debates about DH flared again in 2019 around "computational literary studies"—another extension of contested reading practices taken for DH as a whole. In an essay in *Critical Inquiry*, Nan Z. Da did not resort to characterological critique but statistical analysis to challenge the claims of distant reading.¹¹² Yet the exchanges to follow would sharpen the familiar contrasts of the debate. Across social media and in a coordinated series of responses on the *Critical Inquiry* blog, practitioners circled the wagons to effectively reinscribe an inside/out boundary of belonging.¹¹³ European DH scholars that same year proposed a separate research society and journal for more rigorous computational literary scholarship—provoking, in turn, critiques that DH was again avoiding the most pertinent topics of humanities study, specifically in the context of race, class, and gender. In a keynote lecture at the 2019 Digital Humanities Summer Institute, Jacqueline Wernimont confessed that

> I've been watching the debate around computational literary studies with a fair degree of horror—horror that it continues to be centered as "The DH" in the popular press, horror at the personal attacks, and horror that this is what people are choosing to spend their time fighting over.¹¹⁴

I too, as a sometime DHer, have felt disturbed by this serial horror show. Even, at times, alienated from skeptical colleagues in an English department where I claim membership. In a different guise, I am also interested in its characterological familiarity within a literary history of horror, aligning with perceptions of crisis, and manifesting alongside reorganizations of humanities labor. That history extends through episodes of professionalization within literary authorship and criticism and flares especially when new media seem to unsettle their proper boundaries.

While digital humanities gets declared as new, the debate is an old story, stretching through the twentieth century into nineteenth-century contexts, and given shape by the narrative frameworks of that era. If Victorian literature offered a "vernacular media theory" for its time, it also imparted a "novelistic imagination" to discourse about intellectual labor when pressured by changes in media. As I have argued, we can still see the long shadows of that imaginary in contemporary debates. *Jekyll and Hyde* has been my case study, as it transformed anxieties about late nineteenth-century media shift into an enduring characterological template, deployed across the twentieth century into our own. Its history of adaptations suggests the flexibility and usefulness of that template to confront media shift and frame its implications. Whether present in specific allusions or as part of a gothicized framework, *Jekyll and Hyde* testifies to a durable Victorian afterlife as it continues to shape discourse about literature, media, and interpretive labor. If these eras maintain an uncanny contact, this chapter has also noted some of the transmissions of the time between. We know the Victorians only through that interval, which exerts its own material and conceptual effects on the Victorians' legacy—especially when it becomes digital.

FIVE

THE ARCHAEOLOGY OF VICTORIAN NEW MEDIA

Periodical literature may be compared to a vast wilderness, "without form and void"; its extent unknown, its ramifications unfathomed.... It has been a dream of my life to explore this region, to compass its extent, to open roadways by which it may be conveniently traversed, to lift up some of the once noble forms which lie mouldering in oblivion; to rescue many a bright memory from the mass of decadence in which it has become embedded; to analyze the underlying strata, and to show of what its successive formations have been composed.
—CORNELIUS WALFORD, *The Outline of a Scheme for a Dictionary of Periodical Literature* (1883)[1]

We are now on the brink of a further, exponential expansion of those opportunities as vast new quantities of hitherto inaccessible records and texts become available for digital searching.
—PATRICK LEARY, "Googling the Victorians" (2005)[2]

THE PERIODICAL PRESS WAS THE engine of the Victorian's new print media and its resulting sense of information overload. Elizabeth Miller claims that a "nearly incalculable volume of new print material made for a qualitative, not just quantitative, shift in the identity of print as a medium."[3] Periodicals—including newspapers, magazines, journals, reviews, and more—presented some astounding problems of scale. For one journalist in 1859, cheap print had unleashed a "flood" that "no living man has ever been able completely to traverse," being far "too vast to be dealt with as a whole."⁴ In the chapter's first epigraph, the aspiring bibliographer Cornelius Walford cycles through descriptions of a "vast wilderness," a trackless mouldering waste, a "mass of decadence," and sedimented geological strata—registering the disorientation of industrialized print at scale, as well as Walford's ready Victorian metaphors to colonize, extract, and govern. The century's explosion of periodicals raised difficult questions about how to reckon with it all, whether and how to collect and preserve these materials, and what secondary forms of indexing could allow people to navigate them.

As Patrick Leary suggested in 2005, "we are now on the brink of a further, exponential expansion" of these materials and more, thanks to the engines of digitization. As the digital era seems to take over from print, it renews again the disorientation of superabundant information as well as the attendant problems of accessing, organizing, and preserving it. Scholars are once more confronted with the profusion of the past. Michael Wolff—among the establishing figures of Victorian studies—noted the "staggering" scale of the periodical archive and insisted that "charting the golden stream" would require new forms of reference materials, perhaps only fully realizable in digital forms: "Given the amount of material, it is patently impossible even to imagine anything approaching a thorough-going subject-index of Victorian periodicals except through the massive use of computer scanning."⁵ The digital returns us not only to Victorian print, newly encountered in abundance on the screen, but also to Victorian anxieties and ambitions about the bibliographic control of these expansive, unruly materials. Arguably, the emergence of Victorian studies itself reflects the ambitions of late nineteenth-century bibliographers who sought control over the sprawling textual archive they helped to create.

For these reasons and more, scholars tend to see resonances between these eras. Robert Darnton tallies the mass reproduction of print and the age of digital transition as the two most recent of "four fundamental changes in information technology" that have patterned human history.⁶ Irene Tucker supposes an even closer resemblance: "In rendering all texts equally present and immediately available, the digitalization of the archive materializes something like the confident cultural authority of Victorian Britain."[7] However, there are serious problems with this story. Darnton's framework spotlights "four fundamental changes" by letting the intervening histories fade into the background. New media has this effect, rendering itself new by forgetting or obscuring its constitutive histories. Comparisons across moments of new media can be fruitful—indeed, they have preoccupied most of this book. Yet this chapter offers a corrective by emphasizing the significance of the time between, or what Megan Ward calls the "historical middle" of our relationship to the nineteenth century.[8] In the first chapter, I argued how the nineteenth century helped media imagine its own disembodiment. Here in the last, I want to demonstrate how digitization forgets its own temporal legacies and material dependencies—as well as why and how we might need to reconstruct what it erases in the interval.

Digitization seems to offer access to historical materials as never before, yet fundamentally depends on the time between—the twentieth-century transmission histories that established the very parameters for materials in electronic form, and the social organization of scholarship to examine them. What we call "digitization" is only the nearest link of a tangled chain of remediation, institutional decisions, historical contingencies, and global actors far beyond the Victorian purview. As Nancy Armstrong suggests of the "Victorian archive," "the secrets for which the researcher sifts . . . are products of distinctively twentieth-century research ventures."[9] Those legacies remain embedded in the digital materials that, at whatever scale, condition our knowledge in retrospect, and in no way present "all texts" or make them evenly available. If scholars now stand in an analogous relation to the bewildered nineteenth-century reader, we cannot overlook the transmission of those materials through a century of other media formats, political arrangements, commercial decisions, and academic ventures that now shape our sense of the historical past.

Using a case study of a digitized collection of British newspapers, this chapter tracks how Victorian texts got to now, and how that process established the contours of Victorian studies as a field. I recover a largely hidden transmission history of how Victorian materials arrive in the digital present, following the British Museum's collection of nineteenth-century newspapers from bound library volumes through microfilming and digitization. These materials were selected and processed by a strange confederation of actors, including World War II intelligence agencies, wartime US cultural elites, microfilm companies, and, in their digitization phase, global IT services outsourced to India and Cambodia—all of whom impacted source materials still marketed as "nineteenth-century British." Furthermore, such collections would also establish the institutional conditions for their study. I show how the organization of Victorian studies, in its early days, took shape in a reciprocal relationship to its archives amid their material transformations. Ultimately, I suggest how studying Victorian texts against the *longue durée* of their mediation reveals the lasting impacts of earlier sociotechnical frameworks, invisible labor, and global exchange within the research objects and professional organizations of contemporary scholarship.

An Archaeology of Data

My story starts with a digital humanities researcher wondering what to do with four hard drives that arrived in the mail.[10] This story connects my fumbling experiments as a digital scholar back to the institutional conditions that made them possible, or even which established the terms of my scholarship in Victorian studies. In 2014, the NC State University Libraries announced that they had reached an innovative agreement with the commercial publisher Gale Cengage to license data-mining rights to its digital collections.[11] Within a week, Gale Cengage announced in its own press release that it would generally "make available content from its *Gale Digital Collections* to academic researchers for data mining and textual analysis purposes."[12] In other words, institutional subscribers would be able to request the source files behind Gale's web-based interfaces.[13] The terms of our agreement with Gale included "content mining rights" for digital collections,

FIGURE 4. Hard drives containing "19th Century British Library Newspapers." Source: Photo by Markus Wust, 2015. Used with permission.

allowing for a full range of analytical approaches, such as computer vision and image analytics. The license includes the library's standard subscription to Gale's web-based search interface for these collections as well as physical hard drives containing the source data (for a nominal "cost recovery" charge). Soon the drives arrived by mail.

Excited by this seemingly direct access to the source files, I began to explore what the drives contained. My elation soon drained away as I began sorting through prosaic directories, title manifests, image files, and XML files with text worryingly encoded. Granted, it is unfair to use the first page of a historical newspaper to evaluate a database, as it contains layouts and advertisements that are incredibly challenging for OCR. Alas, that is where I first looked, randomly perusing a front page of the *Huddersfield Chronicle* (April 6, 1850). Its accompanying XML file includes the layers of metadata provided for the newspaper, the issue, and the first article, with each word appeared wrapped in page coordinates along with a 46 percent OCR confidence score.[14]

In using data from Gale Cengage's *British Nineteenth-Century News-*

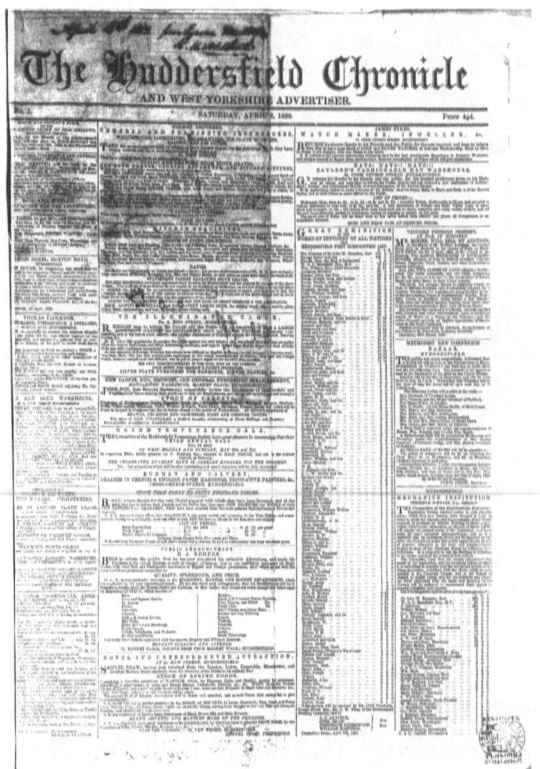

FIGURE 5. Scanned front page of the *Huddersfield Chronicle*, April 6, 1850. Source: HUCE-1850-04-06-0001.jpg from Part II of "19th-century British Library Newspapers," Gale, 2015.

papers collection (*BNCN*), what exactly am I dealing with? As Lisa Gitelman and Virginia Jackson argue, "raw data" is an oxymoron; the phrase obscures the discursive conditions and technical particularities of its own production.[15] If these are the "source files," what, in turn, are the sources of the source files? How did they get this way? If commercial publishers like Gale Cengage are getting into the data and analytics business, scholars must learn what that data comprises and how it has evolved.[16] The efficacy of digitally enabled scholarship depends on a largely missing source history of these collections.

The sense of awe summoned by big data, along with the rhetoric of paradigmatic discovery in digital research, is a symptom of a digital sublime better understood as sublimation. In physics, sublimation occurs when substances skip a physical state change, as when dry ice goes directly from solid to gas without an intermediate liquid stage. It is a useful metaphor for digital resources, which can seem to erase any intermediary state between source object and digital surrogate in the cloud. Thanks to the work of many scholars, today we seldom approach digital scholarly resources so naively. James Mussell, for instance, has called for critical bibliographies of *contemporary* digital objects and delivery platforms to match our study of *historical* text technologies and their materiality. He calls this "historically reflexive media literacy"—a phrase that enables much productive crossover between new media, past and present.[17] Yet its very diachronicity may overlook what has happened in between, the entanglement of digital scholarly resources with histories other than the nineteenth century. Scholars also need to understand what Molly Hardy calls the "prehistory of digitization," in which institutional priorities, material constraints, and historical actors all set the conditions for what eventually became digital collections.[18]

Humanities scholars have specialized in book history and the material transmission of texts, but they are less comfortable, perhaps, with understanding the life cycle of digital resources, particularly those generated by commercial scholarly publishers over the last hundred years. This history is braided through variously sold and reconfigured companies, links big data to microfilming and micropublishing projects from the 1920s onward, and blends labor practices from library acquisitions to the technical work outsourced to the global economy. Gale's hard drives are relatively recent artifacts of that ongoing transmission and also a metaphor for the black boxing of commercial workflows that supply so many of our digitized historical resources. The hard drives do not only carry data but residues of procedures, technologies, and decisions that the data itself does not sufficiently disclose. This record may be difficult to access. It may have been intentionally erased. It may never have been recorded. While DH scholars appreciate the importance of metadata, the legacy and functionality of digital scholarly resources also deeply depend on something else: "paradata." Loosely defined, "paradata" means the procedural contexts, workflows, and intellectual capital generated by groups throughout a project's lifecycle.[19] Paradata might include commentary, rationale, process notes, and records of decisions about projects capturing what its participants chose to include or exclude. As Tim Sherratt elegantly explains, "Big data is made up of many small acts of living."[20] Those acts are imperfect, ephemeral, and (particularly in cases of big scholarly data) embedded in a complex corporate world often careless of its history and jealous of its secrets.

This chapter worries over the largely invisible corporate histories of digital scholarly resources and the question of how (or even if) we might recover, reconstruct, and interpret them. That task presents multiple challenges, including attending to the specific materialities and platform dependencies of texts as they move across different mediums, or through intermediary states, nowadays in "workflows" that are rarely preserved or accessible to outsiders.[21] All these various state changes, process dependencies, and occluded histories have pushed scholars from media history to "media archaeology," which attends more closely to media's materialities and the different notions of history they might express. Media archaeology does not emphasize chronology so much as historical strata or even the plural temporalities in which media take shape. In this sense, "data mining" becomes "data archaeology": the metaphor changes from the extraction of meaning toward trying to recover and reconstitute media objects within their changing ecologies. In her examination of *Early English Books Online*, Bonnie Mak proposes one method we might adopt in our study of digitized nineteenth-century resources: "An archaeology of a digitisation . . . should understand the digitally encoded entity as a cultural object, produced by human labour, and necessarily shaped by—and consequently embodying—historical circumstance."[22] So, rather than doing research with a database of Victorian newspapers, we might research the database itself, looking to its anterior forms, their social circumstances, and mechanisms. Wolfgang Ernst prefers the term "archaeography," which acknowledges the importance of machines in the historiography that Mak attributes to human actors and cultural circumstances.[23] Somewhere on this spectrum, though, we must reckon with the archaeology of digitized scholarly resources.

Mussell knows exactly how significant this problem is, especially for digital materials created or distributed by commercial vendors:

> At present, publishers do not see the value in documenting their methodology (or at least making it available), nor do they provide accessible histories of the content they republish beyond introductory essays about the source material. There is little or no information about where this material is from (which archives?), what has been omitted (multiple editions? supplements?), any intermediary forms (microfilm?), let alone the various transformations that underpin the production of the image and metadata delivered over the web. Given the stake scholars have in this digital material and the fact that it will be used, in one form or another, as it is republished in new resources into the foreseeable future, it is vital that we can account for its history.[24]

Mussell underscores the importance of simply knowing what you are dealing with. How can a given database support valid claims about the nineteenth-century press? How was it conceived, and what does it actually include, exclude, overlook? How do its material legacies, data structure, and interface shape what we can know about its content? As Jensen proposes, all historically minded scholars now need training in "digital archival literacy."[25]

To track the historical witnesses of Victorian media is to approach our digital scholarly resources neither as surrogates nor as remediated objects but as potentially distinctive works.[26] As Laurel Brake suggests, the "digital edition is a copy of a version that is unique among many possible editions."[27] And digital editions have what Conway calls a "secondary provenance" of their long production history.[28] Scholars overlook this not only because of the difficulties of understanding it, but almost by convention, tending not to "[acknowledge] digitised historical texts" in published research, or masking their uses of digital collections as unscholarly intermediaries.[29] But these collections are distinct objects with histories of their own. To analyze their intermediation is, as Paul Eggert puts it, "to understand the text's successive discursive inscriptions, its ideological absorbency."[30] In the case of nineteenth-century British newspapers, their discursive absorptions have included twentieth-century political economies of global conflict, the intelligence community's alliances with scholarly associations and research libraries, gendered and outsourced labor, and commercial techno-futurism. Exploring these histories requires stepping outside of our usual training and engaging with elements of book history, media archaeology, and investigative scholarly journalism.

From Accession to Micropublishing

This section pursues such a method on the hardware and data objects that landed on my desk as *19th-Century British Library Newspapers*. It offers a glimpse at the historical contingencies that shaped the passage of such materials from the nineteenth century to the near present. This is not meant to be an exhaustive survey but a starting point for how we might study Victorian periodicals against the *longue durée* of their mediation—and an argument for why we might need to do so. That time frame includes roughly four phases: the initial production of nineteenth-century newspapers, accession into library volumes, micropublishing, and digitization. Those phases do not necessarily follow discrete moments of change, nor do they offer chronological scenes in which to detect traces of some durable information commodity. Instead, they mark domains of reproduction, more properly conceived as editorial frameworks for the creation of new archives. Nonetheless, we can put them into a simplified historiographical narrative to better understand their relations. Newspapers were printed. Some copies were accessioned. Some of those were microfilmed. Some of those were digitized. Some of those were included in the *British Nineteenth-Century Newspapers* database, a derivative of which was mailed to the NC State

University Libraries. Some of those still linger, in different forms, in the current *British Newspaper Archive* collection online. All the rest is complicated.

The production of nineteenth-century newspapers is well documented in histories and cultural studies of the press. I will pass over it here to focus on the transmission of newspapers through the evolving architectures of scholarly resources, beginning with the accessioning of newsprint by the British Museum in 1822. That date marks the first systematic and institutional attempt to collect British newspapers as such. At that time, the British Museum negotiated a deal with the Board of Commissioners for Stamps (which later amalgamated with the Commissioners of Inland Revenue). The Stamp Office oversaw the longstanding "taxes on knowledge," which, especially after duties increased on periodicals in 1819, profoundly shaped the landscape of newspapers, including what it passed on to the British Museum.[31] The Stamp Office kept copies of stamped newspapers for two years in case they were needed as legal evidence, especially in cases of libel. At the request of the principal librarian, the Stamp Office would "gift" these copies to the museum, a practice that continued until 1869. Already shaped by the political implications of the newspaper tax, these collections were often incomplete and did not include provincial newspapers until 1832. Meanwhile, Irish and Scottish titles were not regularly acquired until after 1849.[32] In 1840, Antonio Panizzi (later the museum's Principal Librarian) proposed to expand collecting to European, colonial, and commonwealth newspapers, making purchases from the "colonial reading rooms" of Peter Lund Simmonds. The museum's Trustees declined, though foreign and colonial papers would continue to be intermittently purchased or received by gift throughout the century.[33]

Histories of colonial copyright deposit have tended to focus on books and government reports, but newspapers sometimes flowed through the same channels. In 1842, the passage of the Imperial copyright act sought to cover works published "in any part of the British Dominions."[34] Yet, like most international copyright legislation, this was difficult if not impossible to enforce. Nor was there infrastructure or funding to secure deposit copies from British territories, or incentive for colonial publishers to conform to such bibliographic control. Herman Merivale, Under Secretary of the Colonial Office, wrote to Panizzi about the "extreme difficulty of complying," as "in the 'British' colonies proper newspapers are almost as numerous and quite as ephemeral as in the United States." Furthermore, even those "proper" newspapers represent "only a fraction" of periodicals being published in various forms.[35] Some colonial offices already kept local newspapers for the purposes of regulation, as in the case of Ceylon's "Ordinance No. 5 of 1839, To regulate the printing and publishing of Newspapers in this Colony," which required a copy of every issue to be sent to the colonial administration.[36] Yet accession to the British Museum was dependent on those administrators' goodwill and the infrequent compliance—or active political resistance—of publishers abroad.

Within the United Kingdom, books were already subject to laws of copyright deposit into the British Museum, but this was not enforced for newspapers until the Newspaper Printer and Reading Room Act of 1869 changed the terms.[37] Publishers would now be required to deposit newspapers within seven days of printing. The Inland Revenue Office would pay for them, keep them for the legal statute of three years, and then deliver them to the British Museum. These papers often show hand annotations in pencil, suggesting they included editorial proofs or even publishers' in-house "receipts" confirming payment for advertisements and some local news.[38] The ongoing gifts and legal deposits over the nineteenth century were supplemented by donations and the British Museum's purchase of sets. At one point, looking to cover gaps in its records, the museum considered a purchasing arrangement with Thomas Holloway, who monitored his extensive advertising of "Holloway's Pills" by requiring a copy of every newspaper issue in which he bought ad space. While his collection was perhaps more extensive than "any other known," he could not guarantee a supply of perfect runs and the deal collapsed.[39] Still, the anecdote suggests an early precedent for the public-private partnerships that would pattern the museum's (and later library's) newspaper collection strategy.

Newspaper accessions were perennially troubled by the museum's storage space and the expense of binding them into volumes. Michael Harris suggests that "by the 1860s the size of the collection had become a matter of routine Victorian amazement and admiration"—as well as a significant source of concern for the museum. Its accessioning policies changed as a result. Along with canceling plans to acquire colonial papers, there was resistance to collecting British provincial papers—the fastest growing sector of the newspaper industry following the stamp tax repeal.[40] Beginning in 1879, the museum collected only the first edition of any given newspaper and for a brief time in the 1880s only bound the "most used newspapers."[41] Each of these initiatives favored the metropolitan press: library usage statistics from 1896 showed 3,000 provincial papers consulted as opposed to 40,000 metropolitan titles, with nearly all newspapers subpoenaed for legal use coming from London. The space issue prompted even more drastic proposals, includ-

FIGURE 6. Bound newspaper volumes in Colindale. Source: Luke McKernan, "Newspaper library #3." Flickr. August 14, 2013.

ing handing over the entire collections enterprise to another institution, redistributing the provincial collections to "local bodies" (which did not even exist), and simply disposing of provincial papers.[42]

In 1905, the storage crisis resulted in the construction of the museum's newspaper repository at Colindale (which was filled within twenty years) and the subsequent construction of the British Museum Newspaper Library in 1932.[43] These were also formative years in the development of microphotography as a storage solution and preservation medium. But microfilm emerged in a significantly different context. Its application to nineteenth-century newspapers at Colindale entwines the British Museum's history with commercial and strategic intelligence interests in microfilming more generally. In the early part of the century, these efforts were led by the work of companies such as Eastman Kodak and University Microfilms Incorporated (UMI), whose cultural preservation efforts were, in turn, mandated and funded by the interests of American cultural elites and intelligence services. The history of UMI (now a part of ProQuest) provides a useful starting place for investigating the complicated relationships that drove such efforts. UMI entangles with Gale's *British Nineteenth-Century Newspapers* database through its extensive connections to twentieth-century microphotography efforts at the British Museum's newspaper archive.

An American company, UMI began in 1938 when its founder, Eugene Power, began photographing rare materials from the Clements Library at the University of Michigan. Power was inspired by a 35 mm camera developed by Captain R. H. Draeger, an officer in the US Navy who had devised the technology as a means to photograph books to read while on assignment in China. While abroad, Draeger simply reprinted the positives from the film and enjoyed the same sort of transportable library that today energizes the marketing of e-book readers. Back in Ann Arbor, Eugene Power cobbled together "parts of two movie and still cameras into the second microfilm-book camera in existence."[44] His first office comprised two rooms in the back of a funeral home where he filmed old books from the English Short Title Catalog, which would eventually become part of *Early English Books*

Online, now owned by ProQuest.⁴⁵ In his autobiography, Power tells the origin story, which reads like the incarnation scene from *Frankenstein*: "I can see that those nights of feverish work amid the caskets and embalming odors of Dolph's Funeral Parlor were the real beginning of University Microfilms."⁴⁶

Though Power characterizes UMI as his own Promethean invention, his work was made possible by a unique confederation of library interests, commercial micropublishing, and intelligence services at the outset of World War II. It was, according to Seth Cayley, a vice president at Gale, a massively coordinated effort that would never again be possible. This point may be disputed, especially considering the phenomenon of Google Books. Nevertheless, it is an argument worth considering—that twentieth-century microfilms are not the accidental intermediaries for commercial digital objects but their institutional precondition.

In 1940, an incendiary bomb destroyed a significant portion of the

FIGURE 7. Postcard of the Majestic Theater and Dolph's Funeral Home on Maynard Street, Ann Arbor, 1929. Source: Dolph's Funeral Home records, Bentley Historical Library, University of Michigan.

King George III's collection in the British Museum, whose missing contents are still indexed in the British Library's catalog.⁴⁷ That same year, a high-explosive bomb hit the museum's original 1905 newspaper repository building at Colindale, affecting 40 percent of its volumes of nineteenth-century English provincial newspapers, of which about 6,000 volumes were completely lost.⁴⁸

The specter of war damage and book burnings in Europe created a wave of interest in microfilming as a preservation strategy that would distribute surrogate copies of newspapers in worldwide depositories. In the United States, institutions such as the Library of Congress, the Social Science Research Council (SSRC), American Council of Learned

FIGURE 8. Bomb damage to the BL newspaper repository in 1940. Source: "The Newspaper Library at War," *BL Newspaper Library Newsletter* no. 12, Spring 1991, p. 3. Courtesy of the British Library Board, shelfmark P.903/690.

Societies (ACLS), and the Council of Library and Information Resources (CLIR) formed committees that agreed that preservation of European and especially British materials was of the utmost importance. In 1930, the SSRC and the ACLS coordinated on a Joint Committee on Materials for Research, appointing World War I veteran and Stanford-educated Robert Binkley as chair. The committee worried about the vulnerability of paper-based historical records and their sometimes chaotic organization: "newsprint was perishable, business records treated as disposable, and ephemera haphazardly kept."[49] Binkley's concluding report, *Methods of Reproducing Research Materials*, was released in 1931 by Edwards Brothers Inc., of Ann Arbor, Michigan, whose director of publications was Eugene Powers.[50] The report advocated for microformats and the production of more expansive bibliographies to index research materials. American academic committees also generated wish lists for such preservation and indexing that featured rare books, manuscripts, and periodicals, and then secured funding from the Rockefeller Foundation to carry out the work abroad. In her study of these developments, Kathy Peiss argues that American preservation efforts during the war were motivated by a broadly shared sensitivity to an endangered European culture as well as by the opportunism of cultural elites in shaping government policy.[51] As Lester Born would later describe such initiatives, "American scholars see the bringing of the resources of the Old world to the New as the principal role for scholarly photocopying."[52]

At the same time, the Office of the Coordinator of Information, soon to become the Office of Strategic Services and later the Central Intelligence Agency, had similar designs on the old world, especially German materials that might be microfilmed. Peiss argues that the "government's need for intelligence had a greater impact on the fate of books than did the organizations whose mandate was cultural protection. The war brought librarians into a relationship with the intelligence-gathering arm of the state through the Office of Strategic Services (OSS), as well as the intelligence units of the armed forces."[53] This relationship also included the commercial agents who supplied the technology, expertise, and ultimately the salable products of preserving cultural heritage, which, in remediated forms, scholars continue to use today. The Office of the Coordinator of Information and the Office of Strategic Services backed Eugene Power on several trips to Europe for copying caches of documents and recent periodicals. For this work, Power turned to a different camera, the Kodak Model D Microfile, otherwise known as a Recordak 35 mm.

Figures 10 and 11 depict microfilm technology from later decades, but they fairly represent this machine and its predominantly women operators, who, like their counterparts of nineteenth-century "typewriters" and twentieth-century computing staff, are mostly absent from micrographic histories.[54] As Power describes it, the Microfile "had a large bed with a glass platen which would press bound newspapers flat and hold them in place to be photographed. Its cradle would shift back and forth in order to get a complete page on each exposure."[55] The look of these setups is familiar to anyone working with a modern overhead scanner, but the Microfile's technique of shifting its cradle may have

FIGURE 9. "Microfilming with a Recordak 35 mm." Source: National Library of Medicine, 1969.

FIGURE 10. "Microfilming at Colindale began in the 1950s." Source: Preservation Advisory Centre, British Library.

informed the decision to identify the page—rather than the opening or two-page spread—as the fundamental unit of display and analysis. Around 1941, Power shipped three Microfile cameras to England for on-site work, but the cargo ship was sunk by a German submarine.[56]

Power would soon successfully develop relationships with the British Museum, the Bodleian Library, and the Cambridge Library, installing his cameras and operators to generate the installment-based products that became *Early English Books Online* and similar collections for sale. Power and UMI also facilitated the micropublishing of British newspapers. During a visit to the United States in 1944, the director and principal librarian of the British Museum, Sir John Forsdyke, became convinced of the value of microphotography as a solution to the museum's escalating newspaper problem. The museum sponsored Forsdyke's visit to UMI in Ann Arbor, where he consulted with Power about what equipment the museum would need. According to Power, he then sketched the microfilming facilities that Forsdyke would soon build.⁵⁷ When the Colindale facility rebuilt temporary structures in 1950, it opened a microfilm annex with equipment the Rockefeller Foundation donated for the purpose. In 1948, the foundation also sponsored three-month fellowships for British Museum staff to train at UMI on large-scale microfilm production, training that was designed to prepare them for photographing the sprawling collections of British newspapers back in Colindale. These visiting staff included D. A. Wilson, who was in charge of the Colindale facilities and soon oversaw the four microfilm cameras from Rockefeller, one of which remained in use through the 1990s.⁵⁸ Setting out on the monumental task of microfilming the collections, Wilson prioritized current British provincial newspapers, important sets of London newspapers, and then historical London newspapers in chronological order from 1801.⁵⁹

It is difficult to say how much of the British Museum's extant print collection of newspapers was filmed. Estimates range between 5 and 30 percent of its print collection exists on microfilm. Beginning with Wilson, the microfilming program necessarily had to make decisions about what to photograph based on the fragility of materials, the coverage of the collection, the interests of potential users, and the budget available for the project. Among the first priorities was to address the material damage from the war, including by borrowing newspaper volumes from other libraries to photograph.⁶⁰ The museum also made microfilms of full sets of UK national newspapers, and expanded to provincial and overseas titles. The development of its microfilming program also "changed the framework within which decisions on retention or disposal were taken." While the newspaper department committed to archiving paper copies of all UK and colonial copyright deposit materials, it established a "disposals policy for foreign newspapers after microfilming" in which certain paper copies were pulped.⁶¹ The department also opened a commercial office to sell positive microfilm copies of its newspapers to other libraries, mostly in the United Kingdom.⁶²

All of these decisions did and did not have downstream effects on the digitization programs to come. The complex question of what microfilm represents and excludes anticipates those very problematics for digitized periodicals resources.⁶³ Just as importantly, microfilm collections also suffer the erasure of their institutional memory and the compounding difficulties of bibliographic control. In his 1982 history of scholarly micropublishing, Alan Meckler explains how librarians did not know about the source histories of microfilm materials and neither, in many cases, did the companies that produced them: "Several, particularly those entrepreneurs who entered the field solely as a commercial venture, simply did not bother to keep papers that might have had some historic value. Others lost or misplaced papers during the course of their careers, especially as business changed hands."⁶⁴ For his book, Meckler had to undertake extensive interviews, tracking the oral histories of an apparently durable cultural heritage medium. A 1964 article in *PMLA*, later reprinted in the 1972 first volume of *Microform Review*, raises an important concern: "The history of scholarship is consequently in large measure a history of the diffusion of the materials for scholarly research."⁶⁵ This article—a report prepared for the ACLS—attempted to survey the landscape of scholarly micropublishing, concluding that the "plain truth is that we have accumulated scattered, incomplete, and almost random collections to which there are few guides and of which there is insufficient use."⁶⁶ Ironically, the article's author is missing from the metadata in JSTOR and miscataloged in the MLA International Bibliography. In fact, he was Lester Born, a classics professor and archivist, who in 1950 would coordinate the microfilm holdings at the Library of Congress. He was also a soldier in the Allied Command's special Monuments, Fine Arts, and Archives section, known as the "Monuments Men," who worked in wartime Europe to secure historic buildings, collections, and books.⁶⁷

From Scanning to Global IT

For today's scholars, nineteenth-century newspapers only exist because of the elaborate transmission history in the intervening years between then and now. In the context of the sturdy bound volumes in the British Library, Brake has characterized the "ephemera" of Victorian periodicals as much more durable than we typically think.⁶⁸ But as media studies scholar Wendy Chun clarifies, the "enduring ephemeral" is rooted in how mediums constitute themselves as "new," promising durable storage that belies the contingencies of memory.[69] Memory—and digital memory especially—is not storage but depends on a technical and social infrastructure that must be actively maintained, largely by institutional commitments to preservation, migration, and access. For nineteenth-century newspapers, understanding the relatively recent shift from microfilm to digitization involves just such complexities in which the military-informational complex cedes to the workings of a global IT economy.

The British Museum—whose library departments became the British Library in 1973—ended its microfilming program with the demolition of the Colindale facility in 2010 to make way for real estate development. When it closed, the facilities at Colindale held about thirty miles of shelved periodicals with over 750 million pages of newspapers, materials that were gradually relocated to the British Library's

FIGURE 11. Demolition of the BL's Colindale building. Source: Clare Newsome. "So farewell, then British Library newspaper archive Colindale." Twitter @ClareNewsome. March 27, 2015. Used with permission.

state-of-the-art facility in Boston Spa, with its dark, low-oxygen storage stacks that one staffer dubbed the "void."[70] The British Library's plans for digitizing its newspaper collections began with a grant application to the Joint Information Systems Committee (JISC), whose funding competition already set the terms for the proposed collection: it had to be large scale, include significant geographical coverage, and be broadly useful. The proposed British Newspapers 1800–1900 project had an initial target of two million pages (about 0.3 percent of the print collection). An advisory group of library staff members and scholars was assembled to establish a "framework of national titles and country-wide coverage with the breadth and depth to form a virtual key to many other provincial newspapers of the same date."[71] In this description, the forty-eight selected titles represent a "virtual key" or representative sample. The funding period aimed to deliver the "scanning of the entire microfilmed content; article zoning and page extraction; OCR of the page images; and the production of the required metadata."[72] This part of the story is admirably documented by the BL's project managers and department heads, including Jane Shaw and Ed King, who continually shared process lessons about large-scale newspaper digitization with the library community in the 2000s.[73] Their published conference papers include an assessment of the image quality and material durability of microfilm slated to become digital facsimiles. While the library's print collection of nineteenth-century newspapers turned out to be in relatively good shape—with only 2 percent unfit for its new Zeutschel microfilm cameras—its microfilm collection of newspapers had problems, largely developed on acetate rolls subject to acidic decay. So the BL decided to digitize newspapers by, whenever necessary, first making *new* microfilms from print copies. This would standardize its digital production and update its microfilm collections to National Preservation Standards. Estimates rose from 50 percent to 90 percent for new filming over the course of the project. Notably, microfilm was not simply a historical intermediary between print and digitization; it was the immediate step in contemporary digitization practices. Making new media regenerated earlier forms of it, too. The BL would later recommend direct scans from original sources, but in the 2000s digital cameras did not yet supply sufficient megapixel capture and, considering the heavy bound volumes of its newspapers, flat-bed scanning was potentially damaging as well as prohibitively expensive. Thus, to avoid "gutter shadow" and to keep pages evenly lit, newspapers were held in book cradles with each page photographed to microfilm.[74] The single page remained the primary unit of image production.

The BL's initial newspaper digitization work occurred in two distinct phases, each of which corresponds to a segment of Gale's collection. The first phrase—which would become known internally as "JISC I," also known as Gale's "Part I"—occurred from 2004 to 2007. A second funding period followed in 2008-9, "JISC II," Gale's "Part II," which expanded the British Newspapers 1800–1900 project to include more regional and local news as well as extending existing titles back through the eighteenth century. This project added a million more pages to the digital collection, though it slightly changed the workflows for the project. Both phases used scans predominantly from new microfilm, though in JISC II one complete paper—the *Standard*—was scanned directly from print at Boston Spa. For each phase, the BL sent its in-house images or new microfilm reels to external vendors for digital scanning and processing. Scans from the films, new as well as old, resulted in multiple digital objects for each newspaper page. In JISC I, this included an "archival master file for each page, in TIFF format, version 6.0 . . . at a resolution of 300 dpi, 8-bit greyscale," as well as service images generated "after the process of article zoning and OCR . . . [and] delivered as greyscale hybrids."[75] As in figure 12, the "hybrid" images combine 1-bit bitonal scans (simple black and white) of textual components with 8-bit grayscale scans of any illustrated content, all to conserve on the eventual file size and to avoid "problems for 56k modem users."[76]

In JISC II, the British Library changed its requirements to grayscale scans at 400 dpi. It received TIFF images of raw scans (one per page, unedited), a lossless JP2 or JPEG2000 master image (cropped and lightly corrected), a compressed JPEG derivative image for service

FIGURE 12. Detail of a hybrid service image from JISC I, showing grayscale illustrations and bitonal text. Source: *Illustrated Police News*, January 28, 1893, in British Nineteenth-Century Newspapers.

copies, and associated XML files.[77] Images from JISC II also look a little different from their earlier counterparts, as "many of the local newspapers are in poorer condition with uneven printing within a run and across individual pages ... This has resulted in deliberately chosen lighter looking scanned images in order to improve the OCR word accuracy."[78] Sometimes digital files can tell their own stories. Ryan Cordell has demonstrated how EXIF metadata extraction software can help reveal the conditions under which such images were produced.[79] Yet that depends on access to the archival master files, which are often distinct from a derivative master, or "mezzanine copy," of the improved image from which other service files are made.[80] Running EXIF software against the derivatives of JPG and TIFF files on Gale's hard drives only reveals the *absence* of evidence for their production. Indeed, as the BL documents, the initial TIFF images from microfilm scans were "destroyed at the end of production," being far too large for the library to ingest in its own long-term object management system.[81] Even the masters are already derivatives.

Remediation is not a one-way street, however. As Ed King explains, "One of the most fascinating aspects of 'first time' large scale digitisation of 19th century newspapers was how little librarians and archivists in the UK knew about the *actual* printing run of any given newspaper in the UK."[82] Ever since the British Museum first started systematically collecting newspapers, as Harris explains, "cataloguing [had] never kept up with accumulation."[83] As the BL logged pages for the JISC I and JISC II digitization projects, they were often improving the library's catalog information about their originals, whose existence in print was frequently unknown or otherwise complicated by variously timed or regionally distributed editions. (When faced with duplicates or multiple editions, the JISC projects selected the last timed edition of a paper for digitization.) Furthermore, the JISC projects included physically stabilizing and repairing original newspapers when necessary, aiding their material preservation in the service of getting good pictures. Thus, digitization ironically regenerates the memory of nineteenth-century newspapers as preserved in other storage media, including stabilized paper as well as new microfilm.

The BL employed several third-party vendors for scanning microfilms and processing digital images. This work included segmenting the pages into articles; creating OCR of the text; encoding page divisions, content, and metadata description into a standardized XML schema; and then delivering service images and XML files back to the library. The specific involvement of these companies is difficult to trace: they often lack records of their own histories, they ascribe to contractual nondisclosure rules, and they typically avoid discussions of outsourcing. For all the BL's admirable transparency, its relations to third-party vendors can be vague: "The allocation of work between in-house operations and third parties is based on where value can best be achieved, balancing the cost effectiveness of competitive tender with the optimum deployment of experience and expertise from the library."[84] The corporate language exemplifies the abstract characterizations of labor and costs that render invisible and palatable the conditions of outsourced work, especially in global contexts. Having taken the "view that the use of human intelligence combined with software applications would give the best quality result," the BL chose a company called Apex CoVantage, which the metadata in the XML files for JISC I (Gale Part I) still names in its <conversionCredit> element.[85] In snapshots of its website from 2006, Apex celebrates its "dual-shore advantage" and "truly global solutions," boasting that it possesses "one of the lowest employee turn-over rates in the outsourcing industry."[86] Nineteenth-century newspapers were processed through a digitization product called "isaac," for which Apex furnishes a corporate video. The video, which includes the British Library's logo at its conclusion, begins with the promise of "unlocking [the] treasures" of historic newspapers, creating cultures of tolerance and peace, offering rich resources for libraries, and increasing revenue streams for content providers. The video illustrates the digitization workflow, highlighting the software's unique processes while also clarifying (explicitly and implicitly) its uses of human labor. The gentle voiceover intones, "Between these steps, a human insures that article boundaries are accurate, adjusting them when necessary." "Article components," it continues, "are then sent through different human-driven workflows."[87] In the background, the video offers glimpses of the "human-driven workflows" as brown-skinned men work at computer terminals in cubicles, cleaning "dirty" materials and validating software suggestions for eventual reassembly and sale in the Anglophone West. Natalia Cecire has pointed to the enforced invisibility of marginalized labor in the scanning operations of the Google Books project, which are occasionally glimpsed as the accidental photography of workers' hands and fingers.[88] Bonnie Mak has argued for a long history of exploitative transcription practices that connect early modern scriptoria to offshore companies currently supplying cheap transcriptions for the Eighteenth Century Collections Online-Text Creation Partnership project.[89] At the very least, Mak suggests, we need to be aware of the enabling conditions of our scholarship, which may increasingly rely on the segmentation and relative invisibility of global labor practices in digitizing historical materials. Otherwise "new" forms of digital scholarship, as Roopika Risam argues, merely extend colonial and neocolonial traditions of knowledge production.[90]

The BL switched vendors for JISC II, choosing Olive Software, a company based in Santa Clara, California, with a research development office in Israel.[91] However, during an early pilot to assure quality, the company failed to produce scans of a similar or better quality than the BL's own. It was soon replaced with the runner-up, Content Conversion Specialists. Although the company is headquartered in Hamburg, Germany, it subcontracts its large digitization projects with companies such as Digital Divide Data, then located in Cambodia.[92] This subcontractor claims to practice socially responsible "impact sourcing," hiring disadvantaged high school graduates as workers and offering them opportunities for higher education (after one year of employment). None of this is recorded in the XML metadata for JISC II files.

For both of its digitization phases, the BL needed Gale to assume responsibility for transforming, hosting, and serving data files on an accessible website. The library initially planned to create its own web services and interface but soon realized that this would be unfeasible. Here—finally—the sharper outlines of *British Nineteenth-Century Newspapers* begin to come into focus. Sometimes building on and sometimes overwriting legacy codes and processes, Gale's product was based on procedures developed at its corporate offices in the United Kingdom, with skilled labor outsourced to India and web development services located at Gale's US headquarters in Farmington, Michigan. Gale further subcontracted work to the company HTC Global Services (also uncredited in the metadata), with its team of 400 people in Chennai, India. According to Gale, these were English-speaking workers with computer science backgrounds who ran the Abby FineReader OCR software, entered and verified metadata, visually mapped distinct articles, and validated the XML. Launched in October 2007, the resulting product was called *19th-Century British Library Newspapers*.

Jane Shaw describes the project as an "innovative and challenging example of a public/private partnership between Gale Cengage Learning, CCS and the British Library," each of which has its own "cultural emphases."[93] Indeed, Gale's emphases would shape the project in important ways.[94] Shaw notes that the BL had already developed its own standards for digitizing microfilm in the face of inconsistencies in similar projects worldwide. A project manager at Gale characterizes the early 2000s as a "wild west" where projects and standards proliferated, and another called it the "gold rush to digital."[95]

In either case, Gale was soon using its own workflows and proposing additional requirements such as using subject categories for articles (with twenty-six options).[96] These decisions consolidate in a master file, called the document type definition (DTD), a set of rules that all the project's XML files must obey. In simpler terms, it constitutes the set of editorially accepted categories—for example, subjects, genres, and document features—within a digital collection. Establishing these parameters was apparently the most contentious aspect of the project, as developers and scholars attempted to model the staggering heterogeneity of formats and content across a century of periodical publishing. The BL's project managers made sure to employ the Metadata Encoding and Transmission Standard and Dublin Core standards, including four structural levels: title, issue, page, and article.[97] For its part, Gale was following the procedures it developed for its recently completed *Eighteenth-Century Collections Online* and, more directly, the *Times Digital Archive*. These near ancestors may have passed on their genetic materials. Andrew Hobbs has criticized scholars for reflexively gravitating to the *Times* and overlooking the provincial press.[98] Not coincidentally, the *Times* was the first British newspaper made commercially available as a digitized scholarly resource.[99] Furthermore, the same workflows and article categories Gale developed for the *Times Digital Archive* quickly came to structure the experience of *19th-Century British Library Newspapers* as a whole. Scholars of the Victorian press have generally noted how metropolitan news was copied throughout the country. Gale's database cemented that legacy at the level of its document type definition against which all its XML has to validate.

For each "work product," Gale took a snapshot of their file production and backed it up. File histories show that the copy we received at NC State University was derived from 2007 (part I), and 2008–9 (part II). Gale also uses an "iron mountain" backup service called Portico, a nonprofit affiliated with the Library of Congress and JSTOR, which will maintain Gale's data even if the company goes bust. But which version will be preserved? Scholars like Charles Upchurch and Natalie Houston have alerted us to pay attention to the versioning of such sources, which can be silently and periodically updated.[100] Even within a given data set, researchers ought to verify coverage. Bob Nicholson has demonstrated how Gale's content swells toward the second half of the nineteenth century and sometimes contains significant gaps within any given issue's run.[101] In the most extensive survey of the collection's contents to date, Kaspar Beelen and colleagues also demonstrated that JISC I and II are not evenly distributed over the nineteenth century, showing disparities in relation to the broader landscape of Victorian newspapers: "Over time, the digital sample makes up a smaller percentage of the total landscape of known papers. And the decline is rather drastic, from 10% around 1850 to less than 2 per in 1900."[102] Furthermore, they claim that while these projects attempted to represent a diversity of political viewpoints, the digitized collections "over-represented politically aligned newspapers at the expense of neutral and independent titles, thereby exaggerating the politicization of the Victorian public sphere and its obeisance to party politics."[103]

In 2010, when the British Library began to expand its newspaper digitization project once again, Gale lost the bid to a genealogy company called Findmypast, which now owns the rights and operations to the renamed and still expanding *British Newspaper Archive*. The specific reasons for the BL's decision to change vendors were not disclosed. Having lost the rights, Gale had to rename their product *British Nineteenth-Century Newspapers*. It packages this in separate parts to sell to libraries with differently sized budgets. According to Ray Abruzzi, then vice president and publisher of Gale's digital collections, the company tries to "right size" its products. Gale could create a five-million-page database, but it would be too expensive for anyone to afford. So they offer two million pages as a way of balancing Gale's production costs against library acquisitions budgets, which are themselves shaped by a library's sense of how much coverage is adequate or representative. To their credit, Gale's managers are remarkably accessible to scholars.

Abruzzi was interviewed for the journal *C19: Interdisciplinary Studies in the Long Nineteenth Century*.[104] Seth Cayley, in the United Kingdom, has published in *Victorian Periodicals Review* and regularly attends the Research Society for Victorian Periodicals conference.[105] Compelled by the scholars he has encountered, Cayley has provided process histories and perspectives for some of Gale's collections, such as his essay on the *Daily Mail* archive.[106]

That kind of valuable paradata exists unevenly. Gale does not have its own archivist or historian. On the phone, Cayley and Abruzzi were both candid about Gale's lack of institutional memory. They pointed out the irony that a company based on archives and history so often lacks its own. Much of this record exists only by word of mouth, and staff sometimes leave. In fact, Abruzzi himself left Gale since I first interviewed him. An emeritus worker could take on the job of company historian in an unpaid capacity. But the corporate masters see this as a luxury. There is no obvious place for Gale to store this institutional memory and no financial benefit in doing so. In 2015, the online "corporate history" page for Gale Cengage had a broken style sheet and a nonfunctional time line By 2016, that history page no longer existed.

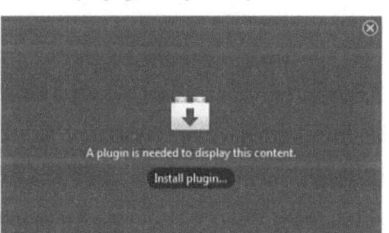

FIGURE 13. Screenshot of "Progress and partnership: Gale history." Source: Gale Cengage Learning, 2015.

Even the British Library's history can be surprisingly contingent. In the introduction to his massive *History of the British Museum Library*, Philip Rowland Harris explains that he began the project because he was concerned that common knowledge would be lost when the library moved to St. Pancras: "The way in which the library operated for over two centuries should be recorded before memories fade."[107] Now-retired employee Ed King pointed me to the BL's internal reports for JISC about *British Newspapers, 1800–1900*, which are now only web accessible through PDFs on the *Internet Archive*.[108]

The British Newspaper Archive

Since 2011, the British Library offers its digital newspaper collections as the "British Newspaper Archive" (BNA), available on site to library users and to individual subscribers online. The transition from Gale to Findmypast reveals a different aspect of how the newspaper archive is changing: this time, not into a new medium, but across a commercial handoff, effectively becoming another edition of these historical texts. That switch shows how digitization is not a one-time process but a transformation that occurs within the evolving circumstances of libraries, publishers, and users, and gets reshaped by different sets of institutional values and technical specifications. The hard drives on my shelf no longer represent what the BL's users now encounter (for the most part). My files have become artifacts, representing *old* digital content, which itself needs consideration about its futures or disposal. Findmypast adds yet another strand in the complex braid of media's propagation, which can be difficult to unpick.

I regret that Findmypast (FMP) has shared so little about its processes. Having reached out without success, what I do know comes from BL employees who remain committed to, as much as contractually possible, the transparency of their collections and open dissemination.[109] Whereas Gale is in the publishing business, FMP is a genealogy company. Its corporate values now guide the continuing digitization of British Library newspapers and the platform for accessing and searching them. The BNA's website includes a page on "How We Do It," offering a selection of technical details about the project, for example, that its five Zeutschel A0 overhead scanners capture digital images at 400 dpi in 24 bit color—which sounds impressive, except the majority of FMP's scanning comes from the BL's existing microfilm collections. These are processed in grayscale at 300 dpi and are then "moved to our operations centre in Dundee, Scotland" for OCR and post-processing. That brief web page (which has not been updated in the ten+ years since it was posted) amounts to all the published paradata for a collection of seventy-five+ million pages of digitized newspapers.[110]

The massive increase in page count from its approximately four-million-page predecessor to the current *British Newspaper Archive* reflects FMP's corporate priorities. Genealogy is the business of *family* history, not newspaper history or even history more broadly. Its market increases with the number of subscribers who search the BNA for family records. Hence, FMP has prioritized the digitization of as many pages (and potential family histories) to cover the broadest geographical areas in the United Kingdom. Like the British Museum's long struggles to define its national, colonial, and foreign coverage, those geographical boundaries profoundly limit exactly whose families have a searchable British history. Page counts have dramatically increased, but coverage also changes, and with it, its historical representativeness. Ironically, the BNA offers diminished coverage of London papers, contrary to their seeming metropolitan dominance. As a result, separate departments within the British Library have undertaken their own digitization projects to supplement what FMP produces, including an admirable Endangered Archives program that expands, though at a necessarily smaller scale, the geographical and cultural horizons of newspaper digitization.

On its website, the BNA advertises its page count front and center in an updated ticker. The emphasis on scale and coverage filters into the digitization workflow, as FMP seeks to digitally publish as much as it can, as quickly as possible. They have worked primarily with BL's extant microfilm collections for faster digitization; no preservation microfilms have been made since that department closed in 2010. More consequentially, FMP has reprocessed all the previously existing scans from the JISC projects. As those images were processed and encoded by previous vendors, FMP found it more efficient to abandon the legacy XML files they inherited and start over with their own workflows. They dealt with the problem of interoperability simply by creating new OCR and encoded XML based on their own data standards (which have not been shared). This effectively creates a new edition of digitized newspapers from the same JISC image scans. Someone searching the BNA not only has access to new content but to different versions of text and metadata for newspapers already extant in the BL's digital collection.

Whereas Gale sold its products to institutional subscribers, sometimes frustrating independent researchers without an affiliation, FMP sells to individual subscribers, primary schools, and public libraries—frustrating others, especially in higher education, who depend on institutional access. Furthermore, access to the BNA can change based on where you search it. Some titles are curiously not accessible to users inside the British Library itself (e.g., the *Illustrated London News*, *The Sphere*, *The Sketch*, *Britannia & Eve*, *Illustrated Sporting & Dramatic News*, *The Graphic*, *The Bystander*, and *The Tatler*). Sometimes just parts of other papers are "not available on British Library or library premises," while still other titles have parts available *only* in those locations (e.g., *Yorkshire Evening Press*, *Westmorland Gazette*, *Hereford Times*, *Finsbury Weekly News and Chronicle*, and so on). The digitized *Woking News & Mail* is not available through the BNA's website at all, viewable from "BL premises only." And these lists and restrictions are changing.

These terms of variable access emerge from the multiple commercial partners that contribute to the British Newspaper Archive. While Findmypast is the BL's contracted provider, renewable every five years, the BNA also includes products from other companies, including ProQuest, the Illustrated News Group, and, yes, Gale, too. In fact, Gale is still licensed to sell packages of British Library newspapers to the higher education market, along with its data mining agreements and even bespoke text analysis platforms for computational and digital humanities research. Those researchers are not FMP's market. Data-level access to the expanded BNA collections is handled on a case-by-case basis by the British Library. Users of the BNA are confined to its web interface, limited by its variable access, and may even encounter differently encoded files, tumbled together from various providers with bespoke digitization processes. Somewhere, the JISC XML files are still circulating in the BNA—though even the BL's news curators cannot say precisely where.

Digitization has now fully replaced microfilm as a preservation strategy. With paper copies of historical newspapers isolated in the vaults at Bath Spa, the BL has instituted a "surrogate first policy" for researchers seeking access.[111] They still deliver papers to researchers on reasonable request. But even the expanded BNA only represents a small percentage of the BL's newspaper collections in print.[112] Gale's and FMP's changing priorities are only the most recent of factors affecting that digital collection. Some parts of the collection are showing their age, or otherwise pressuring digital storage and preservation costs. Discussions about digital preservation are happening across all the BL's departments, including among the newspaper team, about what to save, what to keep, and how to do so. Do older digital versions of the archive, like the JISC collection, have historic value? On the BNA, they've effectively been displaced by the newest digitized version, but should older files be preserved as distinct works unto themselves? This chapter has argued yes, but that's an easier argument to make than a policy to institute within a library's material constraints. Though practices like culling books sometimes shock researchers, libraries must necessarily discard and delete as part of their continuing service. They have a right to forget, too.

Record Keepers and Researchers

These collections formed within the evolving paradigms of librarians, bibliographers, scholars, spies, and salesmen. But the story of digitization has also been shaped by users, too. Users and collections mutually constitute each other. Collections give rise to systematic ways of using them, establishing the horizons of what gets studied and organizing people institutionally. Reciprocally, as Gitelman explains in her history of the paper document, "new tools become tenable only if the attendant social organization of labor changes in concert."[113] The long history of newspaper digitization also includes the reorganization of scholarly labor in libraries, professional academic organizations, and funding bodies. While previous sections have noted the often-invisible labor of creating and maintaining these collections, this section sketches the impact of this material history on scholarly fields. To demonstrate this, I will examine my own field—Victorian studies—whose history, in this context, looks quite different from conventional stories about its mid-twentieth-century emergence. Instead, I argue that Victorian studies is inextricably related to the archives it helped to envision and the media forms that defined them.

In *The Teaching Archive*, Laura Heffernan and Rachel Buurma reorient the history of literary studies away from narratives about methodological battles and intellectual shifts, away from landmark publications and elite names. They look to the lived, everyday experiences of teaching as "determined by local institutional histories."[114] In a similar spirit, we should also acknowledge the constitutive work of librarians, archivists, bibliographers, and scholars who envision and support the archives of a field. In the case of Victorian studies, the field forms in concert with the regeneration of its archives in new mediums, as part of a broader project of record keeping, at the time being redefined by micropublishing and the computerization of bibliographic records. These media forms were thoroughly exercised on nineteenth-century periodicals and newspapers whose scale and informational complexity pushed (and continues to push) the early adoption of digital methods, and the reorganization of scholarly labor around indexing and information retrieval.

Any collection gets conceived within an understanding, however implicit, of its purpose and organization. As newspapers and periodicals amassed over the nineteenth century, so did the problem of storing, sorting, and accessing them. By the late Victorian era, the scale of periodical publishing generated a kind of archive fever—more properly an indexical fervor—in the minds of journalists, librarians, and would-be bibliographers. Was such a sprawling world of print even navigable? As Blair suggests, the problem of too much to know tends to generate new forms of "information management."[115] Facing their swelling mass of print media, Victorians attempted to devise reference tools to catalog and sort it all. Periodical publishing alternately drove the exasperation with that task and the "bibliographical utopianism" of schemes to organize the world of print. Mussell has described various late century projects to create indexes, dictionaries, and reference guides to the periodical archive, including the American William Frederick Poole's *Index to Periodical Literature*, W. T. Stead's *Review of Reviews* and *Index to the Periodical Literature of the World*, Frank Campbell's *Theory of National and International Bibliography*, and Cornelius Walford's never-completed *Dictionary of Periodical Literature*.[116] Of course, these efforts could never achieve their utopian ambitions, either collapsing entirely, adding another obfuscating layer to the information they would govern, or at best achieving an "uneasy truce between bibliographic control and the exuberance of the press."[117] Walford, for his part, devised a paper database of slips, each with multiple categories of information, envisioned as part of a universal catalog. Walford started the work and prepared to release it in monthly parts, but he soon died, and no evidence of the project remains besides his prospectus. As if punished for bibliographic hubris, "his library was soon afterwards struck by lightning and presumably the acres of carefully compiled 'slips' were consumed with the rest of his collection."[118]

The bibliographical utopianism of these projects would be revived a hundred years later, as another enterprising wave of scholars envisioned the value and systematic study of the periodical archive. Michael Wolff, among the founding editors of the journal *Victorian Studies* in 1957, would soon become convinced that the field's self-declared "broad approach" was not broad enough.[119] Within a decade, Wolff proposed that "new sources of research material were needed, and that Victorian periodicals were just what was required."[120] By the late 1960s, Wolff and others had envisioned a stand-alone journal and a separate scholarly society, which became in 1968 the mimeographed *Victorian Periodicals Newsletter* (*VPN*, later *Victorian Periodicals Review*) and in 1969 the Research Society for Victorian Periodicals (RSVP). From the start, *Victorian Studies* foregrounded its historical focus and interdisciplinary methods: a prefatory note in the 1957 first issue declared its "openness to critical and scholarly studies from all the relevant disciplines."[121] But Wolff's other scholarly enterprises were resolutely bibliographical. As he declared, "I should be delighted to have the V_S [Victorian Studies] office used as a clearinghouse for news of bibliographical projects underway and of acquisitions (in book and microform) un-recorded in the Union catalogues, for offers of moral or substantive support, and for practical suggestions."[122] Among Wolff's early contributions to the journal was just such a proposal, later to evolve into the *Wellesley Index*, described in an article, "Charting the Golden Stream: Thoughts on a Directory of Victorian Periodicals."[123] Its epigraph was a long quotation from Cornelius Walford.

This second wave of bibliographical utopianism has more than a family resemblance to the first. At a glance, they share the fascination and awe with the voluminous textual materials of the Victorian press. However, the (re)formation of periodical studies has more to do with twentieth-century media than with nineteenth-century print. Victorian periodical studies only becomes possible in an age of micropublishing and early computerization. Contrary to Walford and Wolff, the "vast wilderness" of Victorian newspapers and magazines does not itself reignite this bibliographic desire. Rather, it emerges within the disorientation and utopian possibilities introduced by the twentieth century's tools of information management. These tools were not determinative but show the social reorganization of scholarly labor around new technologies of reference. In 1930, Robert Binkley published an article about the potentials of microfilm called "New Tools for Men of Letters."[124] The story of RSVP shows its corollary, as new organizations of men (and women) of letters developed around those tools. Wellmon has traced the emergence of a similar phenomenon in nineteenth-century Germany, in which "a similar moment of epistemic confusion and media surplus" creates not just the reference tools to deal with it, but the attendant social organization of intellectual labor that claims authority as the modern research university.[125] As Wellmon helps illustrate, academic institutions are expressions of technologies they attempt to subordinate to their claims of enlightenment. In a way, Victorian studies may owe less to grand claims about its historical significance than to the everyday labor of listing its texts, made possible by twentieth-century tools.

While periodical studies represents only part of that field, it brings into sharp focus the dynamics among academic societies, tools of information management, and the reorganization of scholarly labor that gives a clearer picture of disciplinary formation. From its very inception, RSVP entwines with the contemporaneous mediums that would regenerate its archives. The first issue of *VPN* appeared in January 1968; the first national meeting of Victorian periodicals scholars was held at the CUNY Graduate Center in October 1969.[126] As Rosemary VanArsdel recounts in her history of the organization, "the program opened with discussion of a totally new technology in periodicals research: microfilm. Even more important, however, was an announcement of the formation of RSVP."[127] That word "however" is misleading. The formation of RSVP neither contradicts nor contrasts with the "new technology" of microfilm but emerges precisely in relation. Merrill Distad took note of something else about that first conference: "The opening session, appropriately, consisted of a presentation by Michael Barnett of Columbia University's Library School on 'The Use of Computers in Periodicals Research.'"[128] That Barnett—a chemist and computer scientist—even attended the inaugural conference seems both unusual and "appropriate," given that his career also wound through photocomposition and computerized typesetting as well as library cataloging and database publishing. Such potential uses of computers and microfilm in periodical research preoccupied many of RSVP's early members. As reported about the conference in the subsequent issue of *VPN*, "Two of the most important projects announced at this meeting were James E. O'Neill's effort to list newspapers and periodicals available on microfilm and Dorothy Deering's pioneering computer program for indexing the Victorian press."[129]

In RSVP's mission statements, Wolff and others would continue to emphasize the "sheer intellectual value" of periodicals as windows into the literary and journalistic culture of the Victorian age.[130] Appearing in *Victorian Studies* in 1970, the "RSVP Manifesto" published by Wolff and Joel Wiener claimed that journalism was the distinctive forum of Victorian British writers, and that periodicals offered a vast, relatively unknown, and uncharted resource.[131] Much of RSVP's usual business was helping to envision and build an infrastructure for the systematic study of periodical texts. Patrick Leary has shown how Wolff, Walter Houghton, and Richard Altick all envisioned such projects in the 1950s, linking their "large ideas" for the field to the catalogs they made.[132] These included the *Wellesley Index*, which names authors of otherwise anonymous and pseudonymous articles published in periodicals from 1824 to 1900. According to Christopher Ricks, reviewing the *Index* on its first publication, "it will quietly change the whole nature of Victorian studies."[133] Yet even quieter changes were taking place in the background of such high-profile projects, as periodical scholars reckoned with the implications of newer technologies for list making and information retrieval. While Wolff and Houghton envisioned their index as a card catalog—the same technique as their Victorian predecessors—others were reckoning with how new media would dramatically change such an enterprise.

In an echo of RSVP's first official meeting, its second conference opened with a preliminary workshop on microfilm led by O'Neill. At the workshop, RSVP agreed to have a standing committee on microforms, maintain a list of periodicals available on microfilm commercially and/or in libraries, and create desiderata for future microfilming projects. O'Neill noted how "erratic" such collections could be and suggested how scholars and/or the organization might help produce new materials.[134] To my mind, O'Neill offers a better sense of how bibliographical control runs into the challenges of its escalating, chaotic materials—now in micropublished forms. While Wolff continually emphasized the scale of Victorian journalism, O'Neill and others were reckoning with the opportunities and problems of twentieth-century information management. Writing in 1958 on "The Future of Microfilming" in the *American Archivist*, Ernest Taubes claimed that the "Atomic Age" might, with "just as much justification," be called "the Age of Recordkeeping" instead.[135] The study of Victorian periodicals would not only be facilitated by grand indexes but by the changing nature of recordkeeping and the reorganized labor it required.

The first issue of *VPN* credits Wolff as editor and Dorothy Deering as assistant editor. At the time, Deering was a PhD student at Indiana University and Wolff's research assistant. Deering had already circulated an initial form letter to the mailing list of subscribers to *Victorian Studies*, soliciting subscriptions for the new offshoot.[136] Deering also pioneered how the field's nascent bibliographical projects might be adapted to and expanded by computers. Hans De Groot explains that "the *Wellesley Index* must have been one of the last scholarly projects of its kind put together without the help of a computer."[137] But Deering understood that the "new digital capabilities of preserving and making periodicals accessible are the next step in accessing the Golden Stream that Michael Wolff originally envisioned."[138] Beyond the card catalog system of the *Wellesley*, Deering began to explore how computer punch cards might expand the indexing and sorting of the voluminous Victorian press. Her reports on early experiments note the challenges of translating bibliographic information about Victorian periodicals into metadata. The capacities of punch cards—defined both by the limits of their storage and the extraordinary cross-referencing they could perform at scale—prompted hard questions about what data even to describe and prioritize; how to control for the shifting nature of titles, editors, frequency, and runs in periodicals; and how the inevitable gaps within a computerized collection affected its representativeness.[139] All of these problems continue to define digital scholarship on the Victorian press.

Deering's efforts also show how academic labor, in early DH projects, expanded to agents outside of the usual historiography of the field:

big name scholars with their "large ideas." As Deering reported about the Victorian Periodicals Project (VPP) in 1970: "The pilot computer study was made possible through the facilities of the Indiana Research Computing Center, and the help of Mary Ann Shaw, programmer. I am particularly indebted to the generous assistance of Susan Gliserman, editorial assistant of *Victorian Studies*, who gave much of her time to seeing the program through its early stages."[140] Feminist science and technology studies (STS) scholars have noted how women disappear in the history of computing, even while establishing its foundations and performing much of its labor. But women were instrumental in the digital transformation of Victorian periodicals research from its inception.[141] Also notable, in this case, is Deering's involvement with the early infrastructure for humanities computing projects: first working with a mainframe at Indiana's Research Computing Center, then—on taking a lectureship—with the "generous budget for computing in the humanities" at Purdue University, where she explored transferring VPP's data from cards to tape.[142] Additionally, while major foundations had since moved away from supporting large microfilming projects, Deering found grant support for humanities computing from the Chapelbrook Foundation of Boston and the Council on Library Resources.[143] Such alliances would shape Victorian periodicals research and national funding bodies in tandem.

If wartime endangerment of historical materials helped give rise to professional academic organizations like the ACLS and CLIR, postwar funding for humanities research also took cues from scholarship in nineteenth-century periodicals. Russell Wyland, now a deputy director at the National Endowment for the Humanities (NEH), has made a compelling argument that "the same forces that gave rise to Victorian studies had their equivalent on Capitol Hill with passage of the National Foundation on the Arts and Humanities Act of 1965."[144] Victorian studies—and periodicals research—flourished in the context of the postwar investments in interdisciplinary and "area studies" in US universities. As Hossein Khosrowjah and others have noted, especially of Middle Eastern studies, such initiatives cannot be separated from the strategic interests of US foreign policy and intelligence services.[145] These organizations had already been involved with the microfilming programs that were transforming humanities materials. Now, the US government would help to establish the infrastructure for its further development into scholarly resources. According to Wyland, Victorian studies had good timing, articulating the importance of its subject and the necessity of interdisciplinary methods at the very moment the humanities benefited from such justifications of its public interest. Furthermore, driven by its indexical fervor, periodical studies was defining a series of bibliographic projects ready-made for funding by the newly formed NEH:

> If *VS* functioned independently to prepare scholars with the rhetoric and arguments that would articulate the very goals set out by Congress for the NEH, then the chatty *Victorian Periodicals Newsletter* and its entrepreneurial editor Michael Wolff served as the mouthpiece for the kinds of funding needed for Victorian studies immediately after NEH opened its doors.[146]

Wyland spotlights Wolff's entrepreneurialism and "Houghton's grand enterprise" as signature examples of this phenomenon, though he also acknowledges workaday contributions within the early issues of *VPN*.[147] Yet even more credit is due to the various correspondents of *VPN*'s proposals and reports, not only for the lists, indexes, and resources they proposed but for their imaginative engagement with then-new mediums. If Victorian studies and national humanities funding were mutually constitutive, as Wyland suggests, they also took shape in context of the technologies that redefined this "Age of Recordkeeping." These technologies rekindled the nineteenth century's bibliographic ambitions about its periodical archive, now being regenerated for systematic study in the new media of the twentieth, and pushing the reorganization of scholarly labor toward forms that still define DH today.

Wolff imagined periodical scholars as heirs to Cornelius Walford, "charting the golden stream" with bibliographic indexes to the riches of Victorian journalism. But contemporary periodicals scholars may owe more to Deering. She envisioned historical materials less as a surging river to heroically explore than as network emerging from the conditions of Victorian print media. She understood this, I suspect, as computerization moved the age of recordkeeping (card catalogs, microfilm) toward an age of information storage and retrieval. Her view of the past calibrates to an understanding of what present-day technologies disclose about it, increasingly defined by databases and the networks they constructed and revealed. As she explained of the Victorian Periodicals Project, "increased knowledge about any one periodical (or publisher or writer for a periodical) inevitably sheds light on others, in the vast and endlessly interlocking world of Victorian journalism."[148] Wyland sees Wolff and Houghton's legacy of bibliographic indexes carried forward in twentieth-century funding programs for the humanities. But Deering's legacy follows another stream toward the collaborative labors and grant support for the *digital* humanities. From this standpoint, Deering has an heir in Laurel Brake, among the directors of the Nineteenth-Century Serials Edition (ncse), a digital project funded partly by the United Kingdom's Arts & Humanities Research Council (AHRC) and supported by the Centre for Computing in the Humanities at King's College (now the Department of Digital Humanities), Ed King at the British Library, Olive Software, and a cohort of collaborators and research assistants, many of whom continue to explore the intellectual history and methodological opportunities of digitization. New tools require the social reorganization of academic labor, from Deering's time in humanities computing to the institution of DH as such.

Brake would more fully articulate Deering's insight about the "endlessly interlocking world of Victorian journalism," won from her own experiences creating a digital edition. Brake urged scholars to move away from individual biographies or authors (the organizing kernel of the *Wellesley Index*) toward understanding periodical networks. Computerization reveals in retrospect that "networking can be understood as part of the *structure* of journalism."[149] Importantly, Brake urged an expansive view of networks, beyond individual agents and including "the material characteristics of the media" that constitute them. This insight also affects periodicals scholars "at a moment when investigation of the journalism industry is facilitated through digitisation."[150] In other words, as this chapter has endeavored to show, the concepts we use to study historical texts cannot be separated from the material histories of how they were collected, remediated, and accessed. Nor can those material histories be separated from the social and scholarly reorganization they occasion, and in which researchers continue to practice.

Digital Victorians has staked many of its arguments on anachronism. Yet we cannot step into the past's golden stream except through its meanderings in the interval. Along the way are offshoots and eddies that did not join the mainstream, or were overswept by conventional narratives that preserve institutional prestige. Yet the course of scholarship bends around bigger sociotechnical phenomena, too, often shaped by agents and institutional agencies that can disappear from disciplinary histories while still conditioning much of what scholars do. The long legacy of remediation in nineteenth-century newspapers shows some of these determinative conditions and their effects on the social organization of humanities research. At the same time, even a more capacious history must recognize the exclusions, prejudices, and silences that still persist. While a "digital Victorian" framework makes possible many useful contrasts, it must also make way for other genealogies than just the nineteenth century's to describe new media. As I will suggest in closing, the future of the digital means leaving the Victorians behind.

AFTERWORD

THE DIGITAL VICTORIAN FRAME OF MIND, 1957–2020

This interpenetration of two cultures, this intimate and solicitous refertilization of the past by the present, is a transaction of quite exceptional value; and those concerned have every right to see themselves as engaged in an enterprise at least as novel as that which has set a man-made moon revolving about the face of the earth.
—"LEND-LEASE," *Times Literary Supplement* (1957)[1]

Perhaps among the theories we need are theories of Victorian information (in its historical formation as well as its digital transformations and circulation), theories of the archive, even theories of scholarship itself.
—RICHARD MENKE, "Responses to the V21 Manifesto" (2015)[2]

THE *TIMES LITERARY SUPPLEMENT* (*TLS*) declared Victorian studies to be a historically comparative project from its very outset. Reviewing the first issue of the journal *Victorian Studies* in 1957, the *TLS* noted how its interdisciplinary and transatlantic approach might just revive the era for the twentieth century amid its dramatic technological changes. The final clause refers to the Sputnik satellite, which had launched the previous month, inaugurating the space age. This book has argued that as other technologies and platforms "launch" us toward similar epochal claims, we have again reanimated Victorian concerns in the digital age. According to the *TLS*, the new field of Victorian studies helps identify this "interpenetration of two cultures" and pursues a method for explaining its significance: the "refertilization of the past by the present." Many years later, we may have a different sense of those time frames, yet the historically comparative impulse continues to yield ideas: about the Victorians, and about ourselves. These days, Victorian studies has added *cross*-fertilization to its enterprise. In various forms of "engaged presentism," we can imbue the past with the present to learn something new about each.[3] The lesson is not simply that what is new is old. Seen through anachronism or in novel genealogies, what's new looks different, open to scrutiny and potentially to reform.

Digital Victorians has pursued this reciprocal enterprise to put nineteenth-century media and digital media into each other's orbit. Doing so identifies the role of new media in imagining each as an age of transition, alike in perceiving what media seemed to transform—communication, sociality, memory, materiality—and shifting how writers, publishers, and critics worked to understand these changes. Looking backward, we find the stirrings of modern concepts of information, media, and digitality in these nineteenth-century contexts. These genealogies help recover many of the social and material dependencies that contemporary new media likes to forget. For my purposes, they also illuminate how media change is even imagined, and what conceptual and institutional frameworks arise in tandem. As this book has argued, responses to nineteenth-century media shift—as registered by Victorian writers, then propagated and renewed in the interval—help to historicize the development of digital humanities, broadly construed. Nineteenth-century media offers a long history of imagining technological newness, its consequences for cultural production, and the shifting roles of its casual and professional interpreters.

This book also stretches what we understand digital humanities to be, not just where it comes from but what it might compass now or in the future. The nineteenth century offers examples that look familiar to contemporary DH, as in chapters 3 and 4, but many others, as in chapters 1 and 2, that seem either peripheral or the concerns of other disciplines. Yet Victorians engaged with their new media quite fluidly, and their pre- or proto-disciplinary media culture might inspire our own interdisciplinary pursuits. I have focused on literary, journalistic, and textual responses to nineteenth-century media that exemplify such an array of concerns, and that demand a more capacious analysis than resides in one academic field. Some of our disciplinary attitudes about how to study literature and media, like the divides between literary studies and quantitative analysis or information history, derive from the nineteenth century. This book joins a growing body of scholarship attempting to reconsider those splits and imagine other academic futures.

The second epigraph of this afterword comes from such a moment of disciplinary challenge, as the V21 Collective's 2015 "Manifesto" demanded changes to how Victorian studies was practiced. In response, Richard Menke urged attention both to its "historical formation" and "digital transformations." Menke, like the *TLS*, suggests that the transactions between then and now may let us imagine Victorian studies anew, or even articulate "theories of scholarship itself." His argument appeared in a reply to a blog post whose provocations were debated widely across social media, academic listservs, and then in the field's journals. I've spotlighted his response for that reason, too, as "theories of scholarship" entangle with the platforms and institutional conditions that make them possible. The previous chapter made such a case: the field owes much to micropublishing, computerization, and an expanding infrastructure for humanities research that characterized the early development of Victorian studies. This afterword hazards a related theory of scholarship about the coeval development of Victorian studies and digital humanities in the time since. While that story compasses many different disciplines and institutional changes, nineteenth-century studies has a notable presence within it, perhaps even an "intimate and solicitous" relation, in the *TLS*'s words, to the establishment of digital humanities as a field. In various ways, DH has recapitulated aspects of the nineteenth century, marking a new period of digital Victorianism, for better and worse.

The title of this afterword alludes to Walter Houghton's book, *The Victorian Frame of Mind* (1957), frequently cited in histories of the field.[4]

Arguably, DH has been characterized—at least in part—by a digital Victorian frame of mind, especially during the last few decades of its consolidation. As the introduction proposed, this includes the self-awareness of our respective media cultures as an "age of transition." But beyond that, I also want to underscore the conspicuous "nineteenthcentricity" of DH, to borrow a phrase from Rachel Buurma and Laura Heffernan about trends in literary studies since the 1980s.[5] The nineteenth-century's frame has significantly shaped DH's materials, methods, arguments, and institutional configurations. I certainly do not mean to downplay the extensive engagements of other fields, disciplines, and communities in the formation and reorientation of DH. But its Victorian entanglements offer useful ways of explaining many of its contemporary features. Perhaps they offer as many cautions about recapitulating its politics, while also pointing toward undisciplined and postcolonial futures.

Digital Nineteenthcentricities

In the following brief sketch of these nineteenthcentricies, I risk telling a very partial history of DH to illustrate some of the problems of its institutionalization. That story might begin with the digitization, OCR, and collection of English-language historical materials for study. A combination of factors made nineteenth-century printed materials amenable to digitize and assemble into searchable collections. First, these materials appear historically in a sweet spot between the standardization of English language orthography and the moving wall of copyright restrictions. The regularization of spelling and the deprecation of the "medial S" character ƒ around 1800 allow OCR programs to more effectively generate accurate digital texts to index and search.[6] Yet, just over the horizon of 1900, copyright restrictions tend to close the window on what texts are available to digitize and make available online.[7] This has downstream consequences for what digital collections and/or data DH scholars have tended to experiment with. As Matthew Jockers once complained, "Today's digital-minded literary scholar is shackled in time; we are all, or are all soon to become, nineteenth centuryists."[8] Jockers was arguing for unrestricted computational access to texts still under copyright restrictions, which, to certain degrees, has become possible under provisions of "transformative use" or "nonconsumptive research." But those materials still have to appear digitally in the first place.

The selection of what materials to digitize, as well as to transform into digital projects, also bears the marks of nineteenth-century thinking. As with printed text, nineteenth-century statistical records arrive predisposed for conversion into data. Patrick Leary argues that "the vast quantity of routinely gathered and, for the most part, consistently organized records amassed by the Victorians was a natural fit with the computer's ability to make rapid calculations based on large quantities of records that could be coded into distinct fields." Leary's example is the 1901 UK population census and, one hundred years later, its appearance as a searchable online database: "emblematic of the beginnings of one emerging information society and the applications of computers to its study by another."[9] If punch card computing projects were themselves descendants of Jacquard looms and Babbage and Lovelace's Analytical Engine, so data-driven humanities research might owe much to the quantitative mindset and statistical records of the nineteenth century.[10] In "The Origin Myths of Computing in Historical Research," Adam Crymble traces methods in cliometrics and digital history back to a "groundwork [of] algorithmic thinking had been set decades if not centuries before 1949." Notably, some of the signature projects of each rely on nineteenth-century data, especially about the American Civil War.[11] They may also operationalize nineteenth-century mindsets, or "the desire to count and classify people according to gender and race" whose grim legacies include eugenics and the statistical methods it spawned.[12] Digital projects can uncomfortably align with the longer history of the "devastating thingification of black women, children, and men" rendered into yet still unredeemed by data.[13]

The early development of DH projects and digital collections in literary studies also tended to favor nineteenth-century texts. As Amy Earhart explains, the democratizing rhetoric about the early internet in the 1980s seemed ready-made for the decades-long efforts to expand the literary canon. Earhart documents the flourishing of various "digital recovery projects" in the 1990s—and their disappearance for lack of institutional support.[14] What survived were digital archives of more familiar writers, including William Blake, Walt Whitman, Emily Dickinson, and Dante Gabriel Rossetti—"canonical writers and voices that hew to the norms of the dominant national culture of the nineteenth century," as Roopika Risam argues.[15] Early collections of e-texts made available by Michael Hartt at Project Gutenberg likewise overrepresented that perspective; for example, in 1996, of the roughly 500 titles on offer, well over half were nineteenth-century texts, while others reflected its notions of canonicity.[16] Earhart argues that many of the signature DH projects of nineteenth-century literary studies, aside from their contents, were also built as experiments in new historicist methodologies that would dominate the field.[17]

For reasons of availability, standardization, and recognition, nineteenth-century materials featured prominently in the methodological experiments of early DH. Jerome McGann started the Rossetti Archive, for instance, less to canonize the poet than to test the capacities of a "hypermedia archive" to accommodate Rossetti's work across genres and mediums—including books, sketches, paintings, picture frames, and even furniture. Relatedly, The Orlando Project, spanning women's writing across historical periods, sought to use the web's network architecture to make its argument about feminist literary history.[18] Even earlier, directories of links and web-based resources proliferated, notably including Alan Liu's Voice of the Shuttle, the Romantic Circles project, George Landow's The Victorian Web, Leary's Victoria Research Web, and Mitsuharu Matsuoka's Victorian Literary Studies Archive along with the Gaskell Web. More than link directories, these sites—and many more like them—attempted to envision web-enabled scholarship from the systematic organization of its sprawling resources. In some ways, they reenact the indexical fervor that attended the proliferation of Victorian texts. And, as Andrew Stauffer has argued, their fragility—few of those original links continue to work—echoes the anxiety of nineteenth-century print culture about its own ephemerality.[19]

Nineteenth-century texts and data have also supported formative experiments in text analysis, stylometry, and distant reading. The historical coincidence of the nineteenth century's explosion in print publishing, and its relative accessibility to digitize, established almost a default corpus for text analysis at scale. Consider how Moretti lays out the case for quantitative analysis in *Graphs, Maps, and Trees*: "we all work on a canon of two hundred novels [which] sounds very large for nineteenth-century Britain . . . but is still less than one per cent of the novels that were actually published: twenty thousand, thirty, more, no one really knows."[20] Other prominent scholars in distant reading would likewise pursue nineteenth-century corpora at scale; for example, Katherine Bode's *Reading by the Numbers* challenges the history of the nineteenth-century Australian novel; Ted Underwood's *Distant Horizons* considers genre change in a corpus 1750–1950.[21] Among the first scholars to take advantage of the Google Books corpus were the historians Frederick Gibbs and Dan Cohen, who published their results as "A Conversation with Data" in *Victorian Studies*, in which they attempted to test Houghton's claims in *The Victorian Frame of Mind*.[22] Notable experiments in stylometry attempted to identify the unsigned writings of Abraham Lincoln, or whether Oscar Wilde had authored a work of pornography.[23] Experiments in text reuse algorithms and network analysis, as by Ryan Cordell and David Smith in the *Viral Texts* project, emerged from digitized nineteenth-century US newspapers in the Chronicling America collection.[24] When Lev Manovich coined "cultural analytics" for the large-scale analysis of images, he released the software ImagePlot with a sample data set and tutorial about the paintings of Vincent Van Gogh.[25]

As critics have suggested, DH may have regenerated an exclusionary knowledge project in which nineteenth-century English-language materials came to define humanities research, consolidating in the Global North. While many other kinds of projects proliferated, from many other scholars, the infrastructure for digital scholarship tended to align with some of the nineteenth century's political asymmetries, given the dominance of institutions in the United States, United Kingdom, and Canada, the funding apparatus that supported them, and an imperial monolingualism that penetrates to the very level of code. In the broader context of the last several decades, that phenomenon ran counter to rising scholarly attention to postcolonial and global studies. So much so that Liu called out DH in an important talk in 2011: "How the digital humanities advance, channel, or resist the great postindustrial, neoliberal, corporatist, and globalist flows of information-cum-capital, for instance, is a question rarely heard."[26] In fact, it would soon be prominently heard in critiques of the colonial enterprise that institutionalized DH seemed to mask, with calls to transform and globalize DH; to articulate its many and intersecting forms, including queer, black, postcolonial, and multilingual DH; and to describe its variegated histories beyond a US-centric diffusion model.[27]

While this book also looks to nineteenth-century precursors, it does not mean to enshrine them as DH's only possible history. Instead, it makes its comparisons strategically: to resist claims of disruption, to approach new media capaciously, and to identify as many problematic legacies as possibilities for how the Victorians help us revisit the digital in the present. *Digital Victorians* provides only one alternative in support of broadening the view. As various scholars remind us, "there are multiple possible genealogies for humanities computing and digital humanities."[28] Earhart specifically argues against a monolithic understanding of DH, encouraging the contingencies, positionalities, and local contexts in which dh (lower case) variously manifests.[29] What genealogies we use have consequences. For that reason, Kim Gallon articulates a black DH as a counternarrative to its abiding whiteness, finding its flourishing in domains that haven't conventionally fallen even within DH's big tent.[30] In a similar spirit, the volume *Global Debates in Digital Humanities* seeks "to build a different representation of DH based on cultural, linguistic, political, and ultimately epistemological diversity." The project of "epistemic justice," as its editors note, also includes "conversations in which the digital humanities is not a dominant concept in the development of technological approaches to the humanities."[31] Redefining DH means looking beyond its established boundaries, or considering its different manifestations within highly local contexts.[32] Doing so may yield "a hidden history of intersectionality in digital humanities scholarship" and bring marginalized perspectives forward.[33]

Yet these arguments have an uncanny Victorian resonance too, not in the consolidation of its empire, but in the pursuit of its fracture and postcolonial reconfiguration. As Risam points out, "the histories of postcolonial studies and digital humanities, two subfields that emerged after World War II in response to a radically changing geopolitical and techno-cultural landscape[,] have dovetailed in surprising ways."[34] Each subfield also has a generative relation to Victorian studies. From its outset, postcolonial studies had strong roots in nineteenth-century literature, enlisting Victorianist scholars among its practitioners. Arguably, DH is seeing a similar shift, certainly with the increase of cultural criticism and attention to a broader array of voices and global contexts as well as with the infrastructural changes that may increasingly define its next phase. According to Élika Ortega, DH's new media moment always had the potential to engender cross-cultural encounters, which she and others continue to advocate for.[35] Collectively, DH is moving out of its digital Victorian frame of mind, or broadening its nineteenthcentricity in ways that do not reinforce imperial whiteness.

As in critiques of diversity initiatives, representation alone is not sufficient to address historical exclusions.[36] Risam gestures to a number of projects that, while focusing on nineteenth-century texts and contexts, thoughtfully interrogate the epistemologies of their own knowledge production. For example, she finds Livingstone Online "an exemplary project that takes this responsibility seriously and interrogates its own politics of colonialism."[37] As the project explains, even while digitizing and assembling "the written, visual, and material legacies of the famous Victorian explorer, missionary, and abolitionist David Livingstone (1813–73)," it tries to shift attention to "key aspects of nineteenth-century global history and intercultural encounter."[38] It has also spawned the "One More Voice" project, seeking to recover "non-European contributions from nineteenth-century British imperial and colonial archives." More importantly, the project everywhere foregrounds its own intellectual goals, technical processes, and collaborative enterprise. In a related way, the Colored Conventions Project (CCP) recuperates records of nineteenth-century Black political organizing in the United States. Just as importantly, it is also committed to its own values as a collaborative knowledge project, defined by the commitments of its members, aware of their positionalities and institutional situation.[39] Among the remarkable instances of this: the CCP makes its data set available for download and analysis—if users acknowledge the ethical principles of dealing with that data. These "terms of service" are not legalistic, but they establish a critical perspective on what that data represents and occludes. They also assert the user's respect for and ethical participation in a knowledge community.

The End of Digital Humanities

These examples suggest how even digital projects focused on the nineteenth century can move beyond some of its material, institutional, and conceptual legacies that, at least in this telling, characterized the emergence of DH. They may represent the "undisciplining" of DH, in a form similar to the undisciplining of Victorian studies as proposed in 2020 by Chatterjee, Christoff, and Wong. Undisciplining declared the end of Victorian studies—in the sense of ending a coherent disciplinary formation inaugurated in 1957 that, while nominally about interdisciplinary study, also established the field's "foundation in whiteness, universalism, and liberalism."[40] The trajectory of institutionalized DH may be following a similar path: celebrated for its interdisciplinarity, critiqued for its exclusions, and reconfigured for a more just future. The "digital humanities moment," as Gold declared in 2012, may be reaching its end. Not in the sense of its termination or failure, as in greatly exaggerated reports of its death or the "digital humanities bust."[41] But in reaching, as Mark Algee-Hewitt suggests, "the ends of its beginning."[42]

In the introduction, I argued that DH represented a new media moment for the academy, defined less by technologies or methods than by a broadly shared awareness of a period in transition. In this framework, the Victorians' sense of their "age of transition" corresponds to this later moment of consequential media shift, especially within humanities knowledge practices that understand themselves as new. Yet new things grow old. The world spins down the grooves of change, and one era transitions to the next. As early as 1851, the Victorians named their own era as such, and later knew its ending. At some point, we will see the end of "digital humanities," whether as a phrase or a coherent nomination of a field. As of this writing, it's too early to tell, but "the field has already reached an inflection point."[43] The "digital present" or the "new temporal chapter" announced with DH is passing into retrospect. When that formative era ended (or will end) is debatable, but I think the year 2020 offers a strong candidate, given the massive ruptures of COVID lockdown, international reckonings with racial violence, calls for reform in the academy (including the "Undisciplining" essay), and even the release of GPT-3, with AI soon to eclipse so many conversations about the digital's human impact.

What will happen to DH? Depends on who you ask. Nor will its ending be evenly distributed. Algee-Hewitt suggests that DH has reached the end of its preliminaries and will now either split into an interdisciplinary computational field on its own or else variously merge into existing fields, contributing to domain research with the specific methods that have proved useful therein. In this view, the big tent will break camp, as DHers drift closer to adjacent fields in which they're already making contributions. For instance, as they join media studies and STS scholars to confront the consequences of machine learning and artificial intelligence. Or as sustainers of endangered, community, and indigenous archives. Or as digitally minded book historians and critical makers help grow the small press revival. Or as innovators in scholarly communications join libraries, academic organizations, and nonprofits. Or as compositionists—whose traditions in computers and writing describe another genealogy altogether—reorient approaches to writing, assessment, and pedagogy in context of generative AI. Or as computational humanists move into library and information schools or data science programs. Or as GIS and mapping consolidate in spatial and environmental history. Or even as studies of digital media gradually reshape the contours of existing fields, as in the appearance of Victorian media studies.

Predictably, I like Algee-Hewitt's overview for its unexpected symmetry with another historical pattern. Houghton claimed that the Victorian frame of mind was characterized by "a bundle of various and often paradoxical ideas and attitudes. It is fragmentary and incoherent." And yet to look backward at the chaos, according to Houghton, "is to see our own situation a little more clearly."[44] For some, the nineteenth century was the golden age of amateurism, an "undisciplined culture" before the specialization and segmentation of professions and disciplines we have variously inherited.[45] The novelty years of DH have more than a resemblance to that chaotic amateurism: "the various practices, contexts, and knowledge systems that make up the field are widely varied and often incompatible."[46] In Victorian studies and DH alike, scholars have increasingly pointed out who the big tent leaves out in the cold, and what mentalities and embodiments are excluded or evicted from mainstream frames of mind. Each field is experiencing its next age of transition. The digital Victorian era is over.

What will come next? That's even harder to say. As Booth and Posner suggest, DH will be eclipsed by the "[midcentury metamorphosis to be named]" about which we can only guess.[47] It seems likely that the massive deployment of machine learning and AI across economies, education, and cultural production will increasingly occupy digitally minded humanists and media scholars. What uses will Victorian studies have for these sociotechnical developments yet to come? Still a great deal, perhaps, in attending to the neocolonial networks of power and labor that undergird these economies; to the environmental calamity that industrial-scale computing seems to extend; to the experimentation with machine methods on nineteenth-century materials; to the overlooked legacies of craft and indigenous knowledge; to the prehistories of automatic writing and machinic media. Who knows. Even the future coherence of the Victorian period remains in question. Far worse, academic departments in humanities and world languages are being steadily dismantled. Yet Victorian studies—or whatever it becomes—may help us adapt to these challenges, given the creative thinking its "undisciplined culture" can inspire, and the critical resistance and reconfiguration that undisciplining the field compels. For those who interpret and challenge nineteenth-century legacies, the past will still have usable futures, and its media much to teach.

NOTES

Introduction

1. John Stuart Mill, *Mill: Texts, Commentaries*, ed. Alan Ryan (New York: W. W. Norton, 1997), 5.

2. Alan Liu, "Imagining the New Media Encounter," in *A Companion to Digital Literary Studies*, ed. Ray Siemens and Susan Schreibman (Oxford: Blackwell, 2004).

3. W., "Art VII. Political Retrospect, 1830–1841," *Westminster Review* 37, no. 2 (1842): 427.

4. John Guillory, "The Genesis of the Media Concept," *Critical Inquiry* 36, no. 2 (2010): 321-62, https://doi.org/10.1086/648528.

5. Lisa Gitelman, *Always Already New: Media, History, and the Data of Culture* (Cambridge, MA: MIT Press, 2006).

6. John Durham Peters, *The Marvelous Clouds: Toward a Philosophy of Elemental Media* (Chicago: University of Chicago Press, 2015), 23.

7. Simon Joyce, *The Victorians in the Rearview Mirror* (Athens: Ohio University Press, 2007).

8. For example, James Gleick, *The Information: A History, A Theory, A Flood* (New York: Pantheon Books, 2011); Toni Weller, *The Victorians and Information:*

A Social and Cultural History (Saarbrücken, Germany: VDM Verl. Dr. Müller, 2009); Tom Standage, *The Victorian Internet: The Remarkable Story of the Telegraph and the Nineteenth Century's Online Pioneers* (New York: Walker, 1998).

9. Benjamin Morgan, "Critical Empathy: Vernon Lee's Aesthetics and the Origins of Close Reading," *Victorian Studies* 55, no. 1 (2012): 52; Yohei Igarashi, "Statistical Analysis at the Birth of Close Reading," *New Literary History* 46, no. 3 (2015): 485–504, https://doi.org/10.1353/nlh.2015.0023.

10. Jay Clayton, *Charles Dickens in Cyberspace: The Afterlife of the Nineteenth Century in Postmodern Culture* (New York: Oxford University Press, 2003), 8.

11. Richard Menke, *Literature, Print Culture, and Media Technologies, 1880–1900: Many Inventions* (Cambridge: Cambridge University Press, 2019); Maurice S. Lee, *Overwhelmed: Literature, Aesthetics, and the Nineteenth-Century Information Revolution* (Princeton, NJ: Princeton University Press, 2019).

12. Linda Hughes, "SIDEWAYS!—Navigating the Material(ity) of Print Culture," North American Victorian Studies Association, University of Victoria, BC, October 11, 2007.

13. Carolyn Marvin, *When Old Technologies Were New: Thinking About Electric Communication in the Late Nineteenth Century* (New York: Oxford University Press, 1988); Michèle Martin, *"Hello Central?": Gender, Technology, and Culture in the Formation of Telephone Systems* (Montreal: McGill-Queen's University Press, 1991); Lisa Gitelman, *Scripts, Grooves, and Writing Machines: Representing Technology in the Edison Era* (Stanford, CA: Stanford University Press, 1999).

14. Lisa Gitelman, *Paper Knowledge: Toward a Media History of Documents* (Durham, NC: Duke University Press, 2014), 56.

15. Geoffrey Nunberg, ed., *The Future of the Book* (Berkeley: University of California Press, 1996), 10.

16. Marshall McLuhan, *The Gutenberg Galaxy: The Making of Typographic Man* (Toronto: University of Toronto Press, 1962), 1; see also Gleick, *The Information*, 413. Extending this analogy, librarians have described recent decades as a period of "digital incunabula"; see Gregory Crane et al., "Beyond Digital Incunabula: Modeling the Next Generation of Digital Libraries," in *Research and Advanced Technology for Digital Libraries*, ed. Julio Gonzalo et al., Lecture Notes in Computer Science (Berlin: Springer, 2006), 353–66, https://doi.org/10.1007/11863878_30.

17. Toni Weller, "An Information History Decade: A Review of the Literature and Concepts, 2000–2009," *Library and Information History* 26, no. 1 (2010): 94. See also Geoffrey Nunberg, "Farewell to the Information Age," in *The Future of the Book*, 103–38; Gleick, *The Information*; James R. Beniger, *The*

Control Revolution: Technological and Economic Origins of the Information Society (Cambridge, MA: Harvard University Press, 1986); Aileen Fyfe, "The Information Revolution," in *The Cambridge History of the Book in Britain: Volume VI, 1830–1914*, ed. David McKitterick (Cambridge: Cambridge University Press, 2009), 567–94.

18. James W. Carey, *Communication as Culture: Essays on Media and Society* (Winchester, MA: Unwin Hyman, 1989); John Durham Peters, *Speaking into the Air: A History of the Idea of Communication* (Chicago: University of Chicago Press, 1999), 5.

19. Marvin, *When Old Technologies Were New*, 4.

20. Guillory, "Genesis," 321.

21. David Thorburn and Henry Jenkins, eds., *Rethinking Media Change: The Aesthetics of Transition* (Cambridge, MA: MIT Press, 2003), 1.

22. Standage, *The Victorian Internet*; Shaun Raviv, "The Secret History of Facial Recognition," *WIRED*, January 21, 2020, www.wired.com/story/secret-history-facial-recognition/; Natasha Kitcher, "Electrophone: The Victorian-Era Gadget That Was a Precursor to Live-Streaming," *The Conversation* (blog), accessed January 11, 2021, http://theconversation.com/electrophone-the-victorian-era-gadget-that-was-a-precursor-to-live-streaming-148944.

23. Veronica Alfano and Andrew M. Stauffer, eds., *Virtual Victorians: Networks, Connections, Technologies* (New York: Palgrave Macmillan, 2015), 2.

24. Rachel A. Bowser and Brian Croxall, "Introduction: Industrial Evolution," *Neo-Victorian Studies* 3, no. 1 (2010): 16.

25. Roger Whitson, *Steampunk and Nineteenth-Century Digital Humanities: Literary Retrofuturisms, Media Archaeologies, Alternate Histories* (New York: Routledge, 2017).

26. Lee, *Overwhelmed*, 4.

27. For a good overview of differences in how new media have been defined, see Jonathan Sterne, "Out with the Trash: On the Future of New Media," in *Residual Media*, ed. Charles R. Acland (Minneapolis: University of Minnesota Press, 2007), 16–31.

28. Charles R. Acland, ed., *Residual Media* (Minneapolis: University of Minnesota Press, 2007), xix.

29. Marvin, *When Old Technologies Were New*, 4; see also Lisa Gitelman and Geoffrey B. Pingree, eds., *New Media, 1740–1915* (Cambridge, MA: MIT Press, 2003).

30. Colette Colligan and Margaret Linley, eds., *Media, Technology, and Literature in the Nineteenth Century: Image, Sound, Touch* (Farnham, Surrey, England: Ashgate, 2011), 10.

31. Gitelman and Pingree, *New Media*, xii.

32. Christopher Keep, "The Cultural Work of the Type-Writer Girl," *Victorian Studies* 40, no. 3 (1997): 401–26; Menke, *Literature, Print Culture, and Media Technologies*; Jill Galvan, *The Sympathetic Medium: Feminine Channeling, the Occult, and Communication Technologies, 1859–1919* (Ithaca, NY: Cornell University Press, 2010).

33. Liu, "Imagining."

34. Liu.

35. Alison Byerly, *Are We There Yet? Virtual Travel and Victorian Realism* (Ann Arbor: University of Michigan Press, 2013), 4.

36. Amy R. Wong, "Victorian Media Studies, History, and Theory," *Literature Compass* 15, no. 3 (2018): 5, 6, https://doi.org/10.1111/lic3.12438.

37. Melissa Score, "Interred in Printing House Vaults: Pianotype Composing Machines of the 1840s," *Victorian Periodicals Review* 49, no. 4 (2016): 578–97, https://doi.org/10.1353/vpr.2016.0040.

38. N. Katherine Hayles, "Print Is Flat, Code Is Deep: The Importance of Media-Specific Analysis," *Poetics Today* 25, no. 1 (2004): 67–90.

39. Richard Menke, "New Grub Street's Ecologies of Paper," *Victorian Studies* 61, no. 1 (2018): 60–82.

40. A partial list: Yohei Igarashi, *The Connected Condition: Romanticism and the Dream of Communication* (Stanford, CA: Stanford University Press, 2019); Celeste Langan and Maureen N. McLane, "The Medium of Romantic Poetry," in *The Cambridge Companion to British Romantic Poetry*, ed. James Chandler and Maureen N. McLane (Cambridge: Cambridge University Press, 2008), 239–62; Robert Darnton, "An Early Information Society: News and the Media in Eighteenth-Century Paris," *American Historical Review* 105, no. 1 (2000): 1–35, https://doi.org/10.2307/2652433; Paul Duguid, "The Ageing of Information: From Particular to Particulate," *Journal of the History of Ideas* 76, no. 3 (2015): 347–68; Katherine E. Ellison, *Fatal News: Reading and Information Overload in Early Eighteenth-Century Literature* (New York: Routledge, 2006); David W. Park, Nick Jankowski, and Steve Jones, eds., *The Long History of New Media: Technology, Historiography, and Contextualizing Newness* (New York: Peter Lang, 2011); Ann Blair and Peter Stallybrass, "Mediating Information, 1450–1800," in *This Is Enlightenment*, ed. Clifford Siskin and William Warner (Chicago: University of Chicago Press, 2010), 139–63; Ian F. McNeely and Lisa Wolverton, *Reinventing Knowledge: From Alexandria to the Internet* (New York: W. W. Norton, 2008); Alex Wright, *Glut: Mastering Information through the Ages* (Washington, DC: Joseph Henry Press, 2007); Tom Standage, *Writing on the Wall: Social Media—The First Two Thousand Years* (New York: Bloomsbury, 2013).

41. Liu, "Imagining." See also Simone Natale, "There Are No Old Media," *Journal of Communication* 66, no. 4 (2016): 585–603, https://doi.org/10.1111/jcom.12235.

42. Brian Winston, *Media Technology and Society: A History from the Telegraph to the Internet* (London: Routledge, 1998); Acland, *Residual Media*; Daniel R. Headrick, *When Information Came of Age: Technologies of Knowledge in the Age of Reason and Revolution, 1700–1850* (Oxford: Oxford University Press, 2000).

43. Wolfgang Ernst, *Digital Memory and the Archive*, ed. Jussi Parikka (Minneapolis: University of Minnesota Press, 2012).

44. Jussi Parikka, *A Geology of Media* (Minneapolis: University of Minnesota Press, 2015).

45. Matthew Fuller, *Media Ecologies: Materialist Energies in Art and Technoculture* (Cambridge, MA: MIT Press, 2005); Peters, *Marvelous Clouds*.

46. Whitney Trettien, "Substrate, Platform, Interface, Format," *Textual Cultures* 16, no. 1 (2023): 293.

47. Kathleen Fitzpatrick, "Media Studies and Literary Studies," Kathleen Fitzpatrick (blog), February 13, 2009, https://kfitz.info/media-studies-and-literary-studies/.

48. "Prefatory Note," *Victorian Studies* 1, no. 1 (1957): 3.

49. Catherine Gallagher, "Theoretical Answers to Interdisciplinary Questions or Interdisciplinary Answers to Theoretical Questions?" *Victorian Studies* 47, no. 2 (2005): 254.

50. Liu, "Imagining."

51. Menke, *Literature, Print Culture, and Media Technologies*, 21.

52. Ray Siemens, John Unsworth, and Susan Schreibman, eds., *A Companion to Digital Humanities* (Oxford: Blackwell, 2004).

53. Matthew Kirschenbaum, "Digital Humanities As/Is a Tactical Term," in *Debates in the Digital Humanities*, ed. Matthew K. Gold (Minneapolis: University of Minnesota Press, 2012); Scott Weingart, "A Look Backwards through the Index of Digital Humanities Conferences," The Digital Humanities Long View, UCL Centre for Digital Humanities, Center for Spatial and Textual Analysis, April 17, 2021.

54. Susan Hockey, "The History of Humanities Computing," in Siemens et al., eds., *Companion to Digital Humanities*. For related versions of this origin story, see William G. Thomas II, "Computing and the Historical Imagination," in Siemens et al., eds., *Companion to Digital Humanities*; Stephen Ramsay, *Reading Machines: Toward an Algorithmic Criticism* (Urbana: University of Illinois Press, 2011).

55. Weingart, "A Look Backwards." See also Arun Jacob, "Punching Holes

in the International Busa Machine Narrative," *Interdisciplinary Digital Engagement in Arts & Humanities (IDEAH)*, 2020, https://doi.org/10.21428/f1f23564.d7d097c2; Steven E. Jones, *Roberto Busa, S.J., and the Emergence of Humanities Computing: The Priest and the Punched Cards* (New York: Routledge, 2016); Jamie Skye Bianco, "This Digital Humanities Which Is Not One," in *Debates in the Digital Humanities*, ed. Matthew K. Gold (Minneapolis: University of Minnesota Press, 2012).

56. Rachel Sagner Buurma and Laura Heffernan, "Search and Replace: Josephine Miles and the Origins of Distant Reading," *Modernism/Modernity* 3, no. 1 (2018); Brad Pasanek, "Extreme Reading: Josephine Miles and the Scale of the Pre-Digital Digital Humanities," *ELH* 86, no. 2 (2019): 355–85.

57. Morgan, "Critical Empathy"; Igarashi, "Statistical Analysis"; Natalia Cecire, "Ways of Not Reading Gertrude Stein," *ELH* 82 (2015): 281–315.

58. Weingart, "A Look Backwards."

59. William Pannapacker, "The MLA and the Digital Humanities," *Chronicle of Higher Education*, December 28, 2009.

60. Matthew Kirschenbaum, "What Is Digital Humanities and What's It Doing in English Departments?," *ADE Bulletin*, 2010; Matthew Kirschenbaum, "What Is 'Digital Humanities,' and Why Are They Saying Such Terrible Things about It?," *Differences* 25, no. 1 (2014).

61. Matthew K. Gold, "The Digital Humanities Moment," in *Debates in the Digital Humanities*, ed. Matthew K. Gold (Minneapolis: University of Minnesota Press, 2012), http://dhdebates.gc.cuny.edu/debates/text/2. Similarly, when the *Journal of Cultural Analytics* launched in 2016, in an editorial statement Andrew Piper emphasized the "act of mirroring" and "new recursivity" within DH praxis. Andrew Piper, "There Will Be Numbers," *Journal of Cultural Analytics* 1, no. 1 (2016): 7–8, https://doi.org/10.22148/16.006.

62. Élika Ortega, "Media and Cultural Hybridity in the Digital Humanities," *PMLA* 135, no. 1 (2020): 162, https://doi.org/10.1632/pmla.2020.135.1.159.

63. Anne Burdick et al., *Digital_Humanities* (Cambridge, MA: MIT Press, 2012), 1.

64. David Theo Goldberg and Patrik Svensson, eds., *Between Humanities and the Digital* (Cambridge, MA: MIT Press, 2015), 4.

65. Alan Liu and William G. Thomas II, "Humanities in the Digital Age," in Goldberg and Svensson, *Between Humanities and the Digital*, 35.

66. N. Katherine Hayles, "Final Commentary: A Provocation," in Goldberg and Svensson, *Between Humanities and the Digital*, 504.

67. Goldberg and Svensson, *Between Humanities and the Digital*, 5.

68. Jonathan Sterne, "The Example: Some Historical Considerations," in Goldberg and Svensson, *Between Humanities and the Digital*, 19.

69. Alan Liu, "The Meaning of the Digital Humanities," *PMLA* 128, no. 2 (2013): 410, https://doi.org/10.1632/pmla.2013.128.2.409.

70. Julia Flanders, "The Productive Unease of 21st-Century Digital Scholarship," *Digital Humanities Quarterly* 3, no. 3 (2009), http://digitalhumanities.org/dhq/vol/3/3/000055.html.

71. Alan Liu, "Digital Humanities and Academic Change," *English Language Notes* 47, no. 1 (2009): 17–35.

72. Kirschenbaum, "What Is 'Digital Humanities,' and Why Are They Saying Such Terrible Things about It?"

73. Moya Z. Bailey, "All the Digital Humanists Are White, All the Nerds Are Men, but Some of Us Are Brave," *Journal of Digital Humanities* 1, no. 1 (2011), http://journalofdigitalhumanities.org/1-1/all-the-digital-humanists-are-white-all-the-nerds-are-men-but-some-of-us-are-brave-by-moya-z-bailey/; Kim Gallon, "Making a Case for the Black Digital Humanities," in *Debates in the Digital Humanities 2016*, ed. Matthew K. Gold and Lauren F. Klein (Minneapolis: University of Minnesota Press, 2016).

74. Thomas S. Kuhn, *The Structure of Scientific Revolutions* (Chicago: University of Chicago Press, 1996).

75. Cathy N. Davidson, "Humanities 2.0: Promise, Perils, Predictions," *PMLA* 123, no. 3 (2008): 708, https://doi.org/10.1632/pmla.2008.123.3.707. John Walsh claims that "the industrial revolution of the nineteenth century is the closest analog to the rapid technological and social change of the digital age. John A. Walsh, "Multimedia and Multitasking: A Survey of Digital Resources for Nineteenth-Century Literary Studies," in Siemens and Schreibman, *A Companion to Digital Literary Studies*.

76. Patricia Cohen, "Digital Keys for Unlocking the Humanities' Riches," *New York Times*, November 16, 2010, www.nytimes.com/2010/11/17/arts/17digital.html.

77. Chad Wellmon, "Loyal Workers and Distinguished Scholars: Big Humanities and the Ethics of Knowledge," *Modern Intellectual History* 16, no. 1 (2019): 87–126.

78. Gitelman, *Always Already New*, 6.

79. Gitelman, *Scripts, Grooves, and Writing Machines*, 5, 2.

80. Gitelman, *Paper Knowledge*, 56.

81. Lee, *Overwhelmed*, 11.

82. Mark W. Turner, "Seriality, Miscellaneity, and Compression in Nineteenth-Century Print," *Victorian Studies* 62, no. 2 (2020): 283–94; Clare Pettitt, *Serial Revolutions 1848: Writing, Politics, Form* (Oxford: Oxford University Press, 2022).

83. Burdick et al., *Digital_Humanities*, 4.

84. Roopika Risam, *New Digital Worlds: Postcolonial Digital Humanities in Theory, Praxis, and Pedagogy* (Chicago: Northwestern University Press, 2018), 4.

85. Adeline Koh, "Niceness, Building, and Opening the Genealogy of the Digital Humanities: Beyond the Social Contract of Humanities Computing," *Differences* 25, no. 1 (2014): 93–106, https://doi.org/10.1215/10407391-2420015; Dorothy Kim and Adeline Koh, eds., *Alternative Historiographies of the Digital Humanities* (Punctum Books, 2021).

86. "Professor Sees Parallels between Things, Other Things," *The Onion*, March 16, 2007, www.theonion.com/professor-sees-parallels-between-things-other-things-1819569111.

87. danah boyd and K. Crawford, "Critical Questions for Big Data: Provocations for a Cultural, Technological, and Scholarly Phenomenon," *Information, Communication, and Society* 15, no. 5 (2012): 668, https://doi.org/10.1080/1369118X.2012.678878.

88. Eve Kosofsky Sedgwick, "Paranoid Reading and Reparative Reading; or, You're so Paranoid, You Probably Think This Introduction Is About You," in *Novel Gazing: Queer Readings in Fiction*, ed. Eve Kosofsky Sedgwick (Durham, NC: Duke University Press, 1997), 1–37.

89. Gitelman, *Paper Knowledge*, 137.

90. Miri Rubin, "Presentism's Useful Anachronisms," *Past and Present* 234, no. 1 (2017): 236–44, https://doi.org/10.1093/pastj/gtw057.

91. James H. Sweet, "Is History History? Identity Politics and Teleologies of the Present," *Perspectives on History*, August 17, 2022; Lynn Hunt, "Against Presentism," *Perspectives on History*, May 1, 2002.

92. Marvin, *When Old Technologies Were New*, 154.

93. Carolyn Marvin, "Information and History," in *The Ideology of the Information Age*, ed. Jennifer Daryl Slack and Fred Fejes (Norwood, NJ: Ablex, 1987), 49.

94. Rubin, "Presentism's Useful Anachronisms."

95. Clayton, *Charles Dickens in Cyberspace*, 114.

96. Catherine Hall, "Thinking Reflexively: Opening 'Blind Eyes,'" *Past and Present* 234, no. 1 (2017): 254–63, https://doi.org/10.1093/pastj/gtw059.

97. Sweet, "Is History History?" Ryan Fong, for instance, noted the "the racism, colonialism, anti-Blackness and white supremacy it's trying to be an intellectual fig leaf for." @deephomework, Twitter, August 17, 2022. https://twitter.com/deephomework/status/1560050868996775938.

98. Christina Sharpe, *In the Wake: On Blackness and Being* (Durham, NC: Duke University Press, 2016), 14, 13.

99. John Kucich and Dianne F. Sadoff, eds., *Victorian Afterlife: Postmodern*

Culture Rewrites the Nineteenth Century (Minneapolis: University of Minnesota Press, 2000), xiv.

100. Clayton, *Charles Dickens in Cyberspace*, 104.

101. "Manifesto of the V21 Collective: Ten Theses," *V21: Victorian Studies for the 21st Century* (blog), 2015, http://v21collective.org/manifesto-of-the-v21-collective-ten-theses/.

102. David Sweeney Coombs and Danielle Coriale, "Introduction: V21 Forum on Strategic Presentism," *Victorian Studies* 59, no. 1 (2016): 87.

103. Ronjaunee Chatterjee, Alicia Mireles Christoff, and Amy R. Wong, "Undisciplining Victorian Studies," *Los Angeles Review of Books*, July 10, 2020, https://lareviewofbooks.org/article/undisciplining-victorian-studies/.

104. Priya Joshi, "Globalizing Victorian Studies," *Yearbook of English Studies* 41, no. 2 (2011): 38, 39, https://doi.org/10.5699/yearenglstud.41.2.0020.

105. Joshi, "Globalizing Victorian Studies," 22, original emphasis.

106. Joshi, 20.

107. Sharon Marcus, "Same Difference? Transnationalism, Comparative Literature, and Victorian Studies," *Victorian Studies* 45, no. 4 (2003): 677–86, https://doi.org/10.1353/vic.2004.0029.

108. Matthew Charles Rowlinson, "Theory of Victorian Studies: Anachronism and Self-Reflexivity," *Victorian Studies* 47, no. 2 (2005): 251.

109. Andrew Piper, *Book Was There: Reading in Electronic Times* (Chicago: University of Chicago Press, 2012), xii; see Whitson in "Responses to the V21 Manifesto," *V21* (blog), March 23, 2015, http://v21collective.org/responses-to-the-v21-manifesto-2/; Lynda Nead, *Victorian Babylon: People, Streets, and Images in Nineteenth-Century London* (New Haven, CT: Yale University Press, 2000), 8; Dipesh Chakrabarty, *Provincializing Europe: Postcolonial Thought and Historical Difference* (Princeton, NJ: Princeton University Press, 2008), 243; Megan Ward, "Theorizing the Historical Middle," *V21: Victorian Studies for the 21st Century* (blog), June 1, 2015, http://v21collective.org/megan-ward-theorizing-the-historical-middle/; Caroline Levine, "Historicism: From the Break to the Loop," *Boundary2* (blog), October 6, 2016, www.boundary2.org/2016/10/caroline-levine-historicism/; Devin Griffiths, *The Age of Analogy: Science and Literature between the Darwins* (Baltimore: Johns Hopkins University Press, 2016), 4; Rachel Sagner Buurma and Laura Heffernan, "Interpretation, 1980 and 1880," *Victorian Studies* 55, no. 4 (2013): 615–28; Nathan K. Hensley, "Allegories of the Contemporary," *Novel* 45, no. 2 (2012): 276–300, https://doi.org/10.1215/00295132-1573976; Wai Chee Dimock, "A Theory of Resonance," *PMLA* 112, no. 5 (1997): 1060–71, https://doi.org/10.2307/463483; Eleanor Courtemanche, "Beyond Urgency: Shadow Presentisms, Hinge Points, and Victo-

rian Historicisms," *Criticism* 61, no. 4 (2019): 461–79, https://doi.org/10.13110/criticism.61.4.0461; Lisa Lowe, *The Intimacies of Four Continents* (Durham, NC: Duke University Press, 2015).

110. Adela Pinch, "Recent Studies in the Nineteenth Century," *SEL Studies in English Literature, 1500–1900* 54, no. 4 (2014): 943, https://doi.org/10.1353/sel.2014.0039.

111. N. Katherine Hayles and Jessica Pressman, eds., *Comparative Textual Media: Transforming the Humanities in the Postprint Era* (Minneapolis: University of Minnesota Press, 2013); Marie Cronqvist and Christoph Hilgert, "Entangled Media Histories," *Media History* 23, no. 1 (2017): 130–41, https://doi.org/10.1080/13688804.2016.1270745.

112. Gitelman, *Always Already New*, 8.

113. N. Katherine Hayles, *How We Became Posthuman: Virtual Bodies in Cybernetics, Literature, and Informatics* (Chicago: University of Chicago Press, 1999), 2.

114. Peters, *Marvelous Clouds*, 33.

115. Pamela Thurschwell, *Literature, Technology, and Magical Thinking, 1880–1920* (Cambridge: Cambridge University Press, 2001), 114.

116. Stephen Arata, "The Sedulous Ape: Atavism, Professionalism, and Stevenson's 'Jekyll and Hyde,'" *Criticism* 37, no. 2 (1995): 233–59.

117. Peters, *Speaking into the Air*; Jeffrey Sconce, *Haunted Media: Electronic Presence from Telegraphy to Television* (Durham, NC: Duke University Press, 2000); Galvan, *Sympathetic Medium*.

118. Rachel Sagner Buurma and Laura Heffernan, *The Teaching Archive: A New History for Literary Study* (Chicago: University of Chicago Press, 2021).

Chapter 1

1. H. R., "The Passing Railway Train," *Chambers's Edinburgh Journal*, September 7, 1844, 160.

2. Drew Fairweather, "Internet Train," Married to the Sea, January 13, 2007, www.marriedtothesea.com/index.php?date=011307. Used with permission.

3. "Rapid Communication," *Aberdeen Herald*, January 23, 1847, 3, British Newspaper Archive.

4. Nicholas Royle, *Telepathy and Literature: Essays on the Reading Mind* (Oxford: Basil Blackwell, 1991), 5.

5. Standage, *The Victorian Internet*, xiv.

6. Neal Stephenson, "Mother Earth, Mother Board," *Wired*, December 1996, www.wired.com/wired/archive/4.12/ffglass_pr.html.

7. Weller, "An Information History Decade," 94.

8. Ward, "Theorizing the Historical Middle."
9. Ward.
10. Hayles, *How We Became Posthuman*, 2.
11. Carey, *Communication as Culture*; Nunberg, "Farewell to the Information Age," 103–38; Gleick, *The Information*; Peters, *Speaking into the Air*; Guillory, "Genesis."
12. Hayles, *How We Became Posthuman*, 13.
13. Peters, *Marvelous Clouds*, 33.
14. Beniger, *The Control Revolution*.
15. Marvin, *When Old Technologies Were New*, 8.
16. Marvin, 4.
17. Ruth Livesey, *Writing the Stage Coach Nation: Locality on the Move in Nineteenth-Century British Literature* (Oxford: Oxford University Press, 2016), 2.
18. See also Jonathan H. Grossman, *Charles Dickens's Networks: Public Transport and the Novel* (Oxford: Oxford University Press, 2012).
19. Peters, *Speaking into the Air*, 5.
20. Wolfgang Schivelbusch, *The Railway Journey: The Industrialization of Time and Space in the Nineteenth Century* (Berkeley: University of California Press, 1986), 37.
21. Livesey, *Writing the Stage Coach Nation*, 5.
22. Mary A. Favret, *Romantic Correspondence: Women, Politics, and the Fiction of Letters* (Cambridge: Cambridge University Press, 1993), 197.
23. Thomas De Quincey, "The English Mail-Coach, or the Glory of Motion [Part 1]," *Blackwood's Edinburgh Magazine*, October 1849, 491 (original emphasis). Hereafter cited in line.
24. Ralph Harrington, "The Railway Accident: Trains, Trauma, and Technological Crisis in Nineteenth-Century Britain," Institute of Railway Studies, University of York, 1999, www.york.ac.uk/inst/irs/irshome/papers/rlyacc.htm.
25. Marvin, *When Old Technologies Were New*, 4.
26. Susan Zieger, *The Mediated Mind: Affect, Ephemera, and Consumerism in the Nineteenth Century* (New York: Fordham University Press, 2018), 208.
27. Thomas De Quincey, *Confessions of an English Opium-Eater, and Selected Essays*, ed. David Masson (New York: A. L. Burt, 1856), 257, https://catalog.hathitrust.org/Record/100027485.
28. Jason R. Rudy, *Electric Meters: Victorian Physiological Poetics* (Athens: Ohio University Press, 2009), 52.
29. Peters, *Speaking into the Air*, 228.
30. "Our Journal of This Day," *The Times*, November 29, 1814, 3.
31. "The Success of the Atlantic Cable," *The Times*, July 30, 1866.

32. Patricia Anderson, *The Printed Image and the Transformation of Popular Culture, 1790–1860* (Oxford: Oxford University Press, 1991), 3.

33. Benedict R. Anderson, *Imagined Communities: Reflections on the Origin and Spread of Nationalism* (London: Verso, 1983).

34. "Our Address," *Illustrated London News* 1, no. 1 (May 14, 1842): 1.

35. Jay David Bolter and Richard Grusin, *Remediation: Understanding New Media* (Cambridge, MA: MIT Press, 1999).

36. Elizabeth Losh, "Home Inspection: Mina Rees and National Computing Infrastructure," *First Monday* 23, no. 3 (2018), https://doi.org/10.5210/fm.v23i3.8282; Elizabeth Losh and Jacqueline Wernimont, eds., *Bodies of Information: Intersectional Feminism and the Digital Humanities* (Minneapolis: University of Minnesota Press, 2018), www.jstor.org/stable/10.5749/j.ctv9hj9r9.

37. See the editors' introduction "Reading Infrastructure" in Kelly Mee Rich, Nicole Rizzuto, and Susan Zieger, eds., *The Aesthetic Life of Infrastructure: Race, Affect, Environment* (Evanston, IL: Northwestern University Press, 2022).

38. "The Post Office Van, Calling at the Office of the Illustrated London News," *Illustrated London News*, January 18, 1845.

39. Gitelman, *Always Already New*, 86.

40. Caroline Sumpter, "'The Great Event of Modern History': The Victorian Press Visualizes Its Infrastructure," *19: Interdisciplinary Studies in the Long Nineteenth Century*, no. 35 (2023), https://doi.org/10.16995/ntn.10189.

41. Alison Hedley, "Reflexive Pictorial Journalism: Educating Readers in Media Literacy," *Victorian Review* 43, no. 2 (2017): 189, 190, https://doi.org/10.1353/vcr.2017.0026.

42. Christina Lupton, *Knowing Books: The Consciousness of Mediation in Eighteenth-Century Britain* (Philadelphia: University of Pennsylvania Press, 2012).

43. Nicola Kirkby, "Nineteenth-Century Infrastructures before 'Infrastructure,'" *19: Interdisciplinary Studies in the Long Nineteenth Century*, no. 35 (2023), https://doi.org/10.16995/ntn.11184.

44. Lisa Parks, "'Stuff You Can Kick': Toward a Theory of Media Infrastructures," in Goldberg and Svensson, *Between Humanities and the Digital*, 355.

45. Parks, 357.

46. *1903 Throwing Mail into Bags*, 2009, www.youtube.com/watch?v=cL05Y6MJRs8; *Carriers at Work, U.S. Post Office*, 2010, www.youtube.com/watch?v=cNzTEveUURA.

47. Parks, "Stuff You Can Kick," 358.

48. Lai-Tze Fan, "Material Matters in Digital Representation: Tree of Codes

as a Literature of Disembodiment," *Mosaic: An Interdisciplinary Critical Journal* 51, no. 1 (2018): 37–53.

49. Paul Fyfe, "A Great Exhibition of Printing: The Illustrated London News Supplement Sheet (1851)," *Cahiers Victoriens et Édouardiens*, no. 84 (2016), https://doi.org/10.4000/cve.2928.

50. Thomas Smits, "Making the News National: Using Digitized Newspapers to Study the Distribution of the Queen's Speech by W. H. Smith & Son, 1846–1858," *Victorian Periodicals Review* 49, no. 4 (2016): 598–625, https://doi.org/10.1353/vpr.2016.0041.

51. "Queen's Speech," *Newcastle Journal*, January 23, 1847, 3; quoted in Smits, 604.

52. Smits, 604.

53. Graham Law, "Distribution," in *The Routledge Handbook to Nineteenth-Century British Periodicals and Newspapers*, ed. Alexis Easley, Andrew King, and John Morton (London: Routledge, 2016), 53.

54. "The Queen's Speech," *Bradford Observer*, January 21, 1847, 5; quoted in Smits, "Making the News National," 605.

55. "The People of Liverpool," *Morning Post*, November 25, 1847, 6; quoted in Smits, 607.

56. Smits, 609.

57. *The Times*, December 5, 1853, p. 6; quoted in Weller, "An Information History Decade," 83.

58. Marvin, *When Old Technologies Were New*, 109.

59. Law, "Distribution," 52–53 (my italics).

60. John Plotz, *The Crowd: British Literature and Public Politics* (Berkeley: University of California Press, 2000), 101–26; Anne Frey, "De Quincey's Imperial Systems," *Studies in Romanticism* 44, no. 1 (2005): 41–61; Andrew Franta, "Publication and Mediation in 'The English Mail-Coach,'" *European Romantic Review* 22, no. 3 (2011): 323–30.

61. Kate Thomas, *Postal Pleasures: Sex, Scandal, and Victorian Letters* (New York: Oxford University Press, 2012), 34.

62. With so much attention on how De Quincey describes the transmission of news and idealizes forms of publication, it is surprising that discussions of "The English Mail-Coach" overlook *Blackwood*'s as a form of transmission. Plotz insightfully suggests that De Quincey's nationalist news depends on seriality, but Plotz turns more toward the aesthetic event of the news. Plotz also uses the Masson edition of De Quincey's collected writings, which were extensively revised after their original periodical publication.

63. Margaret Russett argues that De Quincey participates in magazines

to self-consciously construct his minor literary status. See chapter 3, "The magazinist as minor author," in *De Quincey's Romanticism: Canonical Minority and the Forms of Transmission* (Cambridge: Cambridge University Press, 1997), 92–134.

64. Thomas Carlyle, "TC to John A. Carlyle," January 10, 1832, The Carlyle Letters Online, http://carlyleletters.dukejournals.org.

65. Robert Morrison, "William Blackwood and the Dynamics of Success," in *Print Culture and the Blackwood Tradition, 1805–1930*, ed. David Finkelstein (Toronto: University of Toronto Press, 2006), 21–48.

66. Frey, "De Quincey's Imperial Systems," 45.

67. In this line, Charles Rzepka has argued that De Quincey has an "animus against textual mediation"; *Sacramental Commodities: Gift, Text, and the Sublime in De Quincey* (Amherst: University of Massachusetts Press, 1995), 47. Franta suggests that De Quincey "regards print as a false promise"; Franta, "Publication and Mediation," 324.

68. Thomas De Quincey, "The Vision of Sudden Death [Part 2]," *Blackwood's Edinburgh Magazine*, December 1849, 744.

69. Rzepka, *Sacramental Commodities*, 259.

70. Rzepka, 266.

71. Aileen Fyfe, *Steam-Powered Knowledge: William Chambers and the Business of Publishing, 1820–1860* (Chicago: University of Chicago Press, 2012), 48; David Finkelstein, *The House of Blackwood: Author-Publisher Relations in the Victorian Era* (University Park: Pennsylvania State University Press, 2002), 17.

72. Fyfe, *Steam-Powered Knowledge*.

73. Even so, you can find a useful answer to "What Is the Internet?" in Kevin Driscoll, *The Modem World: A Prehistory of Social Media* (New Haven, CT: Yale University Press, 2022).

74. Tung-Hui Hu, *A Prehistory of the Cloud* (Cambridge, MA: MIT Press, 2015), ix.

75. Alan Liu and Scott Pound, "The Amoderns: Reengaging the Humanities," *Amodern* 2 (2013), http://amodern.net/article/the-amoderns-reengaging-the-humanities/.

76. Hu, *Prehistory*, x.

77. Nicole Starosielski, *The Undersea Network* (Durham, NC: Duke University Press, 2015), 68, https://doi.org/10.1215/9780822376224.

78. John Perry Barlow, "A Declaration of the Independence of Cyberspace," Electronic Frontier Foundation, February 8, 1996, https://projects.eff.org/~barlow/Declaration-Final.html.

79. Hu, *Prehistory*, xv.

80. Ian Baucom, *Specters of the Atlantic: Finance Capital, Slavery, and the Philosophy of History* (Durham, NC: Duke University Press, 2005).

81. Jessica Marie Johnson, "Markup Bodies: Black [Life] Studies and Slavery [Death] Studies at the Digital Crossroads," *Social Text* 36, no. 4 (137) (2018): 58, https://doi.org/10.1215/01642472-7145658.

82. Johnson, 69. See also Ruha Benjamin, *Race after Technology: Abolitionist Tools for the New Jim Code* (Cambridge: Polity, 2019).

83. Dhanashree Thorat, "Colonial Topographies of Internet Infrastructure: The Sedimented and Linked Networks of the Telegraph and Submarine Fiber Optic Internet," *South Asian Review* 40, no. 3 (2019): 253, https://doi.org/10.1080/02759527.2019.1599563.

84. Tara McPherson, "Why Are the Digital Humanities So White? Or Thinking the Histories of Race and Computation," in *Debates in the Digital Humanities*, ed. Matthew K. Gold (Minneapolis: University of Minnesota Press, 2012), http://dhdebates.gc.cuny.edu/debates/text/29.

85. McPherson; Hu, *Prehistory*, 15.

86. Losh, "Home Inspection."

87. Marie Hicks, *Programmed Inequality: How Britain Discarded Women Technologists and Lost Its Edge in Computing* (Cambridge, MA: MIT Press, 2017); Lisa Nakamura, "Indigenous Circuits: Navajo Women and the Racialization of Early Electronic Manufacture," *American Quarterly* 66, no. 4 (2014): 919–41, https://doi.org/10.1353/aq.2014.0070; Charlton D. McIlwain, *Black Software: The Internet and Racial Justice, from the AfroNet to Black Lives Matter* (New York: Oxford University Press, 2020).

88. Hu, *Prehistory*, xix–xx.

89. "The Success of the Atlantic Cable," *Times*, July 30, 1866.

90. Starosielski, *The Undersea Network*, 87.

91. Leah Price, *How to Do Things with Books in Victorian Britain* (Princeton, NJ: Princeton University Press, 2012), 108, 110.

92. Stephenson, "Mother Earth, Mother Board."

93. Bowser and Croxall, "Industrial Evolution."

94. Andrew Blum, *Tubes: A Journey to the Center of the Internet* (New York: Ecco, 2012), 3.

95. Blum, 162.

96. Blum, 10.

97. Blum, 3.

98. Blum, 143.

99. Blum, 102.

Chapter 2

1. Gordon S. Haight, ed., *The George Eliot Letters* (New Haven, CT: Yale University Press, 1978), 3: 164.

2. Gleick, *The Information*, 407.

3. Gordon S. Haight, *George Eliot; a Biography* (New York: Oxford University Press, 1968); Rosemarie Bodenheimer, *The Real Life of Mary Ann Evans: George Eliot, Her Letters and Fiction* (Ithaca, NY: Cornell University Press, 1994).

4. Helen Small, "George Eliot and the Cosmopolitan Cynic," *Victorian Studies* 55, no. 1 (2012): 85–105; Rae Greiner, *Sympathetic Realism in Nineteenth-Century British Fiction* (Baltimore: Johns Hopkins University Press, 2012).

5. Alexander Welsh, *George Eliot and Blackmail* (Cambridge, MA: Harvard University Press, 1985).

6. Welsh, 29.

7. Welsh, 33; Luciano Floridi, ed., *The Cambridge Handbook of Information and Computer Ethics* (Cambridge: Cambridge University Press, 2010).

8. For a historical overview, see Chris Wiggins and Matthew L. Jones, *How Data Happened: A History from the Age of Reason to the Age of Algorithms* (New York: W. W. Norton, 2023).

9. For instance, see Sherry Turkle, *Alone Together: Why We Expect More from Technology and Less from Each Other* (New York: Basic Books, 2011); boyd and Crawford, "Critical Questions"; Meg Leta Jones, *Ctrl Z: The Right to Be Forgotten* (New York: New York University Press, 2016).

10. Sherry Turkle, *Reclaiming Conversation: The Power of Talk in a Digital Age* (New York: Penguin, 2015), 9.

11. George Eliot, *The Lifted Veil and Brother Jacob*, ed. Helen Small (New York: Oxford University Press, 2009), 13. Hereafter cited in line.

12. Jill Galvan, "The Narrator as Medium in George Eliot's 'The Lifted Veil,'" *Victorian Studies* 48, no. 2 (2006): 245.

13. Thurschwell, *Literature, Technology, and Magical Thinking*, 13.

14. Richard Menke, *Telegraphic Realism: Victorian Fiction and Other Information Systems* (Stanford, CA: Stanford University Press, 2008), 147.

15. Menke, 137.

16. Menke, 147.

17. George Eliot, *Middlemarch*, ed. Rosemary Ashton (New York: Penguin, 1994), 194.

18. Ann Blair, *Too Much to Know: Managing Scholarly Information before the Modern Age* (New Haven, CT: Yale University Press, 2010).

19. Lee, *Overwhelmed*.

20. Amelia Bonea et al., *Anxious Times: Medicine and Modernity in*

Nineteenth-Century Britain (Pittsburgh: University of Pittsburgh Press, 2019), 5, http://muse.jhu.edu/book/66717/.

21. Quoted in Bonea et al., 3.

22. Max Simon Nordau, *Degeneration* (London: William Heinemann, 1898), 42, https://catalog.hathitrust.org/Record/007668760.

23. David M. Levy, "Information Overload," in *The Handbook of Information and Computer Ethics*, ed. Kenneth E. Himma and Herman T. Tavani (Hoboken, NJ: Wiley, 2008), 497–515.

24. Levy, 505.

25. Levy, 498.

26. Laura Otis, *Networking: Communicating with Bodies and Machines in the Nineteenth Century* (Ann Arbor: University of Michigan Press, 2001), 81.

27. Otis, 81.

28. Greiner, *Sympathetic Realism*, 123.

29. Greiner, 126.

30. Menke, *Telegraphic Realism*, 153.

31. Small, "George Eliot and the Cosmopolitan Cynic," 88.

32. Royle, *Telepathy and Literature*, 4.

33. Small, "George Eliot and the Cosmopolitan Cynic," 88.

34. Greiner, *Sympathetic Realism*, 4.

35. Welsh, *George Eliot and Blackmail*; Bodenheimer, *Real Life of Mary Ann Evans*.

36. Haight, *The George Eliot Letters*, 3: 170; quoted in Robert Douglas-Fairhurst, *Victorian Afterlives: The Shaping of Influence in Nineteenth-Century Literature* (Oxford: Oxford University Press, 2002), 119n107.

37. In Galloway's useful genealogy of networks, a "net" has always been simultaneously a tool as well as a trap. Alexander R. Galloway, "Networks," in *Critical Terms for Media Studies*, ed. W. J. T. Mitchell and Mark B. Hansen (Chicago: University of Chicago Press, 2010), 280–96.

38. Adela Pinch, *Thinking about Other People in Nineteenth-Century British Writing* (Cambridge: Cambridge University Press, 2010), 15.

39. Turkle, *Alone Together*, 19.

40. Turkle, *Reclaiming Conversation*, 9.

41. Blair, *Too Much to Know*.

42. Turkle, *Alone Together*, 1.

43. Turkle, *Reclaiming Conversation*, 21.

44. Turkle, *Reclaiming Conversation*, 4.

45. Nicholas G. Carr, *The Shallows: What the Internet Is Doing to Our Brains* (New York: W. W. Norton, 2010), 220.

46. Carr, 221.

47. Sven Birkerts, *The Gutenberg Elegies: The Fate of Reading in an Electronic Age* (New York: Faber and Faber, 2006), 5.

48. Birkerts, 5.

49. Birkerts, 73.

50. In chapter 4, I hypothesize how and why Victorian gothic tropes have been redeployed in contemporary digital debates.

51. danah boyd, *It's Complicated: The Social Lives of Networked Teens* (New Haven, CT: Yale University Press, 2014), 78.

52. Turkle, *Reclaiming Conversation*, 69.

53. Carr, *The Shallows*, 104. Neither the Victorian novel nor the circumstances of its publication support this claim, as many scholars have argued. See Nicholas Dames, *The Physiology of the Novel: Reading, Neural Science, and the Form of Victorian Fiction* (Oxford: Oxford University Press, 2007); Hughes, "SIDEWAYS!"

54. Dames, *The Physiology of the Novel*, 82. See also his fuller discussion, 16–19.

55. Dames, 104.

56. Mark Bauerlein, *The Dumbest Generation: How the Digital Age Stupefies Young Americans and Jeopardizes Our Future (or, Don't Trust Anyone under 30)* (New York: Tarcher/Penguin, 2008), 199, 57.

57. Bauerlein, 218.

58. boyd, *It's Complicated*, 159.

59. boyd, 159.

60. "Internet.Org by Facebook," 2015, https://web.archive.org/web/20150318155351/http://internet.org/.

61. *Meta! Watch Zuckerberg Reveal Facebook's New Name*, 2021, www.youtube.com/watch?v=KIxPRwgXFQg.

62. boyd, *It's Complicated*, 159.

63. boyd, 203.

64. boyd, 127.

65. Jade E. Davis, *The Other Side of Empathy* (Durham, NC: Duke University Press, 2023), 73.

66. Davis, 92.

67. Nicholas Dames, *Amnesiac Selves: Nostalgia, Forgetting, and British Fiction, 1810–1870* (New York: Oxford University Press, 2001).

68. Turkle, *Reclaiming Conversation*, 23.

69. Davis, *Other Side of Empathy*, 6.

70. Charles Bray, *On Force, Its Mental and Moral Correlates; and on That Which Is Supposed to Underlie All Phenomena: With Speculations on Spiritualism,*

and Other Abnormal Conditions of Mind (London: Longmans, Green, Reader, and Dyer, 1866), 80, https://catalog.hathitrust.org/Record/007652622.

71. Bray, 86–87.

72. The program was quickly renamed "Terrorism Information Awareness" and later the anodyne "Basketball." Shane Harris, "Giving In to the Surveillance State," *New York Times*, August 23, 2012, www.nytimes.com/2012/08/23/opinion/whos-watching-the-nsa-watchers.html.

73. Pinch, *Thinking about Other People*, 59.

74. Bray, *On Force*, 86.

75. Edgar Allan Poe, "The Power of Words," in *The Collected Works of Edgar Allan Poe, Vol. III: Tales and Sketches* (Baltimore: Edgar Allan Poe Society of Baltimore, 2012).

76. Charles Babbage, "Chapter IX: On the Permanent Impression of Our Words and Actions on the Globe We Inhabit," in *Ninth Bridgewater Treatise, a Fragment*, 2nd ed. (London, 1838), 112, 115, https://victorianweb.org/science/science_texts/bridgewater/b9.htm.

77. Balfour Stewart and Peter Guthrie Tait, *The Unseen Universe; or, Physical Speculations on a Future State* (London: Macmillan, 1875), 111, 158, https://catalog.hathitrust.org/Record/001940314, original emphasis.

78. Roger Luckhurst, *The Invention of Telepathy, 1870–1901* (Oxford: Oxford University Press, 2002).

79. William Barrett, *On the Threshold of the Unseen; an Examination of the Phenomena of Spiritualism and of the Evidence for Survival after Death* (London: Kegan Paul, Trench, Trubner, 1917), 110, https://catalog.hathitrust.org/Record/00047306; quoted in Pinch, *Thinking about Other People*, 52.

80. Barrett, *On the Threshold of the Unseen*, 128.

81. Friedrich A. Kittler, *Gramophone, Film, Typewriter* (Stanford, CA: Stanford University Press, 1999); Gitelman, *Scripts, Grooves, and Writing Machines*.

82. George du Maurier, *Peter Ibbetson* (New York: Harper, 1919). Hereafter cited in line.

83. For a fuller exploration of ancestral memory and its links to nineteenth-century racial theories, see Athena Vrettos, "'Little Bags of Remembrance': Du Maurier's Peter Ibbetson and Victorian Theories of Ancestral Memory," *Romanticism and Victorianism on the Net (RaVoN)*, no. 53 (2009), www.erudit.org/en/journals/ravon/2009-n53-ravon2916/029899ar/.

84. See Leighton and Surridge, who situate *Peter Ibbetson*'s visual technologies in the context of Victorian book illustration in *The Plot Thickens: Illustrated Victorian Serial Fiction from Dickens to Du Maurier* (Athens: Ohio University Press, 2019).

85. Zieger, *Mediated Mind*, 147.

86. Zieger, 151.

87. Galvan, *Sympathetic Medium*, 101, 126.

88. Vrettos, "Little Bags of Remembrance," para. 3.

89. Wilkie Collins similarly adapted such theories in the character of Franklin Blake in *The Moonstone*. The novel includes this quotation from a fictitious doctor: "There seems much ground for the belief, that every sensory impression which has once been recognised by the perceptive consciousness, is registered (so to speak) in the brain, and may be reproduced at some subsequent time, although there may be no consciousness of its existence in the mind during the whole intermediate period" (*The Moonstone*, ed. Sarah Kemp [London: Penguin, 1998], 390.)

90. Menke, *Telegraphic Realism*, 146.

91. Malcolm McCullough, *Ambient Commons: Attention in the Age of Embodied Information* (Cambridge, MA: MIT Press, 2013), 15.

92. McCullough, 49.

93. McCullough, 70; Patrick Stokes, *Digital Souls: A Philosophy of Online Death* (London: Bloomsbury, 2021), 67.

94. Samuel Smiles, *Self-Help: With Illustrations of Character and Conduct* (Cambridge: Cambridge University Press, 2014), 296, https://doi.org/10.1017/CBO9781107448933.

95. The apotheosis of using late nineteenth century media to imagine the spiritual afterlife may be Marie Corelli's *A Romance of Two Worlds* (1888). The novel reimagines Christianity as the perfection of "human electricity," which connects us to the beyond "like a sort of spiritual Atlantic cable." *A Romance of Two Worlds: A Novel* (Bernhard Tauchnitz, 1888), 278, http://books.google.com/books?id=BNIsAAAAYAAJ.

96. One notable example: Vannevar Bush proposed a "Memex" machine—a kind of proto-database—to answer the problem of information overload in scientific knowledge. Bush argued that such a machine works associatively, like the mind itself. "As We May Think," *The Atlantic*, July 1945, www.theatlantic.com/magazine/archive/1945/07/as-we-may-think/3881/?single_page=true.

97. Jeffrey Rosen, "The Web Means the End of Forgetting," *New York Times Magazine*, July 21, 2010, www.nytimes.com/2010/07/25/magazine/25privacy-t2.html; see also Kate Eichhorn, *The End of Forgetting: Growing Up with Social Media* (Cambridge, MA: Harvard University Press, 2019).

98. Viktor Mayer-Schönberger, *Delete: The Virtue of Forgetting in the Digital Age* (Princeton, NJ: Princeton University Press, 2009), 272.

99. David Brooks, "The Outsourced Brain," *The New York Times*, October 26, 2007, www.nytimes.com/2007/10/26/opinion/26brooks.html. The unsavory

colonial metaphor of "outsourcing" and external "servants" allows Brooks the fantasy of his digital autonomy: "the magic of the information age is that it allows us to know less. It provides us with external cognitive servants.... We can burden these servants and liberate ourselves."

100. Rosen, "The Web Means the End of Forgetting."

101. Stokes, *Digital Souls*, 13.

102. Turkle, *Reclaiming Conversation*, 311.

103. Wendy Hui Kyong Chun, "The Enduring Ephemeral, or the Future Is a Memory," *Critical Inquiry* 35, no. 1 (2008): 148–71, https://doi.org/10.1086/595632.

104. Mayer-Schönberger, *Delete*, 2; Terry Kuny, "A Digital Dark Ages? Challenges in the Preservation of Electronic Information," in *63rd IFLA Council and General Conference*, 1997.

105. Quoted in Jones, *Ctrl Z*, 104.

106. For a good overview of these issues, see Stokes, *Digital Souls*.

107. Quoted in Grant Bollmer, *Inhuman Networks: Social Media and the Archaeology of Connection* (New York: Bloomsbury Academic, 2016), 129.

108. Adrienne Matei, "What Should Happen to Our Data When We Die?," *New York Times*, July 24, 2021, www.nytimes.com/2021/07/24/style/what-should-happen-to-our-data-when-we-die.html.

109. Bollmer, *Inhuman Networks*, 121.

110. Hu, *Prehistory*, 124.

111. Susan Zieger, "'Du Maurierness' and the Mediatization of Memory," *Victorian Studies* 56, no. 1 (2013): 31–57.

112. Johanna Drucker, "Humanities Approaches to Graphical Display," *Digital Humanities Quarterly* 5, no. 1 (2011), http://digitalhumanities.org/dhq/vol/5/1/000091/000091.html.

113. Shoshana Zuboff, "Big Other: Surveillance Capitalism and the Prospects of an Information Civilization," *Journal of Information Technology* 30, no. 1 (2015): 75–89, https://doi.org/10.1057/jit.2015.5. Rockwell and Berendt note that consumers have gleefully joined in: with the proliferation of health tracking and personal activity apps and genetic testing sites, "surveillance has become spectacle." "Information Wants to Be Free, Or Does It?: The Ethics of Datafication," *Electronic Book Review*, 2017, http://electronicbookreview.com/essay/information-wants-to-be-free-or-does-it-the-ethics-of-datafication/.

114. Jean-François Blanchette and Deborah G. Johnson, "Data Retention and the Panoptic Society: The Social Benefits of Forgetfulness," *Information Society* 18, no. 1 (2002): 34, https://doi.org/10.1080/01972240252818216.

115. Jones, *Ctrl Z*, 7.

116. Jones, 8; Stuart A. Thompson and Charlie Warzel, "Twelve Million Phones, One Dataset, Zero Privacy," *New York Times*, December 19, 2019, https://www.nytimes.com/interactive/2019/12/19/opinion/location-tracking-cell-phone.html; Farhad Manjoo and Nadieh Bremer, "I Visited 47 Sites. Hundreds of Trackers Followed Me," *New York Times*, August 23, 2019, www.nytimes.com/interactive/2019/08/23/opinion/data-internet-privacy-tracking.html.

117. Sconce, *Haunted Media*, 25.

118. Jones, *Ctrl Z*, 2.

119. Eliot, *Middlemarch*, 838.

120. See Igarashi for a related argument about Shelley's "poetry of ambidiversion that allows for both connection and disconnection." *Connected Condition*, 35.

121. Quoted in Dames, *Physiology of the Novel*, 150.

122. Dames, 150.

123. Dames, 125.

124. Pinch, *Thinking about Other People*, 147.

125. George Eliot, *Daniel Deronda*, ed. Terence Cave (London: Penguin, 1995), 348, 349.

126. Eliot, 349.

127. Pinch, *Thinking about Other People*, 63.

128. Pinch, 150.

129. Samuel D. Warren and Louis D. Brandeis, "The Right to Privacy," *Harvard Law Review* 4, no. 5 (1890): 195, 197.

130. Warren and Brandeis, 195.

131. Warren and Brandeis, 214. It's worth noting they aim to protect the "sayings of a man" but the body of a woman. The article closes with a line about invading a man's house and castle.

132. Warren and Brandeis, 211.

133. Warren and Brandeis, 205.

134. Warren and Brandeis, 213.

135. Alan Westin, *Privacy and Freedom* (New York: Atheneum, 1967), 62, 339.

136. Westin, 59.

137. Westin, 313.

138. Warren and Brandeis, "Right to Privacy," 195.

139. Ashley Nicole Vavra, "The Right to Be Forgotten: An Archival Perspective," *American Archivist* 81, no. 1 (2018): 100–111, https://doi.org/10.17723/0360-9081-81.1.100.

140. Jones, *Ctrl Z*, 45.

141. Turkle, *Reclaiming Conversation*, 308.

142. Vavra, "Right to Be Forgotten," 102.
143. Mayer-Schönberger, *Delete*, 1.
144. Michael H. Keller and Gabriel J. X. Dance, "Child Abusers Run Rampant as Tech Companies Look the Other Way," *New York Times*, November 9, 2019, www.nytimes.com/interactive/2019/11/09/us/internet-child-sex-abuse.html.
145. Mayer-Schönberger, *Delete*, 125.
146. *Eric Schmidt at the Personal Democracy Forum*, 2007, www.youtube.com/watch?v=ut3yjR7HNLU.
147. Mayer-Schönberger, *Delete*, 111.
148. Jones, *Ctrl Z*, 113.
149. Bollmer, *Inhuman Networks*, 121; see also Matei, "What Should Happen to Our Data."
150. Keller and Dance, "Child Abusers Run Rampant."
151. Jones, *Ctrl Z*, 86.
152. *Eric Schmidt at the Personal Democracy Forum*.
153. Cory Doctorow, "'Out of Home Advertising': The Billboards That Spy on You as You Move through Public Spaces," *Boing Boing* (blog), November 21, 2019, https://boingboing.net/2019/11/21/to-opt-out-just-die-4.html.
154. Jones, *Ctrl Z*, 78.
155. Stokes, *Digital Souls*.
156. Julie E. Cohen, "What Privacy Is For," *Harvard Law Review* 126, no. 7 (2013): 1904–33.
157. Ina Blom, "Introduction: Rethinking Social Memory: Archives, Technology, and the Social," in *Memory in Motion: Archives, Technology, and the Social*, ed. Ina Blom, Trond Lundemo, and Eivind Røssaak (Amsterdam: Amsterdam University Press, 2016), 27.
158. Rockwell and Berendt, "Information Wants to Be Free."
159. Édouard Glissant, *Poetics of Relation*, trans. Betsy Wing (Ann Arbor: University of Michigan Press, 1997), 120.
160. Turkle, *Alone Together*, 234.
161. boyd, *It's Complicated*, 127.
162. Blanchette and Johnson, "Data Retention."
163. Jones, *Ctrl Z*, 9–13.
164. Davis, *The Other Side of Empathy*, 97.

Chapter 3

1. Henry James, "In the Cage," in *Tales of Henry James*, ed. Christof Wegelin and Henry B. Wonham, 2nd ed. (New York: W. W. Norton, 2002), 229. Hereafter cited in line.

2. Ryan Heuser and Le-Khac Long, "A Quantitative Literary History of 2,958 Nineteenth-Century British Novels: The Semantic Cohort Method," Pamphlets of the Stanford Literary Lab (Stanford, CA: Stanford Literary Lab, 2012), 46, http://litlab.stanford.edu/LiteraryLabPamphlet4.pdf.

3. Marvin, *When Old Technologies Were New*.

4. Jay Clayton, "The Voice in the Machine: Hazlitt, Hardy, James," in *Language Machines: Technologies of Literary and Cultural Production* (New York: Routledge, 1997), 226.

5. Richard Menke, "Telegraphic Realism: Henry James's *In the Cage*," *PMLA* 115, no. 5 (2000): 976.

6. Cecire, "Ways of Not Reading"; Morgan, "Critical Empathy"; Igarashi, "Statistical Analysis."

7. Dames, *Physiology of the Novel*.

8. Cecire, "Ways of Not Reading," 283.

9. Jennifer Wicke, "Henry James's Second Wave," *Henry James Review* 10, no. 2 (1989): 146–51; Otis, *Networking*; Thurschwell, *Literature, Technology, and Magical Thinking*; Nicola Nixon, "The Reading Gaol of Henry James's *In the Cage*," *ELH* 66, no. 1 (1999): 179–201; Clayton, "Voice in the Machine"; Christopher Keep, "Touching at a Distance: Telegraphy, Gender, and Henry James's *In the Cage*," in *Media, Technology, and Literature in the Nineteenth Century: Image, Sound, Touch* (Surrey, England: Ashgate, 2011), 239–55; Menke, "Telegraphic Realism"; Jennifer Sorensen Emery-Peck, "'As She Called It': Henry James Makes Free with a Female Telegraphist," *Henry James Review* 31, no. 3 (2010): 288–96; Galvan, *Sympathetic Medium*.

10. Henry James, *The Novels and Tales of Henry James*, vol. 11 (New York: C. Scribner's Sons, 1908), xviii–xix, https://catalog.hathitrust.org/Record/001423157.

11. James, 11: xix.

12. Leon Edel, "The Architecture of Henry James's 'New York Edition,'" *New England Quarterly* 24, no. 2 (1951): 169–78, https://doi.org/10.2307/361360.

13. Otis, *Networking*, 177.

14. Henry James and Percy Lubbock, *The Novels and Tales of Henry James*, vol. 15 (New York: C. Scribner's Sons, 1907), 251, https://catalog.hathitrust.org/Record/001423157.

15. James and Lubbock, 15: 263.

16. Catherine Nicholson offers a different history of distant reading with early modern commonplace books: mechanisms by which Renaissance readers aggregated and sorted texts, not reading them, but collecting them and sifting with the tools of rhetoric. "Algorithm and Analogy: Distant Reading in 1598," *PMLA* 132, no. 3 (2017): 643–50, https://doi.org/10.1632/pmla.2017.132.3.643.

17. Igarashi, "Statistical Analysis," 486.

18. Hockey, "History of Humanities Computing."

19. Benjamin Morgan, *The Outward Mind: Materialist Aesthetics in Victorian Science and Literature* (Chicago: University of Chicago Press, 2017), 236.

20. T. C. Mendenhall, "The Characteristic Curves of Composition," *Science* 9, no. 214 (1887): 237-49, https://doi.org/10.2307/1764604; Morgan, *Outward Mind*, 235.

21. Mendenhall, "Characteristic Curves," 238.

22. Mendenhall, 239, original emphasis.

23. Mendenhall, 245.

24. Mendenhall, 242.

25. Mendenhall, 245.

26. Jean-Baptiste Michel et al., "Quantitative Analysis of Culture Using Millions of Digitized Books," *Science* 331, no. 6014 (2011): 176-82, https://doi.org/10.1126/science.1199644.

27. Michel et al., 1.

28. Michel et al., 5.

29. Michel et al., 1.

30. Lisa Marie Rhody, "Beyond Darwinian Distance: Situating Distant Reading in a Feminist *Ut Pictura Poesis* Tradition," *PMLA* 132, no. 3 (2017): 659-67, https://doi.org/10.1632/pmla.2017.132.3.659.

31. Igarashi, "Statistical Analysis"; see also Lydia H. Liu, "iSpace: Printed English after Joyce, Shannon, and Derrida," *Critical Inquiry* 32, no. 3 (2006): 516-50, https://doi.org/10.1086/505377.

32. Ted Underwood, "A Genealogy of Distant Reading," *Digital Humanities Quarterly* 11, no. 2 (2017), www.digitalhumanities.org/dhq/vol/11/2/000317/000317.html; Dames, *Physiology of the Novel*, 1-3.

33. Morgan, "Critical Empathy," 52.

34. Morgan, *The Outward Mind*, 252.

35. Morgan, 237.

36. Alan Liu, "Close, Distant, and Unexpected Reading: The Modern Paradigm of Literary Analysis," Australasian Association for Digital Humanities, Australian National University, Canberra, Australia, March 28, 2012, http://aa-dh.org/conferences/conference-2/; Ryan Cordell, "'Taken Possession Of': The Reprinting and Reauthorship of Hawthorne's 'Celestial Railroad' in the Antebellum Religious Press," *Digital Humanities Quarterly* 7, no. 1 (2013), www.digitalhumanities.org/dhq/vol/7/1/000144/000144.html; Alison Booth, "Mid-Range Reading: Not a Manifesto," *PMLA* 132, no. 3 (2017): 620-27, https://doi.org/10.1632/pmla.2017.132.3.620.

37. Franco Moretti, "Conjectures on World Literature," *New Left Review* 1 (February 2000), www.newleftreview.org/?view=2094.

38. Ted Underwood, *Distant Horizons: Digital Evidence and Literary Change* (Chicago: University of Chicago Press, 2019), xi, xxi.

39. Katherine Bode, "The Equivalence of 'Close' and 'Distant' Reading; or, Toward a New Object for Data-Rich Literary History," *Modern Language Quarterly* 78, no. 1 (2017): 77–106, https://doi.org/10.1215/00267929-3699787; Underwood, *Distant Horizons*; Andrew Piper, *Enumerations: Data and Literary Study* (Chicago: University of Chicago Press, 2018).

40. Piper, *Enumerations*, 9.

41. Heuser and Long, "Quantitative Literary History," 46.

42. Morgan, "Critical Empathy," 50.

43. Dames, *The Physiology of the Novel*, 25.

44. Quoted in Cecire, "Ways of Not Reading," 289.

45. Cecire, 291.

46. Cecire, 281, 295.

47. Melissa Terras, "Father Busa's Female Punch Card Operatives," *Melissa Terras' Blog* (blog), October 15, 2013, http://melissaterras.blogspot.com/2013/10/for-ada-lovelace-day-father-busas.html.

48. Buurma and Heffernan, "Search and Replace."

49. Lauren F. Klein, "Dimensions of Scale: Invisible Labor, Editorial Work, and the Future of Quantitative Literary Studies," *PMLA* 135, no. 1 (2020): 25, https://doi.org/10.1632/pmla.2020.135.1.23.

50. Nixon, "Reading Gaol," 194.

51. Nixon, 195.

52. Katherine Bode, *Reading by Numbers: Recalibrating the Literary Field* (New York: Anthem Press, 2012), 7.

53. Nan Z. Da, "The Computational Case against Computational Literary Studies," *Critical Inquiry* 45, no. 3 (2019): 607, 634, https://doi.org/10.1086/702594.

54. For roundups of these critiques, see Genie Babb, "Victorian Roots and Branches: 'The Statistical Century' as Foundation to the Digital Humanities," *Literature Compass* 15, no. 9 (2018): 3, https://doi.org/10.1111/lic3.12487; Bode, *Reading by Numbers*, 7.

55. Dames, *Physiology of the Novel*, 7.

56. Dames, 39.

57. Dames, 39, 212.

58. Edmund Burke Huey, *The Psychology and Pedagogy of Reading: With a Review of the History of Reading and Writing and of Methods, Texts, and Hygiene in Reading* (New York: Macmillan, 1908).

59. Sue Currell, "Streamlining the Eye: Speed Reading and the Revolution of Words, 1870–1940," in Acland, *Residual Media*, 347.

60. Currell, 363.
61. Charles R. Acland, "The Swift View: Tachistoscopes and the Residual Modern," in Acland, *Residual Media*, 363.
62. Quoted in Acland, 377.
63. Currell, "Streamlining the Eye," 346.
64. Huey, *The Psychology and Pedagogy of Reading*, 156.
65. Currell, "Streamlining the Eye," 350.
66. Quoted in Currell, 350.
67. Megan Ward, *Seeming Human: Artificial Intelligence and Victorian Realist Character* (Columbus: Ohio State University Press, 2018), 119.
68. Ward, 98.
69. Ward, 107.
70. Ward, 100, 117.
71. Ward, 99.
72. Otis, *Networking*.
73. Thurschwell, *Literature, Technology, and Magical Thinking*, 29.
74. Thurschwell, 29.
75. Quoted in Acland, "Swift View," 354.
76. Ward, *Seeming Human*, 99.
77. Ward, 99.
78. Adrian Mackenzie, *Machine Learners: Archaeology of a Data Practice* (Cambridge, MA: MIT Press, 2017), 1. Long and So offer a useful definition: "Machine learning refers to a whole suite of statistical algorithms that treat every text as an amalgam of certain quantifiable features. They assume these features are distributed across texts in ways that help to identify differences between them and attempt to learn these features in order to classify or predict the category or group to which a text is likely to belong." "Literary Pattern Recognition: Modernism between Close Reading and Machine Learning," *Critical Inquiry* 42, no. 2 (2016): 250.
79. Mackenzie, *Machine Learners*, 23.
80. Mackenzie, 14.
81. Clayton, "The Voice in the Machine," 226. Indeed, much has been written about her role as "interface" or as an embodiment of telegraphic "mediation"; see Menke, "Telegraphic Realism."
82. Igarashi, "Statistical Analysis."
83. Nixon, "Reading Gaol," 194.
84. Katherine Stubbs, "Telegraphy's Corporeal Fictions," in Gitelman and Pingree, eds., *New Media*, 95; see also Jennifer L. Fleissner, "Dictation Anxiety: The Stenographer's Stake in Dracula," *Nineteenth-Century Contexts* 22, no. 3 (2000): 417–55, https://doi.org/10.1080/08905490008583519.

85. Marvin, *When Old Technologies Were New*, 84.

86. Stubbs, "Telegraphy's Corporeal Fictions," 95.

87. Christopher Keep, "Blinded by the Type: Gender and Information Technology at the Turn of the Century," *Nineteenth-Century Contexts* 23, no. 1 (2001): 149–73, https://doi.org/10.1080/08905490108583536; Jennifer Wicke, "Vampiric Typewriting: Dracula and Its Media," *ELH* 59, no. 2 (1992): 467–93, https://doi.org/10.2307/2873351.

88. Catherine D'Ignazio and Lauren Klein, *Data Feminism* (Cambridge, MA: MIT Press, 2020), 2.

89. Hicks, *Programmed Inequality*.

90. D'Ignazio and Klein, *Data Feminism*, 7–8.

91. Bush, "As We May Think."

92. Li Cornfeld, "Babes in Tech Land: Expo Labor as Capitalist Technology's Erotic Body," *Feminist Media Studies* 18, no. 2 (2018): 205–20, https://doi.org/10.1080/14680777.2017.1298146.

93. Bush, "As We May Think."

94. Simone Natale, "To Believe in Siri: A Critical Analysis of AI Voice Assistants," *Communicative Figurations*, no. 32 (2020).

95. "146 Funny Things to Ask Siri—The Ultimate Siri List," Smarthome.news, 2020, www.smarthome.news/how-tos/apple/funny-things-to-ask-siri.

96. Karen Haslam and Jason Cross, "More Than 50 Fun and Funny Things to Ask Siri," *Macworld*, 2020, www.macworld.com/article/672515/fun-and-funny-things-to-ask-siri.html.

97. Leopoldina Fortunati, "Immaterial Labor and Its Machinization," *Ephemera* 7, no. 1 (2007): 140, 149.

98. Jennifer Rhee, *The Robotic Imaginary: The Human and the Price of Dehumanized Labor* (Minneapolis: University of Minnesota Press, 2018), 31.

99. Marc Hill and Susan Bennett, "I'm the Voice of Siri: And No, Apple Didn't Pay (or Warn) Me," Cracked.com, February 18, 2016, www.cracked.com/personal-experiences-2108-i-am-siris-voice-4-bizarre-realities.html.

100. Tom Standage and Seth Stevenson, "The Box That AI Lives In," Secret History of the Future, accessed September 28, 2018, www.slate.com/articles/podcasts/secret_history_of_the_future/2018/09/a_200_year_old_chess_playing_robot_explains_the_internet.html; Sarah Kessler, *Gigged: The End of the Job and the Future of Work* (New York: St. Martin's Press, 2018).

101. Li Yuan, "How Cheap Labor Drives China's A.I. Ambitions," *New York Times*, November 25, 2018, www.nytimes.com/2018/11/25/business/china-artificial-intelligence-labeling.html; see also Kristy Milland, "A Mechanical Turk Worker's Perspective," *Journal of Media Ethics* 31, no. 4 (2016): 263–64, https://doi.org/10.1080/23736992.2016.1228813.

102. Billy Perrigo, "OpenAI Used Kenyan Workers on Less Than $2 Per Hour to Make ChatGPT Less Toxic," *Time*, January 18, 2023, https://time.com/6247678/openai-chatgpt-kenya-workers/.

103. Kate Crawford and Vladan Joler, "Anatomy of an AI System: The Amazon Echo as an Anatomical Map of Human Labor, Data, and Planetary Resources," AI Now Institute and Share Lab, 2018, www.anatomyof.ai.

104. For a good overview, see Bethany Layne, "'Henry Would Never Know He Hadn't Written It Himself': The Implications of 'Dictation' for Jamesian Style," *Henry James Review* 35, no. 3 (2014): 248–56, https://doi.org/10.1353/hjr.2014.0039. For the typewriter's "dilemma of indeterminate authorial agency," see Gitelman, *Scripts, Grooves, and Writing Machines*, 213.

105. Here, I am arguing with Keep, "Blinded by the Type."

106. Theodora Bosanquet, *Henry James at Work*, ed. Lyall H. Powers (Ann Arbor: University of Michigan Press, 2006), 13.

107. Thurschwell, *Literature, Technology, and Magical Thinking*, 90.

108. See the useful section explaining these interests in Bosanquet, *Henry James at Work*.

109. Bosanquet, 111.

110. Quoted in Thurschwell, *Literature, Technology, and Magical Thinking*, 102n42.

111. Thurschwell, 114.

112. Daniel Mark Fogel, "Theodora Bosanquet, Virginia Woolf, and the Missing Women," *Henry James Review* 39, no. 3 (2018): 307–13, https://doi.org/10.1353/hjr.2018.0029.

113. Leah Henrickson, "Towards a New Sociology of the Text: The Hermeneutics of Algorithmic Authorship" (PhD Dissertation, Loughborough University, 2019).

114. Emily M. Bender et al., "On the Dangers of Stochastic Parrots: Can Language Models Be Too Big?," in *FAccT '21: Proceedings of the 2021 ACM Conference on Fairness, Accountability, and Transparency*, Conference on Fairness, Accountability, and Transparency (FAccT '21), Virtual Event, ACM, 2021, 616, https://doi.org/10.1145/3442188.3445922.

115. Leah Henrickson, "Chatting with the Dead: The Hermeneutics of Thanabots," *Media, Culture, and Society* (2023), https://doi.org/10.1177/01634437221147626.

116. Sarah Allison, "Authorship after AI," *Public Books*, June 25, 2019, www.publicbooks.org/authorship-after-ai/.

117. Sconce, *Haunted Media*, 26.

118. Stokes, *Digital Souls*, 4.

Chapter 4

1. Max Simon Nordau, *Degeneration* (London: William Heinemann, 1898), 171, https://catalog.hathitrust.org/Record/007668760.

2. Wendy Hui Kyong Chun et al., "The Dark Side of the Digital Humanities," in *Debates in the Digital Humanities 2016* (University of Minnesota Press, 2016), https://dhdebates.gc.cuny.edu/read/untitled/section/ca35736b-0020-4ac6-9ce7-88c6e9ff1bba.

3. Robert Louis Stevenson, *The Strange Case of Dr Jekyll and Mr Hyde*, ed. Martin A. Danahay (Peterborough, ON: Broadview, 2005). Hereafter cited as *Jekyll and Hyde* with page numbers in line.

4. Arata, "Sedulous Ape."

5. Menke, *Literature, Print Culture, and Media Technologies*, 21.

6. Menke, 4–5; see also Gitelman, *Paper Knowledge*, x.

7. Menke, *Literature, Print Culture, and Media Technologies*, 11.

8. Guillory, "Genesis," 347.

9. Bolter and Grusin, *Remediation*.

10. Arata, "Sedulous Ape."

11. Menke, *Literature, Print Culture, and Media Technologies*, 140.

12. Apparently, Stevenson's contemporaries criticized his treatment of the individuality of handwriting: F. W. H. Myers complained it showed a "want of familiarity on Stevenson's part 'with recent psycho-physical discussions.'" Quoted in Arata, "Sedulous Ape," 252.

13. Carlo Ginzburg, *Clues, Myths, and the Historical Method*, trans. Anne C. Tedeschi (Baltimore: Johns Hopkins University Press, 1989), 102.

14. Gitelman, *Scripts, Grooves, and Writing Machines*, 224.

15. Arata, "Sedulous Ape," 245–46.

16. Walter Besant and Henry James, *The Art of Fiction* (Boston: Cupples, Upham, 1885), 8, https://catalog.hathitrust.org/Record/003609491.

17. Besant and James, 4.

18. Arata, "Sedulous Ape," 246–47.

19. Besant and James, *Art of Fiction*, 63.

20. Menke, *Literature, Print Culture, and Media Technologies*, 73.

21. George Gissing, *New Grub Street*, ed. John Goode (Oxford: Oxford University Press, 2009), 459.

22. Gissing, 107.

23. Arata, "Sedulous Ape," 251–52.

24. Arata, 241–42.

25. Jodey Castricano, "Much Ado about Handwriting: Countersigning with the Other Hand in Stevenson's *The Strange Case of Dr. Jekyll and Mr. Hyde*," *Romanticism on the Net*, no. 44 (2006), https://doi.org/10.7202/014001ar.

26. Included in the appendices in Stevenson, *Jekyll and Hyde*, 139.
27. Castricano, "Much Ado about Handwriting."
28. Arata, "Sedulous Ape," 233.
29. Sharon Aronofsky Weltman, *Victorians on Broadway: Literature, Adaptation, and the Modern American Musical* (Charlottesville: University of Virginia Press, 2020), n.p.
30. Weltman.
31. Bolter and Grusin, *Remediation*, 34.
32. "Lyceum Theatre," *Daily Telegraph*, London, August 6, 1888, quoted in Martin A. Danahay and Alex Chisolm, eds., *Jekyll and Hyde Dramatized: The 1887 Richard Mansfield Script and the Evolution of the Story on Stage* (Jefferson, NC: McFarland, 2005), 124.
33. Danahay and Chisolm, 15.
34. Danahay and Chisolm, 38.
35. *Pall Mall Gazette*, September 1, 1888, in Danahay and Chisolm, 128–29.
36. Danahay and Chisolm, 34.
37. Danahay and Chisolm, 29.
38. Susan Cook argues that, while photography is not mentioned in the story, it is "steeped in late Victorian visual culture" and the possibilities of double exposure. *Victorian Negatives: Literary Culture and the Dark Side of Photography in the Nineteenth Century* (Albany: State University of New York Press, 2019), 90.
39. Daniel A. Novak, "Richard Mansfield as Jekyll and Hyde: Theatre, Photography, and Composite Time," *Victorian Review* 48, no. 1 (2022): 11, https://doi.org/10.1353/vcr.2022.0017.
40. Jonathan Sterne, *The Audible Past: Cultural Origins of Sound Reproduction* (Durham, NC: Duke University Press, 2003), 265.
41. Galvan, *Sympathetic Medium*, 66.
42. Martin, *"Hello Central?,"* 69.
43. Len Spencer, *Dr. Jekyll and Mr. Hyde* (Philadelphia: Victor 4233, 1904), www.loc.gov/jukebox/recordings/detail/id/659.
44. Jason Camlot, "Early Talking Books: Spoken Recordings and Recitation Anthologies, 1880–1920," *Book History* 6, no. 1 (2003): 151, https://doi.org/10.1353/bh.2004.0004.
45. Sterne, *Audible Past*, 244.
46. Tom Gunning, "'Now You See It, Now You Don't': The Temporality of the Cinema of Attractions," *Velvet Light Trap* 32 (1993): 3–12.
47. Sterne, *Audible Past*, 182.
48. Jason Camlot, "The Three-Minute Victorian Novel: Remediating Dickens into Sound," in *Audiobooks, Literature, and Sound Studies*, ed. Matthew Rubery (New York: Routledge, 2011), 28.

49. Camlot, "Early Talking Books," 158.

50. Quoted in Jason Camlot, *Phonopoetics: The Making of Early Literary Recordings* (Stanford, CA: Stanford University Press, 2019).

51. Camlot, "Three-Minute Victorian Novel," 26.

52. Sterne, *Audible Past*, 242.

53. Luella Forepaugh, George F. Fish, and Robert Louis Stevenson, *Dr. Jekyll and Mr. Hyde; or, A Mis-Spent Life; a Drama in Four Acts* (New York: S. French, 1897), 40, https://catalog.hathitrust.org/Record/001908382.

54. "Dr. Jekyll and Mr. Hyde," *Variety*, April 1920, 93.

55. Frederick James Smith, "The Newest Photoplays in Review," *Motion Picture Classic*, June 1920, 45.

56. Burns Mantle, "The Shadow Stage," *Photoplay*, June 1920, 66.

57. Robert Berensten, "Music Week Demonstration," *American Organist*, 1920, 242.

58. Berensten, 243.

59. Berensten, 243.

60. Julie Hubbert, ed., *Celluloid Symphonies: Texts and Contexts in Film Music History* (Berkeley: University of California Press, 2011), 30; Rick Altman, *Silent Film Sound* (New York: Columbia University Press, 2004), 337.

61. Matthew Rubery, "The First Talking Books in Britain," *Audiobook History* (blog), February 19, 2014, https://audiobookhistory.wordpress.com/2014/02/19/the-first-talking-books-in-britain/.

62. "The Phonograph," *New York Times*, November 7, 1877, 4. Quoted in Matthew Rubery, "Canned Literature: The Book after Edison," *Book History* 16, no. 1 (2013): 218, https://doi.org/10.1353/bh.2013.0012.

63. Rubery, 235.

64. Matthew Rubery, *The Untold Story of the Talking Book* (Cambridge, MA: Harvard University Press, 2016), 155.

65. Rubery, "Canned Literature," 220.

66. Thomas A. Edison, "The Phonograph and Its Future," *North American Review* 126, no. 262 (1878): 533.

67. Rubery, "Canned Literature," 35.

68. Kittler, *Gramophone, Film, Typewriter*, 231.

69. Birkerts, *Gutenberg Elegies*, 145; Rubery, *Untold Story*, 60.

70. Arthur Copland, "Talking-Book or Reading-Book?," *The New Beacon: A Magazine Devoted to the Interests of the Blind*, February 15, 1937, 34, 33.

71. Copland, 34.

72. Matthew Rubery, ed., *Audiobooks, Literature, and Sound Studies* (New York: Routledge, 2011), 3; Birkerts, *Gutenberg Elegies*, 146.

73. Birkerts, *Gutenberg Elegies*, ix.

74. Quoted in Birkerts, 121.

75. For discussion of the quote's popularity and original context, see Gilbert Achcar, "Morbid Symptoms," *International Socialist Review*, 2017, https://isreview.org/issue/108/morbid-symptoms/index.html.

76. Nordau, *Degeneration*, 37, 39.

77. Sarah Allison, *Reductive Reading: A Syntax of Victorian Moralizing* (Baltimore: Johns Hopkins University Press, 2018), 24.

78. Amanda Anderson, *The Way We Argue Now: A Study in the Cultures of Theory* (Princeton, NJ: Princeton University Press, 2006), 9.

79. Anderson, 12.

80. Anderson, 11.

81. Matt Erlin, "Digital Humanities Masterplots," *Digital Literary Studies* 1, no. 1 (2016), https://doi.org/10.18113/P8dls1159753 (original emphasis).

82. Besant and James, *Art of Fiction*, 64.

83. Andrew Piper and Matt Erlin, "Humanities: Let the Hypothesis Testing Begin," *Public Books* (blog), October 22, 2021, www.publicbooks.org/humanities-let-the-hypothesis-testing-begin/.

84. Arata, "Sedulous Ape," 233.

85. Mark Garrett Cooper and John Marx, "Crisis, Crisis, Crisis: Big Media and the Humanities Workforce," *Differences* 24, no. 3 (2013): 151, https://doi.org/10.1215/10407391-2391977.

86. Kirschenbaum, "What Is Digital Humanities and What's It Doing in English Departments?," 59.

87. Cooper and Marx, "Crisis, Crisis, Crisis," 131.

88. Mark Garrett Cooper and John Marx, *Media U: How the Need to Win Audiences Has Shaped Higher Education* (New York: Columbia University Press, 2018).

89. Wellmon, "Loyal Workers."

90. Pannapacker, "The MLA and the Digital Humanities."

91. Amy E. Earhart, "Digital Humanities Futures: Conflict, Power, and Public Knowledge," *Digital Studies / Le Champ Numérique* 6, no. 1 (2016), https://doi.org/10.16995/dscn.1.

92. Stanley Fish, "The Old Order Changeth," *Opinionator Blog, New York Times*, December 26, 2011, http://opinionator.blogs.nytimes.com/2011/12/26/the-old-order-changeth/.

93. Stanley Fish, "The Digital Humanities and the Transcending of Mortality," *Opinionator Blog, New York Times*, January 9, 2012, http://opinionator.blogs.nytimes.com/2012/01/09/the-digital-humanities-and-the-transcending-of-mortality/.

94. Lauren F. Klein, "Distant Reading after Moretti," MLA Convention, New York, January 5, 2018, http://lklein.com/digital-humanities/distant-reading-after-moretti/.

95. Cooper and Marx, "Crisis, Crisis, Crisis," 138.

96. Jonathan Arac, "Anglo-Globalism?," *New Left Review*, no. 16 (2002): n.p.

97. Franco Moretti, *Graphs, Maps, Trees: Abstract Models for a Literary History* (London: Verso, 2005).

98. Moretti, "Conjectures."

99. Allison, *Reductive Reading*, 26.

100. Richard Grusin, "The Dark Side of Digital Humanities: Dispatches from Two Recent MLA Conventions," *Differences* 25, no. 1 (2014): 87, https://doi.org/10.1215/10407391-2420009.

101. Grusin, 80.

102. Grusin, 87.

103. Grusin, 80.

104. Kirschenbaum, "What Is 'Digital Humanities,' and Why Are They Saying Such Terrible Things about It?"

105. Liu, "Digital Humanities and Academic Change," 26.

106. David Golumbia, "Death of a Discipline," *Differences* 25, no. 1 (2014): 172, https://doi.org/10.1215/10407391-2420033.

107. Bianco, "This Digital Humanities Which Is Not One."

108. Judith Butler, "Imitation and Gender Insubordination," in *Inside/out: Lesbian Theories, Gay Theories*, ed. Diana Fuss (New York: Routledge, 1991), 1.

109. Rita Raley, "Digital Humanities for the Next Five Minutes," *Differences* 25, no. 1 (2014): 27, https://doi.org/10.1215/10407391-2419991 (original emphasis).

110. Alison Booth and Miriam Posner, "Introduction—The Materials at Hand," *PMLA* 135, no. 1 (2020): 9, https://doi.org/10.1632/pmla.2020.135.1.9.

111. Ellen Rooney and Elizabeth Weed, "Editor's Note," *differences* 25, no. 1 (2014): iv, https://doi.org/10.1215/10407391-2432538.

112. Da, "Computational Case."

113. Patrick Jagoda, "Computational Literary Studies: A Critical Inquiry Online Forum," *In the Moment* (blog), March 31, 2019, https://critinq.wordpress.com/2019/03/31/computational-literary-studies-a-critical-inquiry-online-forum/.

114. Jacqueline Wernimont, "Sex and Numbers: Pleasure, Reproduction, and Digital Biopolitics," Digital Humanities Summer Institute, Victoria, BC, June 3, 2019, http://jwernimont.com/sex-and-numbers-pleasure-reproduction-and-digital-biopolitics.

Chapter 5

1. Cornelius Walford, *The Outline of a Scheme for a Dictionary of Periodical Literature* (London: Elliot Stock, 1883), 3-4, https://books.google.com/books?id=yZMDAAAAQAAJ.

2. Patrick Leary, "Googling the Victorians," *Journal of Victorian Culture* 10, no. 1 (2005): 15, https://doi.org/10.3366/jvc.2005.10.1.72.

3. Elizabeth Carolyn Miller, "Reading in Review: The Victorian Book Review in the New Media Moment," *Victorian Periodicals Review* 49, no. 4 (2016): 626, https://doi.org/10.1353/vpr.2016.0042.

4. "Cheap Literature," *British Quarterly Review* 29 (April 1859): 316.

5. Michael Wolff, "Charting the Golden Stream: Thoughts on a Directory of Victorian Periodicals," *Victorian Periodicals Newsletter*, no. 13 (1971): 29.

6. Robert Darnton, "The Library in the New Age," *New York Review of Books*, June 12, 2008, www.nybooks.com/articles/archives/2008/jun/12/the-library-in-the-new-age/.

7. Irene Tucker, "Tilling Two Cultures," *Victorian Studies* 60, no. 1 (2017): 86.

8. Ward, "Theorizing the Historical Middle."

9. Nancy Armstrong, "The Victorian Archive and Its Secret," *Nineteenth-Century Contexts* 34, no. 5 (2012): 380, https://doi.org/10.1080/08905495.2012.738075.

10. I told an earlier version of this story in "An Archaeology of Victorian Newspapers," *Victorian Periodicals Review* 49, no. 4 (2016): 546-77, https://doi.org/10.1353/vpr.2016.0039. Additional research has been included here. Readers already familiar with that piece may want to skip ahead to an explanation of Findmypast, the British Newspaper Archive, and the establishment of Victorian studies as a field.

11. Hiscoe, "NCSU Libraries."

12. Massari, "Gale Leads to Advance Academic Research."

13. In Victorian periodicals studies, early precedents for working with commercial data include Frederick W. Gibbs and Daniel J. Cohen, "A Conversation with Data: Prospecting Victorian Words and Ideas," *Victorian Studies* 54, no. 1 (2011): 69-77; Dallas Liddle, "Reflections on 20,000 Victorian Newspapers: 'Distant Reading' The Times Using The Times Digital Archive," *Journal of Victorian Culture* 17, no. 2 (2012): 230-37, https://doi.org/10.1080/13555502.2012.683151; Albert D. Pionke, "Excavating Victorian Cuba in the British Periodicals Database," *Victorian Periodicals Review* 47, no. 3 (2014): 369-97, https://doi.org/10.1353/vpr.2014.0038.

14. I do not mean to mischaracterize this collection as being error prone. Front pages with advertisements offer special challenges for OCR software.

And "anything pre-1900 will be fortunate to exceed 85% accuracy," according to Simon Tanner, Trevor Muñoz, and Pich Hemy Ros, "Measuring Mass Text Digitization Quality and Usefulness: Lessons Learned from Assessing the OCR Accuracy of the British Library's 19th Century Online Newspaper Archive," *D-Lib Magazine* 15, no. 7/8 (2009), https://doi.org/10.1045/july2009-munoz; see also Ian Milligan, "Illusionary Order: Cautionary Notes for Online Newspapers," ActiveHistory.ca, March 26, 2012, http://activehistory.ca/2012/03/illusionary-order/.

15. Lisa Gitelman and Virginia Jackson, "Introduction," in *"Raw Data" Is an Oxymoron*, ed. Lisa Gitelman, (Cambridge, MA: MIT Press, 2013), 1–14.

16. Ray Abruzzi, Luisa Calè, and Ana Parejo Vadillo, "Gale Digital Collections: Ray Abruzzi Interviewed by Luisa Calè and Ana Parejo Vadillo," *19: Interdisciplinary Studies in the Long Nineteenth Century*, no. 21 (2015), http://19.bbk.ac.uk/articles/753/.

17. James Mussell, *The Nineteenth-Century Press in the Digital Age* (New York: Palgrave Macmillan, 2012), 152.

18. Molly O'Hagan Hardy, "Digitization," *Early American Studies: An Interdisciplinary Journal* 16, no. 4 (2018): 637–42, https://doi.org/10.1353/eam.2018.0028. See also Hardy's excellent study of precursors to the American Antiquarian Society's digital collections: "Bibliographic Enterprise and the Digital Age: Charles Evans and the Making of Early American Literature," *American Literary History* 29, no. 2 (2017): 331–51, https://doi.org/10.1093/alh/ajx002.

19. Drew Baker, Anna Bentkowska-Kafel, and Hugh Denard, eds., *Paradata and Transparency in Virtual Heritage*, Digital Research in the Arts and Humanities (Farnham, Surrey, England: Ashgate, 2012).

20. Sherratt, "Stories for Machines."

21. Matthew G. Kirschenbaum, *Mechanisms: New Media and the Forensic Imagination* (Cambridge, MA: MIT Press, 2008); Matthew Kirschenbaum, "Books.Files," *Archives Journal* 5 (2017), www.archivejournal.net/issue/5/notes-queries/books-files/.

22. Bonnie Mak, "Archaeology of a Digitization," *Journal of the American Society for Information Science and Technology* 65, no. 8 (2014): 26, https://doi.org/10.1002/asi.23061.

23. Ernst, *Digital Memory and the Archive*.

24. Mussell, "Teaching Nineteenth-Century Periodicals," 205–6.

25. Helle Strandgaard Jensen, "Digital Archival Literacy for (All) Historians," *Media History* 27, no. 2 (2021): 251–65, https://doi.org/10.1080/13688804.2020.1779047. Along with scholars referenced elsewhere in this chapter, some remarkable case studies include Cecire, "Ways of Not Reading"; Michael

Gavin, "How to Think about EEBO," *Textual Cultures* 11, no. 1-2 (2017): 70-105, https://doi.org/10.14434/textual.v11i1-2.23570; Kaspar Beelen et al., "Bias and Representativeness in Digitized Newspaper Collections: Introducing the Environmental Scan," *Digital Scholarship in the Humanities*, July 14, 2022, https://doi.org/10.1093/llc/fqac037; Cassidy Holahan, "Rummaging in the Dark: ECCO as Opaque Digital Archive," *Eighteenth-Century Studies* 54, no. 4 (2021): 803-26, https://doi.org/10.1353/ecs.2021.0093; Benjamin Lee, "Compounded Mediation: A Data Archaeology of the Newspaper Navigator Dataset," *Digital Humanities Quarterly* 15, no. 4 (2021), www.digitalhumanities.org/dhq/vol/15/4/000578/000578.html; Katherine C. Wilson, "Melodrama Remediated: The Political Economy of Literary Database Paratexts," in *Examining Paratextual Theory and Its Applications in Digital Culture*, ed. Nadine Desrochers and Daniel Apollon (Hershey, PA: Information Science Reference, 2014), 190-208, www.igi-global.com/chapter/melodrama-remediated/122542; M. H. Beals and Emily Bell, "The Atlas of Digitised Newspapers and Metadata," Oceanic Exchanges, 2020, www.digitisednewspapers.net/.

26. In his initial bibliographic analysis of digitized nineteenth-century US newspapers in the "Chronicling America" collection, Cordell argues that such remediations can be properly conceived as new editions and that "acknowledging digitised historical texts as new editions is an important step . . . to developing media-specific approaches to the digital that more effectively exploit its affordances; more responsibly represent the material, social, and economic circumstances of its production; and more carefully delineate with its limitations." "'Q i-Jtb the Raven': Taking Dirty OCR Seriously," MLA, Austin, TX, 2016, http://ryancordell.org/research/qijtb-the-raven/.

27. Laurel Brake, "London Letter: Researching the Historical Press, Now and Here," *Victorian Periodicals Review* 42, no. 2 (2015): 248.

28. Paul Conway, "Digital Transformations and the Archival Nature of Surrogates," *Archival Science* 15, no. 1 (2015): 51-69, https://doi.org/10.1007/s10502-014-9219-z.

29. Abruzzi, Calè, and Vadillo, "Gale Digital Collections"; Tim Hitchcock, "Academic History Writing and Its Disconnects," *Journal of Digital Humanities* 1, no. 1 (2011), http://journalofdigitalhumanities.org/1-1/academic-history-writing-and-its-disconnects-by-tim-hitchcock/.

30. Paul Eggert, *Securing the Past: Conservation in Art, Architecture, and Literature* (Cambridge: Cambridge University Press, 2009), 157.

31. Joel Howard Weiner, "Newspaper Taxes, Taxes on Knowledge, Stamp Taxes," in *Dictionary of Nineteenth-Century Journalism*, ed. Laurel Brake and Marysa Demoor (Alexandria, VA: Chadwyck-Healey, 2009).

32. Ed King, "Legal Deposit of Newspapers at the British Library: Past, Present, and Future," in *Newspapers: Legal Deposit and Research in the Digital Era*, ed. Hartmut Walravens (Berlin: Walter de Gruyter, 2011), 161; P. R. (Philip Rowland) Harris, *A History of the British Museum Library, 1753–1973* (London: British Library, 1998), 31, 70, 131, 271.

33. Harris, *History of the British Museum Library*, 51–52.

34. Ilse Sternberg, "The British Museum Library and Colonial Copyright Deposit," *British Library Journal* 17, no. 1 (1991): 64.

35. Quoted in Sternberg, 69.

36. Sternberg, 73.

37. Eamon Dyas, "The Early Development of the Newspaper Library," *BL Newspaper Library Newsletter*, June 1989.

38. Jane Shaw, "British Newspapers, 1620–1900: Final Report" (JISC and the British Library, August 2009), 31n37, www.webarchive.org.uk/wayback/archive/20140614080134/http://www.jisc.ac.uk/media/documents/programmes/digitisation/blfinal.pdf.

39. Michael Harris, "Collecting Newspapers: Developments at the British Museum during the Nineteenth Century," in *Bibliophily* (Alexandria, VA: Chadwyck-Healey, 1986), 53.

40. Harris, 54.

41. Harris, *History of the British Museum Library*, 276, 345.

42. Harris, 376.

43. Stewart Gillies, "History of British Library Newspapers," British Library, 2008, www.bl.uk/reshelp/findhelprestype/news/historicalblnews/. For an overview of the storage crisis and building needs, see Harris, *History of the British Museum Library*, 376–78.

44. Eugene B. Power, *Edition of One: The Autobiography of Eugene B. Power, Founder of University Microfilms* (Ann Arbor, MI: University Microfilms International, 1990), 29.

45. For detailed studies of the emergence of *Early English Books Online*, see Mak, "Archaeology of a Digitization"; Ian Gadd, "The Use and Misuse of Early English Books Online," *Literature Compass* 6, no. 3 (2009): 680–92, https://doi.org/10.1111/j.1741-4113.2009.00632.x.

46. Power, *Edition of One*, 31.

47. For the story, see Adrian S. Edwards, "Destroyed, Damaged, and Replaced: The Legacy of World War II Bomb Damage in the King's Library," *Electronic British Library Journal*, 2013, www.bl.uk/eblj/2013articles/article8.html.

48. Harris, *History of the British Museum Library*, 555; "The Newspaper Library at War," *BL Newspaper Library Newsletter*, Spring 1991, 3.

49. Quoted in Gitelman, *Paper Knowledge*, 58.

50. Gitelman, 54.

51. Kathy Peiss, "Cultural Policy in a Time of War: The American Response to Endangered Books in World War II," *Library Trends* 55, no. 3 (2007): 370–86.

52. Lester Born, "Planning for Scholarly Photocopying," *PMLA* 79, no. 4 (1964): 86, https://doi.org/10.2307/2699195.

53. Peiss, "Cultural Policy," 377.

54. See Mak, "Archaeology of a Digitization," 15; Marvin, *When Old Technologies Were New*; Terras, "Father Busa's Female Punch Card Operatives"; Hardy, "Bibliographic Enterprise."

55. Power, *Edition of One*, 112.

56. Power, 128.

57. Power, 154.

58. Ed King, personal communication. "New Cameras and Microfilm Readers at Colindale," *BL Newspaper Library Newsletter*, Autumn 1980, 4.

59. Harris, *History of the British Museum Library*, 601–2.

60. Stewart Gillies, "Reference—Newsroom," August 8, 2023.

61. "A Disposals Policy for Foreign Newspapers after Microfilming," *BL Newspaper Library Newsletter*, June 1987, 2.

62. A sample catalog: *Microfilms of Newspapers and Journals for Sale 1979* (London: The British Library Newspaper Library, 1979).

63. For a good overview, see Laurel Brake, "Half Full and Half Empty," *Journal of Victorian Culture* 17, no. 2 (2012): 222–29, https://doi.org/10.1080/13555502.2012.683149.

64. Alan M. Meckler, *Micropublishing: A History of Scholarly Micropublishing in America, 1938–1980* (Westport, CT: Greenwood Press, 1982), xii–xiii.

65. Born, "Planning for Scholarly Photocopying," 77.

66. Born, 86. For another institutional history, see Thomas A. Bourke, "Scholarly Micropublishing, Preservation Microfilming, and the National Preservation Effort in the Last Two Decades of the Twentieth Century: History and Prognosis," *Microform Review* 19, no. 1 (1990): 4–16.

67. Greg Bradsher, "Archivist Monuments Man: Lester K. Born," *The Text Message* (blog), April 8, 2014, http://text-message.blogs.archives.gov/2014/04/08/monuments-man-lester-k-born/; Peiss, "Cultural Policy," 372.

68. Laurel Brake, "The Longevity of 'Ephemera': Library Editions of Nineteenth-Century Periodicals and Newspapers," *Media History* 18, no. 1 (2012): 7–20, https://doi.org/10.1080/13688804.2011.632192.

69. Wendy Hui Kyong Chun, "The Enduring Ephemeral, or the Future Is a Memory," *Critical Inquiry* 35, no. 1 (2008): 148–71, https://doi.org/10.1086/595632.

70. Luke McKernan, "Into the Void," *The Newsroom Blog: British Library*

(blog), January 27, 2015, http://britishlibrary.typepad.co.uk/thenewsroom/2015/01/into-the-void.html#. See also McKernan's wonderfully illustrated "Leaving Colindale," *Luke McKernan* (blog), October 9, 2013, http://lukemckernan.com/2013/10/09/leaving-colindale/.

71. Ed King, "Digital Historic Newspapers Online: Prospects and Challenges," in *Newspapers Collection Management: Printed and Digital Challenges: Proceedings of the International Newspaper Conference, Santiago de Chile, April 3–5, 2007*, ed. Hartmut Walravens (Munich: Saur, 2008), 61. They also had to take copyright restrictions into account in cases where newspapers are still in print. For details of how the British Library addressed such concerns, see Ed King, "British Library Digitisation: Access and Copyright," World Library and Information Congress (Quebec: International Federation of Library Associations, 2008); Paul Fyfe, "Access, Computational Analysis, and Fair Use in the Digitized Nineteenth-Century Press," *Victorian Periodicals Review* 51, no. 4 (2018): 716–37, https://doi.org/10.1353/vpr.2018.0051.

72. Jane Shaw, "10 Billion Words: The British Library Newspapers 1800–1900 Project. Some Guidelines for Large-Scale Newspaper Digitization," in *Libraries—A Voyage of Discovery* (World Library and Information Congress: 71th IFLA General Conference and Council, Oslo, Norway, 2005), 3, www.webarchive.org.uk/wayback/archive/20140615090156/http://www.jisc.ac.uk/uploaded_documents/IFLA_2005.pdf.

73. Edmund King, "Digitisation of Newspapers at the British Library," *Serials Librarian* 49, no. 1–2 (August 2005): 165–81, https://doi.org/10.1300/J123v49n01_07.

74. Shaw, "Final Report," 12, 14.

75. King, "Digital Historic Newspapers Online."

76. Shaw, "10 Billion Words," 10.

77. Shaw, "Final Report," 21–22.

78. Shaw, 11.

79. Cordell, "Taking Dirty OCR Seriously."

80. Many thanks to Jason Groth of the NC State University Libraries for help on these points.

81. Shaw, "Final Report," 16, 30.

82. Email to the author.

83. Harris, "Collecting Newspapers," 55.

84. King, "Digitisation of Newspapers at the British Library," 179.

85. King, "Digital Historic Newspapers Online," 63.

86. See the Wayback snapshot at http://web.archive.org/web/20070717194234/http://www.apexcovantage.com/about_us.aspx.

87. See http://fast.wistia.net/embed/iframe/8a0u0435t1?popover=true.

88. Natalia Cecire, "The Visible Hand," *Works Cited* (blog), May 3, 2011, http://nataliacecire.blogspot.com/2011/05/visible-hand.html.

89. Bonnie Mak, "Confessions of a Twenty-First-Century Memsahib: The Offshore Sweatshops of the Digital Humanities," MLA, Austin, TX, 2016.

90. Risam, *New Digital Worlds*, 4.

91. The website for Olive Software shows signs of age, with several broken links; however, the *Internet Archive* offers snapshots of the site during the company's partnership with the British Library. At that time, the company promoted its "ActivePaper Archive" product for historical newspaper digitization, which offered automated strategies for generating XML. See the Wayback Machine's snapshot, http://web.archive.org/web/20060316022837/http:/www.olivesoftware.com/products/technology.asp.

92. Jane Shaw and Patrick Fleming, "JISC Project Plan," JISC and the British Library, October 2008, 8, www.webarchive.org.uk/wayback/archive/20140614080145/http://www.jisc.ac.uk/media/documents/programmes/digitisation/bl_newspapers_public_plan.pdf.

93. Shaw, "Final Report," 8.

94. Abruzzi, Calè, and Vadillo, "Gale Digital Collections."

95. Conversation with the author.

96. Shaw, "Final Report," 15.

97. King, "Digital Historic Newspapers Online," 65ff. Incidentally, the Library of Congress' *Chronicling America* collection of nineteenth-century US newspapers does not segment by article.

98. Andrew Hobbs, "The Deleterious Dominance of *The Times* in Nineteenth-Century Scholarship," *Journal of Victorian Culture* 18, no. 4 (2013): 472–97, https://doi.org/10.1080/13555502.2013.854519. Coincidentally, Andrew Hobbs (then a PhD student) was quoted in the promotional materials for the JISC I Project Plan as saying it "could well change the face of British historiography." See Shaw and Fleming, "JISC Project Plan," 36.

99. Ian Milligan has made a similar argument about how the availability of digital resources privileges certain papers and modes of Canadian history. See Milligan, "Illusionary Order."

100. Charles Upchurch, "Full-Text Databases and Historical Research: Cautionary Results from a Ten-Year Study," *Journal of Social History* 46, no. 1 (2012): 89–105, https://doi.org/10.1093/jsh/shs035.

101. Bob Nicholson, "Counting Culture; or, How to Read Victorian Newspapers from a Distance," *Journal of Victorian Culture* 17, no. 2 (2012): 243–44, https://doi.org/10.1080/13555502.2012.683331. See also the extensive documentation of coverage and gaps in Shaw, "Final Report," 34ff.

102. Beelen et al., "Bias and Representativeness," 10.

103. Beelen et al., 18.

104. Abruzzi, Calè, and Vadillo, "Gale Digital Collections."

105. Seth Cayley, "Digitization in Teaching and Learning: The Publisher's View," *Victorian Periodicals Review* 45, no. 2 (2012): 210–14, https://doi.org/10.1353/vpr.2012.0017; Seth Cayley and Clare Horrocks, "The Punch Historical Archive, 1841–1992: A Sustainable Brand for the Digital Age," *Victorian Periodicals Review* 48, no. 2 (2015): 238–43, https://doi.org/10.1353/vpr.2015.0024.

106. Seth Cayley, "Creating the Daily Mail Historical Archive" (Gale Cengage, 2013), http://gale.cengage.co.uk/daily-mail-historical-archive/essays.aspx.

107. Harris, *History of the British Museum Library*, xv.

108. In a personal communication, King qualifies my claims, suggesting that "in the context of a national library such as the British Library, institutional memory and files of archived papers relating to the work of previous generations can remain quite strong."

109. Special thanks to Beth Gaskell, Stewart Gillies, Mia Ridge, and Heather Pascal for their generous assistance. The opinions represented here are my own.

110. "How We Do It," British Newspaper Archive, 2023, www.britishnewspaperarchive.co.uk/content/how_we_do_it.

111. Correspondence with Beth Gaskell, July 18, 2023.

112. Yann Ryan and Luke McKernan, "Converting the British Library's Catalogue of British and Irish Newspapers into a Public Domain Dataset: Processes and Applications," *Journal of Open Humanities Data* 7 (2021): 1, https://doi.org/10.5334/johd.23.

113. Gitelman, *Paper Knowledge*, 71.

114. Buurma and Heffernan, *Teaching Archive*, 6.

115. Blair, *Too Much to Know*, 2.

116. James Mussell, "Trading in Death: Miscellaneity and Memory in the British Nineteenth-Century Press," ed. Daniela Gretz, Marcus Krause, and Nico Pethes (Hannover: Wehrhahn Verlag, 2022), 141–64.

117. James Mussell, "Too Much to Read: Victorian Periodicals, Bibliographical Utopianism, and the 'Bad Indexer,'" Research Society for Victorian Periodicals Conference, Kansas City, MO, September 10, 2016.

118. Harris, "Collecting Newspapers," 58.

119. "Prefatory Note," *Victorian Studies* 1, no. 1 (1957): 3.

120. N. Merrill Distad, "The Origins and History of 'Victorian Periodicals Review,' 1954–84," *Victorian Periodicals Review* 18, no. 3 (1985): 87–88.

121. "Prefatory Note," 3.

122. Quoted in Distad, "Origins and History," 88.

123. Wolff, "Charting the Golden Stream."

124. Robert C. Binkley, "New Tools for Men of Letters," *Yale Review* 24 (1935): 519–37.

125. Chad Wellmon, *Organizing Enlightenment: Information Overload and the Invention of the Modern Research University* (Baltimore: Johns Hopkins University Press, 2015), 16.

126. Distad, "Origins and History," 89.

127. Rosemary T. VanArsdel, "The Birth and Growth of Victorian Periodicals Newsletter and the Research Society for Victorian Periodicals," *Victorian Periodicals Review* 51, no. 1 (2018): 188.

128. Distad, "Origins and History," 91.

129. VanArsdel, "Birth and Growth," 190.

130. Michael Wolff, "Reports from the Society's Officers, Including a Report on the Second Annual Conference: President's Report for 1969-70," *Victorian Periodicals Newsletter*, no. 10 (1970): 3.

131. Joel H. Wiener and Michael Wolff, "RSVP Manifesto," *Victorian Studies* 13, no. 4 (1970): 413–14.

132. Patrick Leary, "'I Have Just Had One of Those Large Ideas': Walter Houghton, Richard Altick, and the Origins of The Wellesley Index," *Victorian Periodicals Review* 54, no. 2 (2021): 279–303, https://doi.org/10.1353/vpr.2021.0019.

133. Quoted in Leary, 279.

134. James O'Neill, "Victorian Periodicals and Newspapers in Microform: A Preliminary List, and Proposals," *Victorian Periodicals Newsletter*, no. 7 (1970): 14–28.

135. Ernest P. Taubes, "The Future of Microfilming," *American Archivist* 21, no. 2 (1958): 153.

136. Distad, "Origins and History," 88.

137. Hans De Groot, "An Old Editor Remembers: VPN/VPR at Toronto, 1973-85," *Victorian Periodicals Review* 41, no. 1 (2008): 14.

138. Dorothy Deering, "The Victorian Periodicals Newsletter (VPN), January, April and July 1970," *Victorian Periodicals Review* 41, no. 1 (2008): 9–10.

139. Dorothy Deering, "Computer Programming for the Victorian Periodicals Project," *Victorian Periodicals Newsletter* 3, no. 1 (1970): 29–42.

140. Deering, 29.

141. Even W. T. Stead's *Review of Reviews* was "prepared by his long-term collaborator Eliza Hetherington and her staff of women indexers" (Mussell, "Trading in Death."). That pattern continued through the twentieth century,

including with Deering's work and Esther Rhoads Houghton's contributions to the Wellesley Index (Leary, "I Have Just Had," 284.). Linda Distad was the spouse of *VPR* editor Merrill Distad, who "relied so heavily upon the editorial skills and judgement (not to mention unpaid labour) of his wife, Linda, that by 1979 a sense of decent shame prompted her inclusion upon mastheads and letterheads as 'Assistant Editor.'" (Distad, "Origins and History," 94.)

142. Distad, "Origins and History," 92.

143. Deering, "Computer Programming," 29.

144. Russell M. Wyland, "Public Funding and the 'Untamed Wilderness' of Victorian Studies," *Romanticism on the Net*, no. 55 (2009), https://doi.org/10.7202/039554ar.

145. Hossein Khosrowjah, "A Brief History of Area Studies and International Studies," *Arab Studies Quarterly* 33, no. 3/4 (2011): 131–42.

146. Wyland, "Public Funding."

147. Wyland.

148. Dorothy Deering, "The Victorian Periodicals Project," *Victorian Periodicals Newsletter*, no. 10 (1970): 19.

149. Laurel Brake, "'Time's Turbulence': Mapping Journalism Networks," *Victorian Periodicals Review* 44, no. 2 (2011): 117 (original emphasis).

150. Brake, 124.

Afterword

1. "Lend-Lease," *Times Literary Supplement*, October 18, 1957, 625.

2. "Responses to the V21 Manifesto," *V21* (blog), March 23, 2015, http://v21collective.org/responses-to-the-v21-manifesto-2/.

3. Pinch, "Recent Studies," 943.

4. Walter E. Houghton, *The Victorian Frame of Mind, 1830–1870* (New Haven, CT: Yale University Press, 1957).

5. Buurma and Heffernan, "Interpretation, 1980 and 1880."

6. I admit that one of my favorite teaching tricks is to search Google ngrams for the "f word" and watch students initially struggle to understand why people had such dirty minds prior to 1800.

7. The conditions of copyright and public domain materials are more complicated. See Fyfe, "Access, Computational Analysis, and Fair Use."

8. Matthew Jockers, *Macroanalysis: Methods for Digital Literary History* (Urbana: University of Illinois Press, 2013), 173.

9. Patrick Leary, "Victorian Studies in the Digital Age," in *The Victorians since 1901: Histories, Representations and Revisions*, ed. Miles Taylor and Michael Wolff (Manchester: Manchester University Press, 2004), 202.

10. Geoffrey C. Bowker, "The Ends of Computing," in *The Ends of Knowl-*

edge: Outcomes and Endpoints across the Arts and Sciences, ed. Seth Rudy and Rachael King (London: Bloomsbury, 2023), 27-59.

11. Adam Crymble, "The Origin Myths of Computing in Historical Research," in *Technology and the Historian* (Urbana: University of Illinois Press, 2021), https://doi.org/10.5622/illinois/9780252043710.003.0003.

12. Lauren F. Klein, "Dimensions of Scale: Invisible Labor, Editorial Work, and the Future of Quantitative Literary Studies," *PMLA* 135, no. 1 (2020): 36, https://doi.org/10.1632/pmla.2020.135.1.23.

13. Johnson, "Markup Bodies"; see also Jacqueline Wernimont, *Numbered Lives: Life and Death in Quantum Media* (Cambridge, MA: MIT Press, 2019).

14. Amy E. Earhart, *Traces of the Old, Uses of the New: The Emergence of Digital Literary Studies* (Ann Arbor: University of Michigan Press, 2015), 63.

15. Risam, *New Digital Worlds*, 51.

16. See a snapshot at https://web.archive.org/web/19961123224629/http://promo.net/pg/ev/table/author.html.

17. Earhart, *Traces of the Old*, 39. Earhart contrasts these projects with a very different editorial sensibility in medieval studies. For many, McGann's approach became a landmark: "Donald Waters, Andrew W. Mellon Foundation program officer, identifies McGann's 1983 *A Critique of Modern Textual Criticism* as the text that launched literary digital humanities" (Earhart, 21, 41).

18. Susan Brown et al., "The Story of the Orlando Project: Personal Reflections," *Tulsa Studies in Women's Literature* 26, no. 1 (2007): 135-43.

19. Andrew Stauffer, "Romanticism's Scattered Leaves," *Romanticism on the Net*, no. 41-42 (2006), http://id.erudit.org/iderudit/013155ar.

20. Moretti, *Graphs, Maps, Trees*, 4.

21. Bode, *Reading by Numbers*; Underwood, *Distant Horizons*.

22. Gibbs and Cohen, "A Conversation with Data."

23. "Honest Abe: Duquesne Computer Scientist to Authenticate Lincoln Writings," *Duquesne University Times* (blog), May 9, 2012, https://applications.duq.edu/times/2012/05/09/honest-abe-duquesne-computer-scientist-to-authenticate-lincoln-writings/.

24. Ryan Cordell and David Smith, "The Viral Texts Project: Mapping Networks of Reprinting in 19th-Century Newspapers and Magazines," 2012, www.viraltexts.org/.

25. Lev Manovich, "Cultural Analytics," *Software Studies Initiative* (blog), January 2014, http://lab.softwarestudies.com/p/cultural-analytics.html.

26. Alan Liu, "Where Is Cultural Criticism in the Digital Humanities?," in *Debates in the Digital Humanities*, ed. Matthew Gold (Minneapolis: University of Minnesota Press, 2012), 490-509, http://dhdebates.gc.cuny.edu/debates/text/20.

27. For a glimpse at several such approaches, see Losh and Wernimont, *Bodies of Information*.

28. Jones, *Roberto Busa*, 16.

29. Earhart, "Digital Humanities Futures."

30. Gallon, "Making a Case." As Alondra Nelson has similarly explained, "afrofuturism" names and legitimizes a long tradition of sociotechnical experimentation by black artists. See "Introduction: Future Texts," *Social Text* 20, no. 2 (2002): 1–15.

31. Domenico Fiormonte, Sukanta Chaudhuri, and Paola Ricaurte, eds., *Global Debates in the Digital Humanities* (Minneapolis: University of Minnesota Press, 2022), xii.

32. Roopika Risam, "Navigating the Global Digital Humanities: Insights from Black Feminism," in *Debates in the Digital Humanities 2016*, ed. Matthew K. Gold and Lauren F. Klein (Minneapolis: University of Minnesota Press, 2016), 359–67, http://dhdebates.gc.cuny.edu/debates/text/80.

33. Risam, *New Digital Worlds*, 24.

34. Risam, 26.

35. Ortega, "Media and Cultural Hybridity."

36. Risam, *New Digital Worlds*, 25; Chandler Puritty et al., "Without Inclusion, Diversity Initiatives May Not Be Enough," *Science* 357, no. 6356 (2017): 1101–2, https://doi.org/10.1126/science.aai9054.

37. Risam, *New Digital Worlds*, 18.

38. Adrian S. Wisnicki and Megan Ward, "Livingstone Online: An Introduction," Livingstone Online, 2018, https://livingstoneonline.org/about-this-site/livingstone-online-introduction.

39. "Colored Conventions Project Principles," *Colored Conventions Project* (blog), 2020, https://coloredconventions.org/about/principles/.

40. Chatterjee, Christoff, and Wong, "Undisciplining Victorian Studies."

41. Timothy Brennan, "The Digital-Humanities Bust," *Chronicle of Higher Education*, October 15, 2017, www.chronicle.com/article/the-digital-humanities-bust/.

42. Mark Algee-Hewitt, "The Ends of Digital Humanities," in *The Ends of Knowledge: Outcomes and Endpoints across the Arts and Sciences*, ed. Seth Rudy and Rachael King (London: Bloomsbury, 2023), 74.

43. Algee-Hewitt, 74.

44. Houghton, *Victorian Frame of Mind*, xiii, xv.

45. Clayton, *Charles Dickens in Cyberspace*, 8.

46. Algee-Hewitt, "Ends of Digital Humanities," 74.

47. Booth and Posner, "Introduction," 9.

INDEX

Bold page numbers refer to figures.

Acland, Charles, 7, 119
adaptation, 29–30, 138, 148–61, 170
affect, 36, 39–42, 61, 80, 96, 167–68
age of transition. *See under* Mill, John Stuart
Algee-Hewitt, Mark, 225–27
Allison, Sarah, 133, 161, 166
Amazon, 99, 130
American Historical Association (AHA), 18, 20
American Telephone & Telegraph Company (AT&T), 152–**53**
anachronism, 3, 17–25, 31, 67–68, 215–17. *See also* presentism
Anderson, Amanda, 161
Arata, Stephen, 29, 137, 145–47
archival literacy, 179

archives, 101, 164, 172–74, 181–91; digital, 179, 191–207, 221; and memory, 83, 96–101, 192
artificial intelligence, 7, 91, 123–25; generative AI, 29, 133–35, 226–27; machine learning, 29, 105–6, 116–17, 120, 125–26, 255n78
audiobooks, 29, 138, 158–60
authorship: and AI, 106, 132–33 (*see also* automatic writing); attribution (*see* stylometry); profession of, 29, 54, 137, 143–48, 162–63; pseudonymous, 66–67, 76
automatic writing. *See* spiritualism

Babbage, Charles, 83, 88
Barlow, John Perry, 59

275

INDEX

Barrett, William, 83-84
Barrymore, John, 156-57
Bauerlein, Mark, 79
Beniger, James, 36
Besant, Walter, 145, 163
bibliography. *See* critical bibliography; indexing
Binkley, Robert, 187, 208
Birkerts, Sven, 78, 160
Blackwood's Edinburgh Magazine, 53-56, 241n62
Blair, Ann, 73, 207
Blum, Andrew, 26, 63-65
Bode, Katherine, 116, 222
Bollmer, Grant, 91, 98
Bolter, Jay, 45, 47, 140, 150
Booth, Alison, 227
Born, Lester, 187, 191
Bosanquet, Theodora, 28-29, 131-34
boyd, danah, 78-79, 101
Brake, Laurel, 179, 191, 214
Brandeis, Louis, 28, 95-97, 100
Bray, Charles, 66, 69, 81-82
British Library, **183**, 184-90, **186**, **192**-205
British Museum, 30, 181-90
British Newspaper Archive (BNA), 200, 202-5
Brooks, David, 89-90, 249n99
Busa, Fr. Roberto, 12, 115, 233n54, 234n55
Bush, Vannevar, 128, 248n96
Buurma, Rachel, 12, 22, 31, 115, 206, 219
Byerly, Alison, 9

Camlot, Jason, 154-55
Carey, James, 6, 34
Carlyle, Thomas, 54

Carr, Nicholas, 78-79
Castricano, Jodey, 147
Cecire, Natalia, 105, 114, 197
Chatterjee, Ronjaunee, 21, 225
Christoff, Alicia Mireles, 21, 225
Chronicle of Higher Education, 13
Chun, Wendy Hui Kyong, 136, 192
Clayton, Jay, 19, 22, 125
close reading, 79, 112, 147, 163, 165
cloud. *See* Internet
Collins, Wilkie, 248fn89
colonialism, 17, 65, 181-82, 197, 223; postcolonialism, 31, 224-25
Colored Conventions Project, 225
communication: as a field, 6, 8-9; history of, 6, 8, 33-42, 52, 92-93, 104; networks (*see* network); technologies, 1, 24-25, 67, 70-72, 75, 139, 143, 154 (*see also* phonograph; telegraph; telephone)
computational literary studies, 168-69. *See also* distant reading
Cooper, Mark, 163, 166
Copland, Arthur, 159
copyright, 95, 190, 219, 268n71; history of, 56, 181-82
Cordell, Ryan, 195, 222, 265n26
Corelli, Marie, 248n95
cosmopolitanism, 76, 80
critical bibliography, 10, 53, 177
Crymble, Adam, 220
cultural analytics, 222, 234n61
culturomics, 111-12
Currell, Sue, 118-19

Da, Nan Z., 116, 169
Dames, Nicholas, 80, 89, 94, 105, 114, 117
Danahay, Martin, 150

INDEX   277

Darnton, Robert, 172-73
data, 29, 92; ethics, 68-69, 77, 96-102, 225; history of, 60, 67, 176, 220, 244n8; metadata, 175, 195, 199, 204, 211; mining, 174-76, 204, 263n13; paradata, 178, 201; surveillance, 91-93, 96-98
database, 178-79, 220
Davis, Jade, 80, 101
De Quincey, Thomas, 26, 53-56; "The English Mail-Coach," 38-42, 53, 55-56, 62
Deering, Dorothy, 209, 211-12, 214
degeneration, 73, 78, 136-37, 158-60, 168
dictation, 127, 130-31
digital humanities: alternative genealogies, 16-17, 23, 223; black DH, 15, 17, 223; *Companion to Digital Humanities*, 12-13: "dark side," 29-30, 136, 138, 161-70, 223; *Debates in Digital Humanities*, 13; definition/naming, 3-4, 12-17, 161, 164-67, 214, 217-18; end of, 31, 165, 167, 225-27; funding, 212-14; global DH, 17, 223-24; predigital history, 3, 5, 16, 24, 28-29, 217-18, 235n75. *See also* distant reading
digital preservation, 90, 199-202, 205
digitization: digital editions, 179, 202-4, 221, 230n16, 265n26; of historical materials, 30, 172-180, 193-205, 211, 214. *See also* optical character recognition
disability, 159
disembodiment. *See* disintermediation
disintermediation, 62, 152-54, 159, 177; and the cloud, 32-34, 58, 91;

origins of, 26, 34-35, 41-52; politics of, 43-44, 46, 59-61, 65
distant reading, 121-23, 125-27, 166, 222; critiques of, 113, 116, 165, 254n54; gendered labor, 105-9, 114-15, 125-27; history of, 4, 12, 28, 103-6, 110-16, 252n16
doxxing. *See* privacy
du Maurier, George: *Peter Ibbetson*, 27, 69, 84-89, 91-93

Earhart, Amy, 164, 220-21, 223
Early English Books Online, 178, 184, 189
electricity, 39, 43-44, 81-82. *See also* galvanism
Eliot, George, 27, 66; *Daniel Deronda*, 93-94; *Middlemarch*, 72, 75, 93-94; *The Lifted Veil*, 27, 67, 69-78, 94
empathy, 69, 80-81, 101; crisis of, 69, 77-78. *See also* sympathy
ephemera, 191-92, 221-22
Erlin, Matt, 161-62
Ernst, Wolfgang, 10, 179
Evans, Marian. *See* Eliot, George

Facebook, 79-80, 100
Findmypast. *See* British Newspaper Archive
Fish, Stanley, 165
Frankenstein, 40, 42, 185
Frey, Anne, 53, 55
Fyfe, Aileen, 56

Gale Cengage, 174-77, **175**, 194, 198-**201**, 204
Gallon, Kim, 15, 223
Galvan, Jill, 70, 86, 152

galvanism, 39–44
generative AI. *See* artificial intelligence
Gissing, George: *New Grub Street*, 10, 146
Gitelman, Lisa, 2, 5, 16, 24, 47, 84, 176, 206
Gleick, James, 6, 34, 66
Gold, Matthew K., 13, 225
Google, 78–80, 97–99
Google Books, 111, 185, 197, 272n6
gothic, 30, 138, 141, 148, 161, 163, 165, 168
Greiner, Rae, 75
Grusin, Richard, 45, 47, 140, 150, 167
Guillory, John, 6, 34, 139

handwriting, 29, 137, 141–44, 258n12
Hardy, Molly, 177
Harris, Michael, 183, 196
Hayles, N. Katherine, 14, 23, 26, 34
Hedley, Alison, 48
Heffernan, Laura, 12, 22, 31, 115, 206, 219
Heuser, Ryan, 103, 113
Hobbs, Andrew, 199, 269n98
Hockey, Susan, 12, 110
Houghton, Walter, 210, 218–19, 222, 227
Hu, Tung-Hui, 58, 61
Huey, Edmund, 118–19, 124
hypermediacy. *See* remediation

Igarashi, Yohei, 105, 110, 112, 250n120
Illustrated London News (*ILN*), 45–50; "The Post Office Van," 46–50, **47**
illustrated periodicals, 26, 44–50. *See also* newspapers

immediacy. *See* remediation
In the Cage (James), 28, 103–9, 114, 118–30, 252n9
indexing, 171–72, 187, 206–15, 221
industrial revolution, 15–16, 235n75
information history, 6, 17, 34–37, 52, 57, 67–68, 72, 216, 220, 232n40
information overload, 69, 73–80, 87, 93, 107, 207
infrastructure: network, 26, 36, 58–65, 192 (*see also* internet); of the press, 42–43, 46–57, 210; studies of, 26, 36, 48–49, 52, 62
interdisciplinarity: as method, 9–11, 208, 212–13, 218; in nineteenth century, 4, 24, 217–18, 227–28
internet: the cloud, 58, 61, 91, 99; infrastructure, 35, 57, 60–65, 242fn73

James, Henry: "The Art of Fiction," 114, 145, 162–63; "The Figure in the Carpet," 110; *In the Cage*, 28, 103–9, 114, 118–30, 252n9; relations to secretaries, 130–32, 134
Javal, Louis Émile, 118
Jockers, Matthew, 219–20
Johnson, Jessica Marie, 60, 220
Joint Information Systems Committee (JISC), 193–202, 204–5
Jones, Meg Leta, 92, 97–99, 101
Joshi, Priya, 21

King, Ed, 193, 196, 202
Kirschenbaum, Matthew, 13, 15, 163, 167
Kittler, Friedrich, 84, 124, 159
Klein, Lauren, 115
Koh, Adeline, 17

labor: academic labor, 31, 132, 163–70, 177–78, 205–15; invisible, 29, 46, 61, 90, 114–5, 125–34, 152, 188, 197, 212, 271n141; reproductive immaterial labor, 129; secretarial, 29, 106, 130–34
Le Khac, Long, 103, 113
Leary, Patrick, 171–72, 210, 220
Lee, Maurice, 7, 17, 73
Lee, Vernon, 13, 112
Liu, Alan, 3, 10–11, 13–14, 58, 167, 221, 223; new media encounter, 1, 7–9, 11, 13, 24
Livingstone Online, 224–25
longue durée, 21, 30, 174, 180
Losh, Liz, 46, 61

machine learning. *See* artificial intelligence
magic lantern, 71, 85
mail coach, 37–42, **47**, 49–51
Mak, Bonnie, 178, 197
Mansfield, Richard, 148–52, **151**
Marvin, Carolyn, 5–6, 8, 19, 36–37, 39, 43, 52, 127
Marx, John, 163, 166
Mayer-Schönberger, Viktor, 89–90, 98
McCullough, Malcolm, 87
McGann, Jerome, 221
McLuhan, Marshall, 6
McPherson, Tara, 60
Mechanical Turk, 130
Meckler, Alan, 191
media: concept of, 2, 6, 34–42, 89, 139; mass media, 40, 45, 95, 137, 146–60, 163, 166, 171–72; obsolescence, 9, 29, 158. *See also* new media; social media

media archaeology, 9–10, 30, 57, 174–80, 264fn25
media history, 23, 43, 143, 161, 232n40; computer history, 61, 127; as a field, 4–5, 8–10, 16, 33, 52
media shift, 3, 24, 137–39, 154, 158–60, 168, 172–73. *See also* new media: encounter
media studies: comparative, 16, 23, 177; as a field, 4, 9–11, 57
Memex, 128, 248n96
memory: ambient, 69, 86–89, 248n89; digital, 89–93, 192, **201**; and spiritualism, 27, 81–86; telecom operators, 105, 122, 127
Mendenhall, Thomas, 13, 28, 110–12
Menke, Richard, 10–12, 71–72, 104, 138–39, 141, 216, 218
Meta. *See* Facebook
microfilm: digitization of, 193–98, 203; history of, 177, 184–91, **188–89**, 193–94, 203, 209–11; preservation, 186–87, 193–94, 203, 267n66
Miles, Josephine, 12, 115
Mill, John Stuart, 79, 111; age of transition, 1–2, 6, 19, 226–27
Modern Language Association (MLA), 30, 165–68
Moretti, Franco, 113, 165–66, 222
Morgan, Benjamin, 105, 111–14
multilingualism, 17
Mussell, James, 177, 179, 207

Nakamura, Lisa, 61
National Endowment for the Humanities (NEH), 212–13
neoliberalism, 30, 79, 89, 167, 223

network: communications, 61–65, 75–77, 99, 214; definition of, 53, 58–59, 245n37; infrastructure, 26–27 (*see also* internet); periodicals as, 214–15

new media: definition of, 6–10, 19, 143, 192, 231n27; encounter, 1, 7–9, 11, 13–15, 19, 24; history of, 2–3, 5–7, 37, 139, 171–73, 180, 232n40; industry, 2 (*see also* Amazon, Facebook, Google)

newspapers: collection of, 180–91, **183**; digitization, 173, **175–76**, 180, 191–205, **195**, 264n25; distribution, 46, 48–52, 55–56; microfilming, 174, 184–91

Nordau, Max, 73, 136–37, 160

Nunberg, Geoffrey, 5–6, 34

offshoring, 196–98, 249n99

omniscience, 27, 69, 72, 75–77, 82, 94

O'Neill, James, 209–10

Onion, The, 18

optical character recognition (OCR), **176**, 193–98, 204, 219, 263n14

organ music, 157–58

Ortega, Élika, 13, 224

Otis, Laura, 74–75, 109, 124

Panizzi, Antonio, 181–82

Pannapacker, William, 13, 164

paralysis, 73–74, 76, 78, 93

Parks, Lisa, 48–49

Peiss, Kathy, 187

periodicals, 36, 46, 48, 52–56, 171. *See also* illustrated newspapers; newspapers

Peters, John Durham, 2, 6, 34, 41–42

phonograph, 71, 83, 86, 154–56. *See also* audiobooks

photography: as a medium, **151**–52, 259n38; as memory technology, 71, 81–86, 95. *See also* microfilm

physiology, 35, 41–42, 72, 105, 117–19

Pinch, Adela, 22, 77, 82, 94

Piper, Andrew, 22, 113, 162, 234n61

Poe, Edgar Allen, 83

Posner, Miriam, 227

post office, 46–49, 103–4, 108. *See also* mail coach

Power, Eugene, 184–90

presentism, 3, 17–23, 34, 216–17; historians and, 18–20; strategic, 20–22

Price, Leah, 62

printing press, 42–43

privacy: doxxing, 27, 66–67; right to be forgotten, 28, 94–102; right to privacy, 28, 69, 95–96, 101; surveillance, 27, 59, 67, 82, 88, 91–92, 96–100, 249n113

psychoanalysis, 86, 124

Punch, 147

Queen Victoria, 49–51

railway, 32–33, 37–39, 50–52

Raley, Rita, 168

reading, 146–49, 159–60; physiology of, 117–20, 124. *See also* close reading; distant reading; speed reading

remediation, 30, 45, 65, 139–41, 149–50

replication (experimental), 145–46, 162–63

Research Society for Victorian Periodicals (RSVP), 208–15. See also *Victorian Periodicals Newsletter*

right to be forgotten. *See under* privacy
Risam, Roopika, 17, 197, 221, 224
Royle, Nicholas, 33, 76
Rubery, Matthew, 158–60
Rubin, Miri, 18–19

Scheinfeldt, Tom, 15–16
Sconce, Jeffrey, 92, 133
secretaries. *See under* labor
Sharpe, Christina, 20, 60
Shaw, Jane, 193, 198
Siri. *See* voice assistants
Small, Helen, 76
Smiles, Samuel, 88
Smits, Thomas, 50–52
social media, 77–80, 89–92, 97–100, 130, 169, 218
Society of Authors, 145
speed reading, 105, 117–22, 124–25; tachistoscope, 118–20
Spencer, Len, 154–56
spiritualism: automatic writing, 29, 131–34, 146; mediums, 41–42, 98, 131–34, 139–40, 248n95; telepathy, 27, 69–70, 81–86, 124; theories of memory, 27, 69, 81–93, 98
stage coach. *See* mail coach
Standage, Tom, 7, 33
Starolsielski, Nicole, 58, 62
statistics, 112, 116
Stauffer, Andrew, 7, 221–22
steampunk, 7, 63
Stein, Gertrude, 13, 114
Stephenson, Neil, 26, 33, 62–63
Sterne, Jonathan, 14, 154, 156
Stevenson, Robert Louis: *The Strange Case of Dr Jekyll and Mr Hyde*, 29, 136–60, 170
Strange Case of Dr Jekyll and Mr Hyde, The (Stevenson), 29, 136–60, 170;
audio recording, 155–56; film adaptation, 156–58; stage play, 148–51, 155
strategic presentism. *See* presentism
stylometry, 110–11, 222. *See also* Mendenhall, Thomas
surveillance. *See under* data; privacy
Sweet, James, 18, 20
sympathy, 27, 70, 72, 74–81, 87, 94

tachistoscope, 118–20
technological determinism, 16, 24–25, 124, 179
telegraph: encoding, 71–72, 110; gendered labor, 104–7, 110, 115, 120–22, 127; marine, 43–44, 52, 60, 63, 248n95; as news carrier, 50–52; optical, 85, 87; precursor to internet, 2, 33, 60
telepathy, 27, 69–70, 81–86, 124. *See also* spiritualism
telephone, 152–54, **153**
Thorat, Dhanashree, 60
Thoreau, Henry David, 64, 79
Thurschwell, Pamela, 124, 131–32
Times (London), 42–43, 52, 61
Times Literary Supplement (TLS), 216, 218
too much information (TMI). *See* information overload
transmission narrative, 62–65
Turkle, Sherry, 77–80, 90, 97, 101
typewriter, 9, 127, 131–32, 143, 257n104

Underwood, Ted, 112–13, 222
undisciplining. *See under* Victorian studies
University Microfilm Incorporated (UMI), 184–90, **185**

Victorian Periodicals Newsletter (VPN), 209–12
Victorian studies: as a field, 10, 30–31, 172, 174, 206–8, 216–25, 227–28; globalizing, 21–22; and presentism, 20–22; undisciplining, 20–21, 225–26; V21 Collective, 20, 216, 218; *Victorian Studies* (journal), 11, 207–12, 216. *See also* Research Society for Victorian Periodicals
virtual reality, 85
voice assistants, 128–32

W. H. Smith & Sons, 50–52
Walford, Cornelius, 171–72, 207–8, 213
Ward, Megan, 22, 33–34, 123–25, 173

Warren, Samuel, 28, 95–97, 100
Weingart, Scott, 13
Weller, Toni, 6
Wellesley Index, 208, 210–11, 214
Wellmon, Chad, 16, 163–64, 208–9
Welsh, Alexander, 67–68, 76
Weltman, Sharon Aronofsky, 149
Wernimont, Jacqueline, 46, 169
Westin, Alan, 96
Westminster Review, 1, 9
Wolff, Michael, 172, 207–14
Wong, Amy, 9, 21, 225
wood engraving. *See* illustrated periodicals
World War II, 185–91, **186**
Wyland, Russell, 211–14

Zieger, Susan, 40, 86

STANFORD TEXT TECHNOLOGIES

Martin Paul Eve
Theses on the Metaphors of Digital-Textual History

Geoffrey Turnovsky
Reading Typographically: Immersed in Print in Early Modern France

Collin Jennings
Enlightenment Links: Theories of Mind and Media in Eighteenth-Century Britain

Bridget Whearty
Digital Codicology: Medieval Books and Modern Labor

Michael Gavin
Literary Mathematics: Quantitative Theory for Textual Studies

Michelle Warren
Holy Digital Grail: A Medieval Book on the Internet

Blaine Greteman
Networking Print in Shakespeare's England: Influence, Agency, and Revolutionary Change

Simon Reader
Notework: Victorian Literature and Nonlinear Style

Yohei Igarashi
The Connected Condition: Romanticism and the Dream of Communication

Elaine Treharne and Claude Willan
Text Technologies: A History

The authorized representative in the EU for product safety and compliance is:
Mare Nostrum Group
B.V Doelen 72
4831 GR Breda
The Netherlands

www.ingramcontent.com/pod-product-compliance
Lightning Source LLC
Chambersburg PA
CBHW022000220426
43663CB00007B/894